THE FUTURE OF LIBERATION THEOLOGY

The Future of Liberation Theology envisions a radical new direction for Latin American liberation theology. One of a new generation of Latin American theologians, Ivan Petrella shows that despite the current dominance of 'end of history' ideology liberation theologians need not abandon their belief that the theological rereading of Christianity must be linked to the development of 'historical projects' – models of political and economic organization that would replace an unjust status quo. In the absence of historical projects liberation theology currently finds itself unable to move beyond merely talking about liberation toward actually enacting it in society.

Providing a bold new interpretation of the current state and potential future of liberation theology, Ivan Petrella brings together original research on the movement with developments in political theory, critical legal theory and political economy to reconstruct liberation theology's understanding of theology, democracy and capitalism. The result is the recovery of historical projects, thus allowing liberation theologians to once again place the reality of liberation, and not just the promise, at the forefront of their task.

Con el estómago lleno todos somos mejores
Los Olvidados

The Future of Liberation Theology

An Argument and Manifesto

IVAN PETRELLA

ASHGATE

Published by
Ashgate Publishing Limited
Gower House
Croft Road
Aldershot
Hampshire GU11 3HR
England

Ashgate Publishing Company
Suite 420
101 Cherry Street
Burlington, VT 05401-4405
USA

Ashgate website: http://www.ashgate.com

British Library Cataloguing in Publication Data
Petrella, Ivan
   The future of liberation theology : an argument and
   manifesto
   1.Liberation theology
   I.Title
   230'.0464

Library of Congress Cataloguing-in-Publication Data
Petrella, Ivan, 1969-
   The future of liberation theology : an argument and manifesto / Ivan Petrella.
     p. cm.
   Includes bibliographical references.
   ISBN 0-7546-4051-5 (alk. paper)
    1. Liberation theology. I. Title.

   BT83.57.P465 2003
   230'.0464--dc22

                        2003063726

ISBN 0 7546 4051 5

Printed and bound in Great Britain by TJ International Ltd, Padstow, Cornwall

Contents

Acknowledgements   vi
Introduction   vii

1   Liberation Theology Today: the Missing Historical Project   1

2   Liberation Theology as the Construction of Historical Projects   24

3   Liberation Theology, Democracy and Historical Projects   46

4   Liberation Theology, Capitalism and Historical Projects   69

5   Liberation Theology, Institutional Imagination and Historical Projects   93

6   Liberation Theology as the Construction of Historical Projects Revisited   121

7   Conclusion   144

Appendix
The Present and Future of Latin American Liberation Theology:
a Manifesto in Eight Parts   146

References   150
Index   171

Acknowledgements

Many thanks to Maruja and my folks for helping fund the lack of material productivity the gestation and writing of such a project seemed to require, Francis Fiorenza, Gordon Kaufman and Roberto Unger for their insight and guidance; Lori Pearson and Jeannine Hill Fletcher for a great writing group; Karina Galperin who I trust (it remains in her best interest as well…) will never reveal what really went on for seven years on Garden Street; el Tincho for no particular reason, and Bapi without whose comments, editing, patience, companionship and soup this book would not have been finished; Rowman and Littlefield for allowing me to use my article 'Latin American Liberation Theology, Globalization and Historical Projects: from Critique to Construction', from *Latin American Perspectives on Globalization: Ethics, Politics, and Alternative Visions*, ed. Mario Saenz (Lanham, MD: Rowman and Littlefield Publishers, Inc., 2002); Nelson Leirner and Galeria Brito Cimino for letting me use the former's provocative work on the cover as well as Sarah Lloyd and Frances Britain for helping carry this project to fruition.

Introduction

The time to reinvent liberation theology is now. Latin American liberation theology was born with the promise of being a theology that would not rest with merely talking about liberation but would actually help liberate people from material deprivation. It thus had two parts: a rereading of Christianity from the perspective of the oppressed and the construction of 'historical projects'; models of political and economic organization that would replace an unjust status quo. These two parts were inseparable in the pursuit of liberation. However, today the 'end of history' and the demise of socialism have deprived liberation theology of its preferred historical project. Liberation theologians appear incapable of developing a different project in its place and so resign themselves to rehashing their rereading of Christianity. Small wonder that liberation theology seems stagnant; small wonder that many think liberation theology is dead.

This book shows that such an abdication of intellectual ambition and social responsibility is unwarranted. If liberation theology is to do more than talk about liberation it must continue making the development of historical projects an integral part of the theological task. Thus the central contribution of this book lies in the demonstration that liberation theology can again place the development of historical projects at the heart of its self-understanding. What I take to be liberation theology's distinctive mark – the relating of theological concepts and ideals to institutions through the construction of historical projects – is thus recovered. Only then can the 'liberation' in liberation theology be more than an academic catchphrase. My purpose throughout, therefore, is not to criticize a flailing theology. My purpose is constructive: the refashioning of liberation theology for a new century but an old challenge, the liberation of the poor. Allow me to note that while my argument centers on Latin American liberation theology it has implications for liberation theologies generally. Indeed, I believe that most contemporary liberation theologies are 'liberation' theologies in name only. They cannot deliver on what they promise.

In the process of developing my wider constructive argument, I make six contributions to the study and task of liberation theology. First, I present liberation theology's three main responses to the fall of socialism. Today these responses remain unknown in the North Atlantic academy and unsystematized among the liberation theologians themselves. Second, I present liberation theology's two main methodological statements (only one of them known in the North Atlantic academy) and show that in their current form they are obstacles to the development of historical projects. Third, I compare liberation theology's understanding of democracy with that of mainstream North American social science, and update for the North Atlantic academy liberation theology's views on this topic beyond the early 1990s. Fourth, I present liberation theology's three main approaches to capitalism while suggesting that such approaches are another central obstacle in the development of historical projects. Two of these approaches remain unacknowledged in the North Atlantic academy and unsystematized within liberation theology itself. Fifth, I bring together for the first time liberation theology and Roberto Unger's social theory to provide the former with a new way to approach capitalism and society that makes possible historical projects. Finally, I relate my revised liberation theology to selected trends within contemporary theology.

The argument develops in the following fashion. In Chapter 1 I present liberation theology's three main responses to the fall of socialism: reasserting core ideas, revising basic categories and critiquing idolatry. In the process, I recover the intimate relationship between thinking about concepts such as the preferential option for the poor and liberation and thinking about institutions, a central element of early liberation theology once embodied in the notion of a 'historical project'. I argue that the loss of a historical project means the loss of a particular way of thinking about theological concepts which combined attention to both their ideal element and the concretization that might approach that ideal. I claim that the recovery of this link between ideals and institutions is the means to counter the cooption of liberation theology's language by opponents such as the International Monetary Fund and 'new liberationists', address the paucity of its constructive political proposals and strengthen its critique of idolatry

Chapter 2 argues that liberation theology must reassess the role of the social sciences and the placement of theology in its methodological statements. Currently the social sciences' only role within liberation theology lies as an aid for understanding the causes of oppression. Their use is pre-theological, theology proper lies in the rereading of Christian tradition and in the critique of idolatry. I argue that this restriction of the social sciences and delimitation of theology functions to enshrine liberation theology's inability to construct historical projects as good theology. It masks a vice as a virtue. Instead, I suggest that the construction of historical projects, and thus a constructive use for the social sciences, must be seen as intrinsic to doing liberation theology as theology. A less restrictive understanding of theology within liberation theology is required.

Chapter 3 argues that liberation theology can build on its insight that the analysis of democracy cannot be separated from the analysis of the economic basis of society. Here liberation theology opposes the dominant social science approach to democracy in Latin America, which subscribes to a minimalist procedural definition of democracy. I show that there are three phases in liberation theology's understanding of democracy: democracy via revolutionary socialism, democracy via the base communities and the current analysis of stagnant democracy. While the first two approaches contain elements critical of their context and constructive in relation to the future, the third approach is symbolic of our time in its inability to envision a more positive future.

In Chapter 4 I argue that liberation theology's approaches to the concept of capitalism – dependency theory, world system theory, the 'undertheorizing' of capitalism – have proved a hindrance to the development of new historical projects. I show that liberation theology theorizes capitalism as an abstractly defined, hegemonic and indivisible totality. Two consequences ensue: either there is no escape outside a radical revolutionary upheaval of existing society or, given the impossibility of revolution, only a willful and defiant resistance is possible from within hegemonic capitalism. In both cases, the imagination of historical projects remains paralyzed.

Chapter 5 argues that liberation theology can reread the fall of socialism as an opportunity to try out alternative approaches to capitalism. Drawing on recent post-structuralist social theory, comparative political economy and critical legal theory, I argue that without socialism as its opposed unified totality, capitalism too is deprived of its abstract unity. An approach that focused on the piecemeal traits hiding behind concepts such as capitalism and democracy would avoid dualisms such as capitalism/socialism, capitalism/life and even market/state. Instead, I appropriate Roberto Unger's practice of 'institutional imagination,' the step-by-step construction of political and economic alternatives, and his notion of 'alternative pluralisms,' the idea that representative democracies, market economies and civil societies can take different institutional forms. The task is thus no longer to counterpose two systems, such as capitalism/socialism or bourgeois democracy/participatory democracy, against each other but to find the gradual steps that will democratize access to political and economic opportunity. In this way the dual traps of resistance within an ultimately unchangeable system and millenarian revolutionary fervor are overcome.

In the final chapter I relate my reconstructed liberation theology to political theology, radical orthodoxy and Latina and Black theology. First, I argue that Johann Baptist Metz's separation of theology and historical projects functions to create a space where theology is excused from dealing with the reality of massive social misery. In his work theology, despite his own intentions, becomes an ideological crutch for an unjust status quo. Second, I evaluate radical orthodoxy's reconstruction of liberation theology. I argue that while radical orthodoxy may claim to refashion liberation theology for the 21st century, it is merely another example of the cooption previously attempted by the Vatican and the IMF. Within the radical orthodoxy reconstruction, the only thing left of liberation theology is its terminology. The words are there in letter only: the spirit is lost. Finally, I examine Maria Pilar Aquino's version of Latina theology and Dwight Hopkins' brand of Black theology from the perspective afforded by my argument. I suggest that as currently designed, their theologies are incapable of fulfilling their own promise of liberation. Their theologies too need to be reconstructed if they are to move from talking about liberation to actually being capable of furthering liberation where it matters most, in society. While I hope my argument may contribute to that task, the task itself is their own.

CHAPTER 1

Liberation Theology Today: the Missing Historical Project

Latin American liberation theology was born at the crossroads of a changing Catholic church and the revolutionary political–economic ferment of the late 1960s and early 1970s.[1] In the first case, the Second Vatican Council (1962–65) opened the door for a fundamental rethinking of the relation between Christian faith and the world by asserting the value of secular historical progress as part of God's work. Papal social encyclicals such as *Mater et Magistra, Pacem in Terris* and *Populorum Progressio* focused not just on worker's socioeconomic rights but also on the rights of poor nations in relation to rich nations. In addition, Vatican II gave greater freedom to national episcopates in applying church teaching to their particular contexts. In the second case, the Cuban revolution, the failure of the decade of development and Kennedy's 'Alliance for Progress', as well as the exhaustion of import substitution models of development led to the rejection of reformist measures to ameliorate the massive poverty that plagued Latin America.[2] Political and economic views became increasingly radical as groups of priests, workers and students organized in militant revolutionary groups that espoused socialism. At the same time, starting with Brazil in 1964, a succession of military coups led to the imposition of national security states. These two trends, religious and political, came together at the Second General Conference of Latin American Bishops (CELAM) at Medellin, Colombia in 1968. Documents from this meeting began by analyzing Latin America's social situation.[3] They argued that the continent suffers from an internal and external colonialism caused by a foreign exploitation that creates structures of institutionalized violence. Mere development, the documents asserted, could not overcome this condition of dependency. The concept of liberation emerged as an alternative.[4]

Liberation theology's foundational texts, those of its inception and expansion, were written from within this worldview.[5] They share the following presuppositions: (a) a sharp dichotomy between revolution and reformist political action, the first seen as necessary while the second is deemed as ineffectual or as an ideological smokescreen that supports the status quo; (b) the poor were seen as the primary, and at times exclusive, agents of social change; (c) a sharp dichotomy between socialism and capitalism, socialism as the social system that could remedy the injustice of the latter; and (d) priority was given to politics in the narrow sense of struggle over state power, with little attention to issues of gender, ecology, race and popular culture.

But liberation theology's historical context – that is, the sociopolitical and religious context within which liberation theologians work – has changed dramatically since the late 1960s and 1970s.[6] At the ecclesial level, the main changes lie in the rise of Pentecostal groups and the Vatican's clampdown on liberation theology by silencing theologians and replacing progressive bishops with conservative ones.[7] At the same time, however, Vatican documents have incorporated central liberationist concepts such as the preferential option for the poor and liberation. On the political and economic fronts, the first change lies in the collapse of socialism. In my mind, all the other changes need to be understood in relation to the demise of the socialist alternative. For liberation theology, the fall of the Berlin Wall represents the loss of a practical alternative to capitalism.[8] In fact, the prospect of an alternative seems to have disappeared from view. One has to go back to the beginning of industrial capitalism in the 19th century to find a similar period.[9] A second change lies in the perceived decline of the nation state's ability to control economic activity within its own boundaries. The third change lies in the upsurge of culture as a politically contested site and the subsequent downgrading of the traditional political sphere, the struggle for state power.[10]

Liberation theology finds itself on the defensive and is perceived as struggling to respond adequately to this new context. In this chapter I present and assess the three ways liberation theologians have responded to this situation: reasserting core ideas, revising or reformulating central categories and the critique of idolatry. Perhaps because the bulk of the material remains untranslated, these moves remain unrecognized in the North Atlantic academy; surprisingly however, they have yet to be properly theorized by the liberation theologians themselves. The chapter is divided into two parts. First, I present and critique the three positions; I will suggest that they all suffer from a common defect – the inability to devise concrete alternatives to the current social order. They are thus ultimately incapable of fulfilling liberation theology's promise, the promise of a theology that, not content merely to discourse about liberation, actually seeks to further liberation. Second, I turn to liberation theology's foundational texts to recover the idea of a historical project and suggest that the lack of this concept in recent work is both a symptom and a cause of its current impasse.

Current Responses in Liberation Theology

Liberation theologians have developed three moves in response to the fall of socialism and shift in their historical context. I call these moves 'reasserting core ideas', 'reformulating or revising basic categories', and 'critiquing idolatry', whether of the market or of modernity at large. While the same theologian may make more than one move in the same work, the differences in emphasis remain pertinent enough to separate analytically each position.

Reasserting Core Ideas

This position disentangles liberation theology's core ideas – concepts such as the preferential option for the poor, the reign of God and liberation – from Marxism as a social scientific mediation and socialism as a historical project.[11] It builds on a number of essays that sought to separate liberation theology from the death of socialism symbolized by the fall of the Berlin Wall.[12] The argument is simple and can be stated in three steps: (a) liberation theology was never intrinsically tied to any particular social–scientific mediation or historical project; (b) the discrediting of a particular mediation and/or historical project thus cannot affect liberation theology's core intuitions or ideas; (c) the current worldwide situation of growing inequality makes liberation theology's central intuitions as necessary as ever.

This position admits a change in the context within which liberation theology is done. According to Gustavo Gutiérrez:

> In the past years we have witnessed a series of economic, political, cultural and religious events, on both the international and the Latin American plane, which make us think that important aspects of the period in which liberation theology was born and developed have come to an end.... Before the new situations many of the affirmations and discussions of that time do not respond to today's challenges. Everything seems to indicate that a new period is beginning.[13]

Gutiérrez then separates the essential from the inessential in liberation theology:

> Theologies necessarily carry the mark of the time and ecclesial context in which they are born. They live insofar as the conditions that gave them birth remain. Of course, great theologies overcome, to an extent, those chronological and cultural boundaries, those of lesser weight – no matter how significant they might have been for a time – remain more subject to time and circumstance. We are referring, certainly, to the particular modes of a theology (immediate stimuli, analytical instruments, philosophical notions, and others), not to the fundamental affirmations concerning revealed truths.[14]

For Gutiérrez, in the particular case of liberation theology, that essential revealed truth 'revolves around the so-called preferential option for the poor. The option for the poor is radically evangelical, and thus constitutes an important criterion to separate the wheat from the chaff in the urgent events and currents of thought in our days'.[15] Notice that Gutiérrez distinguishes the revealed truths of theology from the vehicles that carry those truths. There is thus a distinction to be drawn between liberation theology's revealed content and the socioanalytical tools used to explicate that content. The discrediting of a particular mediation does not touch the preferential option for the poor as the core of liberation theology.

Jon Sobrino, like Gutiérrez, begins his reassertion of core ideas by stressing the need to rethink liberation theology in the light of current events.[16] He then proceeds to make the notion of 'liberation' the central element: 'What is specific to liberation theology goes beyond particular contents and consists of a concrete way of exercising intelligence guided by the *liberation principle*.'[17] For Sobrino 'liberation is not just a theme, even if the most important, but a starting point: it ignites an intellectual process and offers a permanent pathos and particular light. This ... is the fundamental aspect of liberation theology'.[18] Sobrino too, therefore, separates essential from inessential elements in liberation theology. Liberation is not a 'content' but a guiding light and principle. Liberation, therefore, cannot be tied down to any particular political program or philosophical analysis but precedes and guides them. They come afterwards; their failure does not disprove the guiding principle.[19]

José Maria Vigil provides a final example of the reassertion of core ideas. He stresses that liberation theology never had its own model of society, but had and continues to have a Christian utopia that orients its work within history.[20] For this reason, 'the crisis of the model of society inspired by socialism will inevitably reflect back on liberation theology, but at the level of its practical references rather than its principles'.[21] For Vigil, a 'strategy of liberation has failed, not Liberation itself'.[22] For him, 'if we wanted to express the paradigm in a word we would choose this one: the Reign! That would be liberation theology's paradigm, because it is, in reality, Jesus' paradigm!'[23] Vigil, given the separation between essential and inessential elements in liberation theology, draws the same conclusion as Gutiérrez and Sobrino: 'We will be able to (and will have to) update as much as necessary at the level of theology's mediations, but we have the feeling that the paradigm itself remains undefeated.'[24]

To recapitulate the first position outlined: one strategy pursued by theologians in the face of the shift in their political, economic and cultural context lies in the reassertion of liberation theology's core ideas. The theologian separates a central element, whether it be the preferential option for the poor, liberation or the Reign of God, and asserts that despite all this element remains untouched. The impulse behind this position is correct. It is true that liberation theology, despite what many critics claim, rarely fully identified with any mediation or historical project. Thus the discrediting of such a mediation does not touch the heart of liberation theology with its focus on the poor, the construction of God's reign and liberation. Liberation theologians are right to argue that in an increasingly divided world these elements remain as necessary as ever. The way these elements are defended, however, exacts too high a cost. What allows this position to work is the emptying of the idea defended. It is no longer clear what the preferential option for the poor, the Reign of God and liberation mean in practice without the incorporation of some sort of social scientific mediation, whether Marxist or not; without such mediation it remains impossible to provide alternatives to the current global order.

All three theologians tacitly acknowledge the need for new mediations but make no headway in their incorporation. Sobrino writes that 'liberation theology makes of God's Reign its central content and conceives itself as the adequate theory for its construction'.[25] Construction, however, requires more than the reactive and rearguard defense of a set of theological concepts. Gutiérrez, drawing on indigenous culture's focus on solidarity and reciprocity, calls for an ethic of solidarity that can inspire a popular economics.[26] The vagueness of the proposal, however, does little to advance the claimed necessary refashioning of liberation theology for this millennium.[27] While necessary, and presupposed by the other positions to be reviewed, this move remains incomplete.

Revising Basic Categories

Position two, the revision of some of liberation theology's basic categories, takes the first move reviewed a step further. It accepts the thesis that liberation theology's central ideas remain essential in today's context. However, unlike position one, position two begins to reformulate aspects of early liberation theology – the focus on revolution, the understanding of the poor as history's driving force, the emphasis on capturing state power – in order to open a space for the implementation of new sociopolitical, economic and cultural mediations.

Pedro Trigo is the most influential exponent of this position.[28] The centerpiece of his reformulation lies in staking out an alternative to both early liberation theology's revolutionary worldview and what he perceives as the contemporary market-oriented neoliberal worldview. For Trigo, liberation theology made 'the people' (*el pueblo*) the revolutionary subject of the underside of history.[29] This people was conceived as the engine of revolutionary change and historical salvation, a unified subject whose interests were those of humanity at large. This understanding of a historical subject, according to Trigo, lies discredited. The contemporary social imaginary, however, is that of a marketplace where each individual buys and sells different products, from appliances to eschatological and political salvation. Every alternative to this marketplace, whether political, economic or cultural, already falls within it. For this social imaginary, therefore, there is no underside of history.[30] In principle everyone is included, although some have more influence than others. While the first option dangerously exaggerates the role of the poor in history, creating a monolithic subject with a blank check to refashion society in a totalitarian fashion, the second option is a model based on the exchange of goods and services the poor do not possess. Tacitly excluded from the market, the poor are in fact excluded from society. For Trigo, if these are the only two social imaginaries available – the people as revolutionary subject and engine of history or a market model in which the poor are apparently included but in reality excluded – then 'liberation theology has no future'.[31]

Trigo's proposal begins by rejecting the market model of society and basing a new social imaginary on the concept of 'humanity'.[32] The market model is 'based on the image of an athletic track, in which each athlete runs on his own'.[33] In this model relationships are secondary and derivative of individuals. As the absolute standpoint, the individual voluntarily chooses whether to enter into a social contract with others. Instead, Trigo argues that humanity, as a collective, is primary, that 'each human being, from the very beginning of his or her life, is found in a fundamental unity with everyone else.... Society is a bodily reality, a social body'.[34] For Trigo, the notion of humanity as a social body means that human life possesses an unavoidable social dimension.[35] By 'the underside of history', Trigo thus means the perspective of those who have been marginalized. Since relation is primary, marginalization requires having been actively excluded from society, while in the market model where the individual is primary and stands up and against society, marginalization stems from the refusal to establish social bonds. The underside of history, therefore, is the standpoint of those excluded from the social body, witnesses to the violation of a common humanity.

While the concept of humanity is the centerpiece of Trigo's rejection of the market imaginary, the concept of 'everyday life' is the cornerstone of his reformulation of liberation theology. As seen, Trigo rejects the notion of the poor as a revolutionary subject. Such a notion implies that the poor live only at extraordinary moments in history, and discounts the everyday processes of survival, resistance and creation present in marginalized communities. Such a notion also ignores the role of popular culture in sustaining community. Instead, Trigo insists that everyday life is the preferred venue through which the poor act: 'As we have been describing the historical strength of the poor, it becomes clear that its privileged sphere is everyday life and its densest result is to recreate, heal and strengthen the social fabric.'[36] Resistance, in this case, is 'not an ideological declaration of principles nor can be reduced to a political program. Resistance occurs in everyday life, it is found in the cyclical rituals of community life'.[37] While liberation theology has traditionally privileged the political sphere, Trigo's reformulation widens the area of possible resistance and change:[38] 'We insist that the historical strength of the poor is not exercised in politics as a privileged realm but in the sphere of everyday life recreating, healing and strengthening the social fabric.'[39] The flourishing of civil society – through the creation of myriad social organizations independent of the state but coordinated among themselves – is more important than the conquest of governmental power.[40] The poor are no longer the exclusive privileged subjects of liberation; they are, however, an integral part of a subject that must be wider in scope, including the world's poor communities as well as professionals from both the poor and rich nations, 'the international of life'.[41]

To recapitulate position two: this position accepts the thesis that liberation theology's core ideas – the preferential option for the poor, liberation and the Reign of God – remain relevant in the current historical context. Position two goes beyond position one, however, in reformulating other aspects of liberation theology. To date, that reformulation focuses on the rejection of a unified revolutionary subject of history, the refusal to accept the dichotomy of reform and revolution, and an espousal of popular culture and civil society as the privileged arenas for liberation. Each point is important. The rejection of the poor or the people as a unified revolutionary subject avoids an idealization of the poor as a class as well as the temptation toward revolutionary violence. No class fully embodies history.

Rejecting an understanding of the poor as a unified subject also forces the recognition that social progress requires an alliance across different social groups both within the nation and worldwide, hence Trigo's 'international of life'. The rejection of the dichotomy between revolution and reform makes piecemeal change, often belittled by liberation theologians, as valid as it is necessary. Revolution is also usually understood as requiring an intellectual vanguard that will lead the people and thus suffers from an ingrained elitist bias. This too is rejected, placing change in the hands of communities on the ground.[42] Finally, the turn toward civil society stems from the previous two points. It is in civil society that different groups come together – women, indigenous peoples, the underclass, ecological activists – to demand rights. Here wider social alliances can take place.[43]

While position two's intent to revise and construct is valid, current attempts suffer from a number of problems. First, the exaltation of civil society as the new venue for radical politics may well be the product of wishful thinking. Trigo, for example, claims that 'this network of communities and groups constitutes the creation of the historical power of the poor, fed by faith and popular religion. As it becomes denser it diversifies until it covers educational, formative, recreational, productive, and health aspects, as well as religious ones. And this diversity is kept connected by a deepening of the fraternal relations that are cultivated starting from the community'.[44] Scannone too claims that 'the universal phenomena of the rise of civil society is also found in our Latin America',[45] but social science literature on Latin America documents the increasing political apathy of the majority of the population.[46] The disarticulation of social groups rather than their growth seems to be the trend. Second, the exclusive focus on civil society downplays the continued importance of structural, political and economic change. For Trigo, the solidarity of inhabitants of the rich countries:

> with the poor of the world must reach and transform their own cultural being. It is not a matter of their giving their free time or their economic surplus but that they be different citizens within their own nations, their political communities, and culture. They have to rediscover in their histories an alternative tradition and recreate it to become what they are (political and cultural beings) in a different manner, that is, to put forth in those communities potentialities left aside or untried, so that those political and cultural communities can transform themselves.[47]

While it is true that fundamental change requires a conversion in outlook, the focus on civil society exhibits a puzzling lack of political and economic analysis. Position two also goes too far in downplaying the importance of state power. The ability of civil society to flourish is tied to the legal regulatory framework of the state.[48] Reform needs to occur from the top down as well as from the bottom up. Finally, it remains an open question whether the focus on civil society and the fostering of myriad social organizations is not, in reality, the expression of liberation theology's political defeat.[49] Today, at a time when no wide ranging alternatives to capitalism appear on the horizon, there seems to be no other choice than to call for conversion and concertation at the community level. The exaltation of civil society and corresponding demotion of liberation theology's political ambition, therefore, comes dangerously close to making a virtue out of necessity.

Critiquing Idolatry

Position three develops a critique of the idolatrous nature of capitalism and modernity more generally. Like the first position reviewed, this position's argument can be stated in three steps: (a) for liberation theology God is a God of life; (b) an idol is a God to whom lives are sacrificed; (c) capitalism and modernity are examples of idols since they take priority over human life.[50] Franz Hinkelammert is the most influential exponent of this strand of liberation theology.[51]

In his essay, 'Liberation Theology in the Economic and Social Context of Latin America: Economy and Theology, or the Irrationality of the Rationalized', Hinkelammert examines the different ways liberation theology has been combated throughout its development. He then identifies a recent shift in the strategy through which liberation theology is opposed.[52] Today, he argues, opposition no longer takes the form of denouncing liberation theology for its attempts to begin to realize God's kingdom materially, but instead takes the form of coopting its understanding of the relation between God's kingdom and history as well as its basic terminology. Hinkelammert takes as his example a speech delivered by Michael Camdessus, then head of the International Monetary Fund, at a Congress for French Christian businessmen. Camdessus explains:

> Surely the Kingdom is a place: these new Heavens and this new earth of which we are called to enter one day, a sublime promise; but the Kingdom is in some way geographical, the Reign is history, a history in which we are the actors, one which is in process and that is close to us since Jesus came into human history. The Reign is what happens when God is King and we recognize Him as such, and we make possible the extension, spreading of this reign, like a spot of oil, impregnating, renewing and unifying human realities. 'Let Thy Kingdom come.'[53]

Note the conception of history at work in Camdessus' speech. God's reign is a promise, but a promise that is part of history, a history that has a time and a place in this world. God's reign, moreover, is one that is brought about at least partly by our own actions; we are also responsible for the extension of that Kingdom. The conception of history in relation to God is the same as liberation theology's. Camdessus continues by addressing the businessmen present directly:

> Our mandate? ... It is a text of Isaiah which Jesus explained; it says (Luke 4, 16–23): 'The spirit of the Lord is upon me. He has anointed me in order to announce the good news to the Poor, to proclaim liberation to captives and the return of sight to the blind, to free the oppressed and proclaim the year of grace

granted by the Lord.' And Jesus had one short response: 'Today this message is fulfilled for you that you should listen.' This today is our today and we are part of this grace of God, we who are in charge of the economy (the administrators of a part of it in any case): the alleviation of suffering for our brothers and the procurers of the expansion of their liberty. It is we who have received the Word. This Word can change everything. We know that God is with us in the work of spreading brotherhood.[54]

In his speech, Camdessus makes the IMF God's vehicle on earth. He takes central tenets of liberation theology – the focus on the poor, the Reign of God, liberation – to develop a theology whose practical political outcome is support for the very same structural adjustment policies denounced by liberation theologians. Hinkelammert draws two crucial consequences. First, 'the fact that these two contrary theologies [the theology of the IMF and liberation theology] cannot be distinguished on the level of a clearly theological discussion stands out. At this level liberation theology does not visibly distinguish itself from the anti-theology presented by the IMF. The conflict seems to be over the application of a theology shared by both sides'.[55] Second, 'imperial theology is in agreement with the preferential option for the poor and with the economic and social incarnation of God's Kingdom. It presents itself as the only realistic path for fulfilling those demands ... the option for the poor can no longer identify any specification and natural affinity for liberation theology. Now the question is over the realism of the concretization'.[56]

In response to this situation, Hinkelammert outlines a critique of neoliberal market economy's utopianization of the market. The critique takes two steps, one that points out the internal contradictions within capitalism itself and another that expresses that contradiction and its consequences in theological terms. In the first place, Hinkelammert argues that capitalism's understanding of efficiency, measured as it is exclusively according to profitability, is both inefficient and irrational. For Hinkelammert, 'the exclusion of a growing number of persons from the economic system, the destruction of the natural bases of life ... are the nonintentional results of this reduction of rationality to rentability. The market laws of total capitalism destroy society and its natural environment'.[57] Capitalism, therefore, is not a rational system. On the contrary, it is irrational in that it is self-destructive. Any system whose laws threaten the economic and ecological basis of human life is irrational; the market cannot be universalized without destroying the human and natural foundation upon which it is based. Second, drawing from Paul's 'Letter to the Romans', Hinkelammert develops the theological interpretation of his critique: 'Paul makes visible that the law ... leads those who fulfill it or who are obliged to fulfill it to death'.[58] Liberation theology can draw from Paul's understanding of the relationship between the law and human life:

> Christian freedom returns, therefore, in the sense pronounced by Paul, as a freedom that is sovereign before the law. The free subjects are free to the degree that they are able to make the law relative with respect to their own needs....

Considering market-based law, freedom consists precisely in being able to
subordinate and even to break the law, if the needs of the subject demand it.[59]

Hinkelammert places two Gods and two laws against each other. Liberation
theology's God is a God of life and thus its ultimate law lies in what benefits human
beings. Such a God never imposes a law that ends in death. Freedom, in fact, is the
freedom to break those laws that lead to death. But opposite the God of life lurks
capitalism as God. The extension of capitalism's law of profitability requires the
increasing poverty of the great majority of humankind; capitalism requires human
sacrifices to flourish. For Hinkelammert, sovereignty from the law differentiates
liberation theology's preferential option for the poor from imperial theology's. In
liberation theology, life comes first and the law is judged by its contribution to
human wellbeing. In imperial theology – the theology of capitalism – the market
law of profitability is the standard by which life is measured. Here the law is never
relativized. It stands absolute even before increasing human misery and ecological
destruction.

To recapitulate position three: this position's starting point is the recognition that
modernity is idolatrous rather than secularized.[60] It thus makes the critique of
modernity's idols – capitalism, the market, socialism – the central task.[61] Critique
takes place by unmasking the sacrificial logic behind the idol.[62] For liberation
theology, God is a God of life. Idols, on the other hand, require human sacrifices.
Idolatry is present when upholding a law is placed above human life. Christian
freedom lies in refusing to follow laws that lead to death. Sin, in this case, comes
from upholding the law. So, in the case of capitalism, profitability requires laying
off workers. Profit takes priority over life. Socialism too suffered from the same
logic. Here profitability was pursued by the forced uprooting of entire communities
and their reorganization according to laws that were supposed to lead to greater
efficiency.[63] Position three's strength lies in recognizing that theology cannot be
limited to a narrowly defined religious sphere: the most dangerous idols, those that
affect the greatest number of people, hide behind a secular disguise that must be
unmasked.[64]

Note that Hinkelammert's analysis of the cooption of liberation theology's
terminology reveals the limited contribution of position one: reasserting core ideas.
The heart of position one was the attempt to protect liberation theology's core ideas
from the fall of socialism. But today even liberation theology's opponents espouse
those ideas. The International Monetary Fund wholeheartedly accepts the
preferential option for the poor, liberation and the construction of God's reign.[65]
Liberation theology's basic ideas do not need safeguarding at the level of their
reassertion. What they require is redefinition through the incorporation of new
social scientific and cultural mediations. As Hinkelammert highlights, the problem
becomes one of differentiating the same theological concept – be it liberation, the
preferential option or the reign of God – by imbuing it with different political,
economic, social and cultural content. The attempt to revise basic categories moves

in this direction but does not go far enough. Hinkelammert's solution, however, is inadequate as well. His argument develops life as the absolute criterion by which society is judged. But liberation theology's opponents would agree with this criterion. The disagreement begins with the problem of what institutions best serve the goal of enabling human life.[66] The real question comes after the critique of idolatry: what do we do instead? What can we propose? In addition, the concept of an idol is the negative counterpart to a positive affirmation. If the idol is the only available option it is not really an idol but becomes necessary: it becomes a god. To show the idol as idol, alternatives are needed. Criteria must be able to distinguish between viable options. A key problem, therefore, lies in the lack of viable options.[67]

The Missing Historical Project

Missing from all three positions – the reassertion of core ideas, the revision of basic categories and the critique of idolatry – is a concept once central to liberation theology, the notion of a 'historical project'. The rest of this chapter, and the book as a whole, seeks to outline an alternative position that recovers for this concept the central place and role it had during liberation theology's heyday. Within liberation theology, historical projects brought together thinking about theological categories or ideals such as the preferential option and liberation and thinking about institutions. More specifically, historical projects served the following purposes. First, they were the key way that liberation theology sought to pursue liberation concretely. Liberation had a material and social element that had to be incarnated in the political and economic institutions that make up society. Second, historical projects were the means to give content to liberation theology's theological terms. It was through the development of historical projects that liberation theologians thought through their theological terms, giving them a greater degree of specificity and thus protecting themselves from groups who ostensibly thought alike but in practice espoused different goals. The third function of the historical project, therefore, was one of differentiation between groups that at face value held the same ideals but differed in the understanding of their practical import. The problem of differentiation and cooption that Hinkelammert identifies is not a new problem but one that was understood and resolved through historical projects. Finally, historical projects combated two types of idolatry, the idolatry of society as it stands and the idolatry of future revolutionary plans.

In his classic *Doing Theology in a Revolutionary Situation*, José Míguez Bonino explains:

> 'Historical project' is an expression frequently used in our discussions as a midway term between an utopia, a vision which makes no attempt to connect itself historically to the present, and a program, a technically developed model for the organization of society. A historical project is defined enough to force

> options in terms of the basic structures of society. It points in a given direction.
> But frequently its contents are expressed in symbolical and elusive forms rather
> than in terms of precise technical language.... It is in this general sense that we
> speak of a Latin American socialist project of liberation.[68]

For Bonino, in the late 1960s and early 1970s, the historical project included seven
elements.[69] First, it involved a rejection of 'developmentalist' attempts to solve Latin
American political and economic woes through further integration into the
international capitalist system. Latin America must break away and follow a path
independent from (but not necessarily isolated from) the 'Empires'. Second, element
one is only viable with a parallel social revolution within Latin American society
itself. The great majority of Latin Americans need to be mobilized politically to
remove from power the oligarchic elites that cooperate with foreign interests. Third,
while acknowledging the dangers in such a move, Bonino claims that a strong
centralized state is required to overcome foreign and local resistance to such a
program. Fourth, change needs to occur not just from the top down but from the
bottom up. The people themselves must be awakened to their condition of oppression
and thus also to the need they have to participate in their own emancipation. This
process is termed *conscientization* or *politicization*. Fifth, owing to the fact that a
transfer of power among segments of the population is necessary, primary emphasis
is given to the political sphere. Changes in all other spheres, whether technical,
cultural, social or economic, are subordinate to the political.[70] Sixth, the historical
project involved the search for an authentic Latin American socialism that met the
needs of the continent. Bonino stresses that liberation theology rejects all dogmatism
(Marxist or otherwise) in this search. No model (Eastern Europe or Cuba) is a
stereotype to be copied. Seventh, development must be understood as wider than
mere economic change. In the end, 'liberation is the process through which and in
which a "new man" must emerge, a man shaped by solidarity and creativity over
against the individualistic, distorted humanity of the present system'.[71]

   These, therefore, are the elements Bonino sets up as liberation theology's
historical project. My interest, however, lies not in the specific content of the
historical project but in the role it played in liberation theology's self-definition.
Despite having fallen from use, the notion of a historical project was central to
liberation theology's own understanding of itself. Bonino's debate with Jürgen
Moltmann – liberation theology and political theology – serves as one example.[72]
As the major European progressive theology of the time, German political theology
was a source for liberation theology. At the same time, however, liberation theology
consciously defined itself *against* political theology. Liberation theology's
disagreement with political theology revolves around the relationship between
God's reign and politics and at the center of this dispute lay the notion of a historical
project. This was the main dividing issue. Bonino asks: 'Do historical happenings,
i.e., historical human action in its diverse dimensions – political, cultural, economic
– have any value in terms of the Kingdom which God prepares and will gloriously

establish in the Parousia of the Lord?'[73] He notes that Moltmann and Metz explicate the relationship between politics and God's reign with terms like 'anticipation', 'sketch', and 'analogy'. The result is that there is no causal connection between the two. Bonino concludes: 'In other words, historical action is not really significant for the Kingdom; at most, it may succeed to project provisory images which remind us of it. These images must not be taken too seriously in order to avoid absolutizing them. The historical significance of the expectation of the Kingdom is preeminently to protect us from any too strong commitment to a present *historical project!*' (emphasis added).[74] Note how Bonino understands the connection between a historical project and God's reign as much closer than does Moltmann.[75] For Moltmann, God's reign serves a critical function that keeps us from turning any earthly project into an idol. There is thus an absolute distinction between God's reign and a historical project. For Bonino and liberation theology, however, such an absolute distinction pushes theology into the hands of the status quo: 'we believe that European theologians must de-sacralize their conception of "critical freedom" and recognize the human, ideological contents it carries. When they conceive critical freedom as the form in which God's eschatological Kingdom impinges on the political realm, they are simply opting for *one* particular ideology, that of liberalism'.[76] Liberation theology's first point against political theology, therefore, is that there is no standpoint that escapes thinking in terms of historical projects. For the simple reason that theological concepts have political import, every theology is tied to a historical project, whether that project is explicitly stated or not. The very attempt to stand above and relativize all human politics ends by supporting one particular historical project, that of the status quo.

Bonino also argues that liberation theology's central theological terms cannot be properly understood independent of a historical project. Referring to Moltmann's *The Crucified God*, Bonino states, 'Moltmann ... names five "demonic circles of death" under which man suffers: poverty, violence, racial and cultural deprivation, industrial destruction of nature and meaninglessness or Godforsakenness. Consequently, justice, democracy, cultural identity, peace with nature and meaningful life are the concrete contents of historical hope. Quite clearly this brings us to the area of politics.'[77] Bonino adds:

> Can we remain satisfied with a general description of the 'demonic circles of death', without trying to understand them in their unity, their roots, their dynamics, i.e., without giving a coherent socio-analytical account of this manifold oppression? Are we not taking lightly the stark historical reality of the cross when we satisfy ourselves with an impressionistic description of man's alienation and misery? In other words, it seems that, if theology means to take history seriously, it must incorporate – with all the necessary *caveats* – a coherent and all-embracing method of sociopolitical analysis.[78]

It is only by this incorporation that the 'failure to give a concrete content to "identification with the oppressed"' can be avoided.[79] Bonino further insists:

> it is indeed possible and necessary to underline a continuum, a direction and a purpose in God's historical action...which is conveyed through such expressions and symbols as 'justice', 'peace', 'redemption', in their concrete biblical 'illustrations'. At the same time, *it is equally necessary to stress the fact that such insights cannot be operative except in terms of historical projects* which must incorporate, and indeed always do incorporate, an analytical and ideological human, secular, verifiable dimension. (Emphasis added.)[80]

The historical project, therefore, is needed to give content to theological terms. Without the historical project terms such as liberation, the preferential option for the poor or the reign of God lack concrete content.

Hugo Assmann also places the development of a historical project at the center of liberation theology's self-understanding. For him:

> *We must go back to essentials, and stress what distinguishes theological reflection in Latin America from that of the affluent nations.* This, to my mind, lies in the fact that we have assimilated – somewhat confusedly, maybe, but still characteristically and effectively – three levels of approach necessary for historical reflection on faith as the practice of liberation. If theological reflection is to be historically and practically valid, then it has to operate on these three levels, which are: 1. The level of social, economic and political analysis; the level, that is, of an attempt at rational interpretation of the reality of history – which in itself implies an ethical and political decision in the very selection of the instruments of analysis, since these can never be completely neutral. 2. The level of opting for particular political theories and approaches. These could be 'imposed' by the results of the initial work of analysis, but their choice is also determined by an ethical element not derived from the analysis itself: man's capacity for making himself responsible for history. 3. The level of strategy and tactics. The general political theories require planned implementation, and this implies obedience and discipline – to borrow traditional terms – within an effective form of political action. (Emphasis added.)[81]

For Assmann, therefore, the political dimension of faith 'implies a consciousness of *the fact that the real act of faith, as a concrete bodily realization of a praxis placed within the historical process, always includes an option related to historical projects*' (emphasis added).[82] He insists that 'the abstract option has to be translated into real action according to the circumstances. There can be no real commitment to liberate one's country on the general level alone'.[83] He is well aware of the danger of vacuity in the rhetoric of 'liberation'. Without a historical project, the very language of 'liberation' loses its specificity and can be taken up by groups with agendas different from that of liberation theology.[84] Indeed, Assmann suggests that the deepest divisions in the Latin American church revolve not around concepts such as the preferential option or liberation, but around fundamental differences in the historical projects through which those concepts are to be enacted in practice.[85]

Gustavo Gutiérrez also suggests that the political and economic level embodied by the historical project plays a key role in differentiating between different Christian groups and different theologies. He writes:

In our context the central question is not how to talk about God in a world come of age, as it was for progressive theology ... Our question is how to tell the non-person, the non-human, that God is love and that love makes us all brothers and sisters. The experience and reflection of faith that starts from here will not situate itself only on a religious plane, like that which starts from the critique of atheism. In this context the hiatus is not in the first place between believers and non-believers, but between oppressors and oppressed. And among the oppressors are those 'who call themselves Christians' as Bartolome de las Casas would say. *In contradistinction to what happens at the level of the critique of religion by modernity, where the religious creates a division between persons that share the same lifestyle and the same social world, here oppressors and oppressed 'share' the same faith. But they are separated on the economic, social and political planes; here, in this sphere, one group exploits the other*. (Emphasis added.)[86]

Christian groups are differentiated through the particular type of historical project, self-consciously developed or not, they espouse. This division between believers also translates to a division between types of theology which is at least partly a political division: 'The rupture between traditional and progressive theologies with liberation theology is not just theological. There is first a political rupture without which liberation theology's effort to rethink the struggle of the poor and oppressed of this world cannot be understood'.[87] Once again, for Gutiérrez modern theology situates the theological debate on the terrain of religion's philosophical presuppositions. Liberation theology's problems are different. The issue of the non-person 'moves ... at the economic, social and political levels. It is not a non-theological discussion, as some who seek an easy way out seem to think, but a different type of theology. The hiatus is here given with clarity in the real world, where people live and die, believe and hope, without hiding social conflict behind generic affirmations of false universalism'.[88]

Among liberation theology's founding fathers, Gutiérrez best systematizes the relationship between the concept of liberation and historical projects. In *A Theology of Liberation* he outlines three levels of liberation.[89] On a first level, he writes, liberation 'expresses the aspirations of oppressed peoples and social classes, emphasizing the conflictual aspect of the economic, social and political process which puts them at odds with wealthy nations and oppressive classes'.[90] On a second level, liberation is applied to an understanding of history. Here 'man is seen as assuming conscious responsibility for his own destiny ... The gradual conquest of true freedom leads to the creation of a new man and a qualitatively different society'.[91] On a third and final level, liberation allows for a different approach to biblical sources. Now, 'Christ is presented as the one who brings us liberation. Christ the Savior liberates man from sin, which is the ultimate root of all disruption of friendship and of all injustice and oppression'.[92] For Gutiérrez, while these levels can be held analytically distinct they are really part of a single process. Holding them together allows the theologian to avoid 'idealist and spiritualist approaches, which are nothing but ways of evading a harsh and demanding reality, and second, shallow analyses and programs of short-term effect, initiated under the pretext of meeting immediate needs'.[93] Note, therefore, that the notion of liberation needs to bring together two elements. On the one hand, it must be given enough specificity so that it actually directly addresses, rather than glosses over, real oppression and suffering. On the other hand, however, liberation cannot be just a governmental program of immediate assistance. While liberation is not just political, there is an irreducible political element to the concept.

Later in his argument, Gutiérrez connects his notion of liberation to the idea of a historical project. For Gutiérrez, '*the mediation of the historical project* of the creation of a new man assures that liberation from sin and communion with God in solidarity with all men – manifested in political liberation and enriched by its contributions – does not fall into idealism and evasion' (emphasis added).[94] At the same time, because the historical project is not merely a political program but also a movement towards an ultimately just society '*this mediation* [the historical project] keeps us from any confusion of the Kingdom with any one historical stage, from any idolatry toward unavoidably ambiguous human achievement, from any absolutizing of revolution' (emphasis added).[95] The historical project is thus intimately linked to the idea of liberation. It is, in fact, what allows the notion of liberation to address current society and yet not be reduced to a particular political program. It protects us from a dual idolatry – of society as it now stands by providing an alternative vision, and idolatry of any future social form by remembering that any such vision is ultimately provisional and incomplete.

Bonino, Assmann and Gutiérrez all make of the notion of a historical project a defining point of liberation theology's self-understanding. For all of them liberation theology must think through its theological categories and ideals in relation to institutions, the development of historical projects emerges as central to the task of liberation theology as theology. For Bonino, the place of historical projects in theology is the centerpiece of his dispute with political theology. In his view, theology cannot find a position above a historical project. The historical project is either explicitly developed and theorized or is implicitly hidden. In the latter case, the project usually ends by tacitly supporting the status quo. For Assmann too, the connection between theology and a historical project differentiates liberation theology from other theologies. Gutiérrez develops these insights in a more systematic fashion. He links the notion of a historical project to the concept of liberation. Without a historical project, liberation and its three intertwined elements either loses its connection to the real world or too quickly identifies itself with a political program. The historical project protects theology from the idolatry of society as it stands and the idolatry of future, short-term, revolutionary plans. Without a historical project liberation theology's key concepts lose specificity, become vacuous and are easily taken over by other groups.[96] For all three the only way to truly understand and begin to realize their theological categories and realize their religious ideals is to think them through in relation to historical projects.

Conclusion

Liberation theology's challenge, famously expressed by Gustavo Gutiérrez, comes from the non-person or the non-human, the human being who is not recognized as such by the prevailing social order.[97] Let me here give a dramatic example of what Gutiérrez had in mind. It would take six billion dollars of additional yearly investment to ensure basic education in all developing countries; eight billion dollars a year are spent on cosmetics in the United States. It would take nine billion to ensure clean water and sanitation for all; 11 billion are spent on ice cream in Europe. It would take 13 billion dollars to guarantee basic health and nutrition for every person in the developing world; 17 billion are spent on pet food in Europe and the United States combined. It would take approximately an additional 40 billion dollars to achieve universal access to basic social services, 0.1 per cent of the world's income, a rounding error, would cover the bill for basic education, health, nutrition, clean water and sanitation for every single person on the planet. Yet currently, while the world's richest nations possess only one-fourth of the world's population, they consume 70 per cent of the world's energy, 75 per cent of its metals, 85 per cent of its wood and 60 per cent of its food.[98] Gutiérrez's choice of the term 'non-human' is not a rhetorical flourish intended to provoke; it is a literal description of a terrible reality. The people the above data refer to are quite literally lacking personhood, they are quite literally non-human, in the basic sense that their needs do not count at all for the way the world's resources are distributed.

Yet the three main moves in contemporary liberation theology are not up to the severity of this challenge. These trends – reasserting core ideas, revising central categories and critiquing idolatry – share a common flaw: they are incapable of moving from critique to the construction of alternatives that could give concepts such as 'liberation' and 'the preferential option for the poor' renewed vigor. In this chapter, a first step in addressing this situation, I went back to liberation theology's foundational works to show that in the past it was the concept of a historical project that gave concrete content to liberation theology's terminology. It is through the recovery of this concept that liberation theology can resolve its two main (and interrelated) dilemmas: its political paralysis and the cooption of its vocabulary. It is by thinking about theological ideals in relation to thinking about institutions that liberation theology can develop alternatives to the current order and thus respond to the challenge posed by the non-human.

Of course, the shift in the political, economic, social and cultural context within which liberation theologians work has been massive. Today there just is no ready-made historical project such as socialism on the horizon that liberation theology can embrace. This situation, however, need not be a cause for abandoning the development of new historical projects. In fact, the rest of this book will show that the main obstacles toward such development do not come from the shift in context but rather are internal to liberation theology itself. Here is cause for hope. Liberation theology can adapt the stoic distinction between what depends on us and what does not to focus less on the external constraints and more on its own internal deficiencies.[99] This book does just that to develop one path toward recovering the key role historical projects played in liberation theology.

Notes

1 I provide a cursory measure of historical background so the reader can better grasp the shift in liberation theology's context. I draw on Arthur McGovern, *Liberation Theology and Its Critics: Toward an Assessment* (Maryknoll, NY: Orbis Books, 1989), 4–11. McGovern's first chapter is the best quick introduction to the movement's history until the early 1980s. Another fine book with a longer and more detailed historical survey is Christian Smith, *The Emergence of Liberation Theology: Radical Religion and Social Movement Theory* (Chicago: University of Chicago Press, 1991). A good overview in Spanish can be found in Enrique Dussel, *Teología de la Liberación: Un Panorama de Su Desarrollo* (Ciudad de Mexico: Potrerillos Editores, 1995).

2 For a good, succinct examination of import substitution industrialization (ISI) see Ray Kiely, *Industrialization and Development: A Comparative Analysis* (London: UCL Press Limited, 1998), 83–97. For an evaluation of the current state of development studies see Ray Kiely, *Sociology and Development: The Impasse and Beyond* (London: UCL Press Limited, 1995) and Richard Peet and Elaine Hartwick, *Theories of Development* (New York: The Guilford Press, 1999).

3 The documents can be found in Joseph Gremillion (ed.), *The Gospel of Peace and Justice: Catholic Social Teaching Since Pope John* (Maryknoll, NY: Orbis Books, 1976).

4 As McGovern notes, liberation combined a sociopolitical sense with the biblicotheological sense of God acting in history to save people from all enslavement (McGovern, *Liberation Theology*, 9).

5 One can divide liberation theology into four phases: its gestation (1962–68), a period of rapid growth (1968–79), its consolidation (1979–87) and one of revision (1987–present). See João Batista Libanio, 'Panorama de la Teología de América Latina en los Ultimos Veinte Años,' *Cambio Social y Pensamiento Cristiano en América Latina*, ed. José Comblin, José I. González Faus and Jon Sobrino (Madrid: Editorial Trotta, 1993), 57–78.

6 Two of liberation theology's major congresses were held at the Escorial in Spain, one in 1972 and the other in 1992. The differences in the historical context and the expositions of the liberation theologians themselves comes out in a comparison of the two offshoot volumes. See *Fe Cristiana y Cambio Social en América Latina* (Salamanca: Ediciones Sigueme, 1973) and José Comblin, José I. González Faus and Jon Sobrino (eds), *Cambio Social y Pensamiento Cristiano en América Latina* (Madrid: Editorial Trotta, 1993). See also José Comblin, *Called for Freedom: The Changing Context of Liberation Theology*, trans. Phillip Berryman (Maryknoll, NY: Orbis Books, 1998)

7 Michael Löwy, for example, argues that 'the main challenge to liberationist Christianity is Rome's neo-conservative offensive in Latin America' (Michael Löwy, *The War of Gods: Religion and Politics in Latin America*, New York: Verso, 1996), 131.

8 For one expression of this sentiment, see José Gomez Caffarena, 'Diálogos y Debates', *Cambio Social y Pensamiento Cristiano en América Latina*, ed. José Comblin, José I. González Faus and Jon Sobrino (Madrid: Editorial Trotta, 1993), 330. For another expression, this time from a philosopher, see Santiago Castro-Gomez, *Crítica de la Razón Latinoamericana* (Barcelona: Puvill Libros, S.A., 1996), 16.

9 Ramesh Mishra, *Globalization and the Welfare State* (Cheltenham: Edward Elgar Publishing Limited, 1999), 1–3.

10 See Comblin, *Called for Freedom*, xv–xix, for a more detailed exposition of each one of these points.

11 Cardinal Joseph Ratzinger: 'The fall of the European governmental systems based on Marxism turned out to be a kind of twilight of the gods for that theology'. Joseph Ratzinger, 'Relación Sobre la

Situación Actual de la Fe y la Teología', *Fe y Teología en América Latina* (Santa Fe de Bogota, Colombia: CELAM, 1997), 14. Position one is a response to such statements.

12 See, for example, Leonardo Boff, 'A Implosão Da Socialismo Autoritario e a Teología Da Libertação', *Revista Eclesiastica Brasileira*, 50(197) (March 1990), 76–92; and Frei Betto, 'A Teología Da Libertação: Ruiu Com o Muro de Berlim?', *Revista Eclesiastica Brasileira*, 50(200) (December 1990), 922–9, Frei Betto, 'O Socialismo Morreu. Viva o Socialismo!', *Revista Eclesiastica Brasileira*, 50(197) (March 1990), 173–6, Frei Betto, 'El Fracaso del Socialismo Aleman y los Desafios de la Izquierda Latinoamericana', *Pasos*, 29 (May–June 1990), 1–7.

13 Gustavo Gutiérrez, 'Una Teología de la Liberación en el Contexto del Tercer Milenio', *El Futuro de la Reflexion Teologica en América Latina* (Bogota, Colombia: CELAM, 1996), 102–3; see also Gustavo Gutiérrez, 'La Teología: Una Función Eclesial', *Paginas* XIX(130) (December 1994), 15; and Gustavo Gutiérrez, 'Renovar "la Opción por los Pobres"', *Revista Latinoamericana de Teología*, 36 (September–December 1995), 269–90.

14 Gutiérrez, 'Una Teología de la Liberación en el Contexto del Tercer Milenio', 107.

15 Ibid., 109.

16 Jon Sobrino, 'La Teología y el "Principio Liberación"', *Revista Latinoamericana de Teología*, 35 (May–August 1995), 115.

17 Ibid., 116.

18 Ibid., 118.

19 See also Jon Sobrino, 'Que Queda de la Teología de la Liberación', *Exodo*, 38 (April 1997), 48–53, for a short piece where Sobrino ties the heart of liberation theology to the preferential option for the poor.

20 José Maria Vigil, 'Cambio de Paradigma en la Teología de la Liberación?', *Alternativas*, 8 (1997), 29.

21 Ibid.

22 Ibid., 37.

23 Ibid., 43.

24 Ibid., 45.

25 Sobrino, 'La Teología y el "Principio Liberación"', 129.

26 Gutiérrez, 'Una Teología de la Liberación en el Contexto del Tercer Milenio', 156.

27 Gutiérrez, ibid., 159, n77, cites Luiz Razeto's interesting work but does not incorporate it into his analysis. See Luis Razeto, *Economía Popular de Solidaridad* (Santiago: Area pastoral social de la conferencia episcopal de Chile, 1986) and Luis Razeto, *Crítica de la Economía, Mercado Democratico y Crecimiento* (Santiago: Programa de economía del trabajo, 1994), among other works.

28 See as a central programmatic statement, Pedro Trigo, 'El Futuro de la Teología de la Liberación', *Cambio Social y Pensamiento Cristiano en América Latina*, ed. José Comblin, José I González Faus and Jon Sobrino (Madrid: Editorial Trotta, 1993), 297–317 and Pedro Trigo, 'Imaginario Alternativo al Imaginario Vigente y al Revolucionario', *Iter. Revista de Teología (Caracas)* 3 (1992), 61–99.

29 For a scathing critique of this concept by one of liberation theology's founding fathers, see Hugo Assmann, 'Apuntes Sobre el Tema del Sujeto', *Perfiles Teologicos para un Nuevo Milenio*, ed. José Duque (San José: DEI, 1997), 115–46.

30 Trigo, 'El Futuro de la Teología de la Liberación', 299–300.

31 Ibid., 300.

32 See also Victor Codina, *Creo en el Espíritu Santo. Pneumetología Narrativa* (Santander: Sal Terrae, 1994).

33 Trigo, 'El Futuro de la Teología de la Liberación,' 300.

34 Ibid., 301.

35 Ibid.

36 Ibid., 310.

37 Ibid., 312.

38 Here Trigo is reminiscent of the Michel Foucault that does not forget that the attempt to overcome the sovereign view of power is geared toward opening up a space for the emergence of alternative

communities. See Michel Foucault, *Discipline and Punishment: The Birth of the Prison*, trans. Alan Sheridan (New York: Vintage-Random House, 1979); Michel Foucault, *An Introduction* (New York: Random House, 1980), vol. 1 of *The History of Sexuality*, trans. Robert Hurley; and Michel Foucault, *Power/Knowledge: Selected Writings and Other Interviews 1972–1977*, ed. Colin Gordon, trans. Colin Gordon, Leo Marshal, John Mepham and Kate Soper (New York: Pantheon, 1980).

39 Trigo, 'El Futuro de la Teología de la Liberación', 314.

40 So Trigo writes: 'In the same way that bankers ... feel no temptation to become politicians because they know that the political dimension of their economic power is so decisive that it can place politicians at their service, so too the political power of the people resides in the political dimension of its social organizations. If these organizations are numerous, self-created, unified within themselves and coordinated between themselves, then the people's political clout is much greater than it would be as a political party and even as government'. Trigo, 'El Futuro de la Teología de la Liberación', 315.

41 Trigo, 'El Futuro de la Teología de la Liberación', 316.

42 See Trigo, 'El Futuro de la Teología de la Liberación', 316, for an implicit critique of liberation theology as potentially elitist.

43 Juan Carlos Scannone has noted that liberation theology is currently shifting towards what was called the 'Argentine School' of popular pastoral practice that privileges the use of historical–cultural analysis as mediation over socioeconomic categories. Scannone's work in the 1990s draws heavily on Trigo and serves as another example of the move toward privileging civil society and popular culture as the preferred venues for liberation theology. See Juan Carlos Scannone sj, 'El Comunitarismo Como Alternativa Viable', *El Futuro de la Reflexión Teologica en América Latina* (Colombia: CELAM, 1996), 195–242. On the shift away from state power toward civil society, see also Pablo Richard, 'Caos o Esperanza. Fundamentos y Alternativas para el Siglo XXI', *Diakonia* 74 (June 1995), 59–67. Pablo Richard provides another example of option two. See Pablo Richard, 'Teología de la Solidaridad en el Contexto Actual de Economía Neoliberal de Mercado', *El Huracan de la Globalización*, ed. Franz Hinkelammert (San José, Costa Rica: DEI, 1999), 223–38. For another example of this trend, that includes essays by liberation theologians and sympathetic commentators, see G. De Schrijver (ed.), *Liberation Theologies on Shifting Grounds: A Clash of Socio-Economic and Cultural Paradigms* (Louvain, Belgium: Leuven University Press, 1998). I would also place the ecologically oriented work of Leonardo Boff in category two. See Leonardo Boff, *Cry of the Earth, Cry of the Poor*, trans. Phillip Berryman (Maryknoll, New York: Orbis Books, 1997) and Leonardo Boff, *Ecology and Liberation: A New Paradigm* (New York: Orbis Books, 1995). Finally, for an essay that relates liberation theology to anarchism as a possible mediation, see Rui Manuel Gracio das Neves, 'Neoliberalismo, Teología de la Liberación y Nuevos Paradigmas', *Alternativas*, 9 (1998), 57–96.

44 Trigo, 'El Futuro de la Teología de la Liberación', 310.

45 Scannone sj, 'El Comunitarismo Como Alternativa Viable', 210.

46 On this see R.N. Gwynne and Cristobal Kay, *Latin America Transformed: Globalization and Modernity* (London: Arnold, 1999).

47 Trigo, 'El Futuro de la Teología de la Liberación', 316.

48 For a critique of the focus on civil society in political science, see Ash Amin, 'Beyond Associative Democracy', *New Political Economy*, 1(3) (1996), 309–33.

49 See Chapter 1 of Terry Eagleton, *The Illusions of Postmodernity* (Oxford: Blackwell Publishers Ltd, 1996) for this argument in reference to the North American and European literary and academic left.

50 This position can be read as taking its starting point from Ireneous' dictum: *Gloria Dei vivens homo, gloria autem hominis visio Dei.*

51 Franz Hinkelammert, *The Ideological Weapons of Death: A Theological Critique of Capitalism* (Maryknoll, NY: Orbis Books, 1986), his only book in English translation. For a recent collection of interviews and essays in his honor scc José Duque and German Gutiérrez, *Itinerarios de la Razón Crítica: Homenaje a Franz Hinkelammert en Sus 70 Años* (San José: DEI, 2001).

52 For the English version, see Franz Hinkelammert, 'Liberation Theology in the Economic and Social Context of Latin America: Economy and Theology, or the Irrationality of the Rationalized',

Liberation Theologies, Postmodernity, and the Americas, ed. David Batstone, Eduardo Mendieta, Lois Ann Lorenzten and Dwight N. Hopkins (New York: Routledge, 1997), 25–52. For the Spanish version, see Franz Hinkelammert, *Cultura de la Esperanza y Sociedad Sin Exclusión* (San José, Costa Rica: DEI, 1995), 355–87. For others examples of this position see Hugo Assmann, *La Idolatría del Mercado* (San José, Costa Rica: DEI, 1997) and Jung Mo Sung, *Deseo, Mercado y Religion* (Santander: Editorial Sal Terrae, 1999); Jung Mo Sung, 'Economía y Teología: Reflexiones Sobre Mercado, Globalización y Reino de Dios', *Alternativas*, 9 (1998), 97–118; Jung Mo Sung, *Economía: Tema Ausente en la Teología de la Liberación* (San José, Costa Rica: DEI, 1994); Jung Mo Sung, *Neoliberalismo y Pobreza* (San José, Costa Rica: DEI, 1993) and Jung Mo Sung, *La Idolatría del Capital y la Muerte de los Pobres* (San José, Costa Rica: DEI, 1991).

53 Hinkelammert, 'Liberation Theology in the Economic and Social Context of Latin America', 39.

54 Ibid., 40.

55 Ibid., 44.

56 Ibid., 44–5.

57 Ibid., 45.

58 Ibid., 46–7.

59 Ibid., 47.

60 See Sung, *Economía: Tema Ausente en la Teología de la Liberación*, for an excellent study that sees the acceptance of the secularization thesis by some segments of liberation theology as the root of its economic impasse.

61 For a collection of essays that exemplifies this position see, Pablo Richard *et al.*, *The Idols of Death and the God of Life* (Mayknoll, New York: Orbis Books, 1983).

62 José Míguez Bonino explains: 'As the economist–theologian Franz Hinkelammert cogently argues, the human subject vanishes and only the "fetish" (capital? property? the economic laws?) remains in control. Repression, torture, disappearances, the withdrawal of social, educational and health services, the cultural or physical genocide of native Indians, the suppression of all expressions of public opinion – these are not the result of the whim or the cruelty of bloodthirsty tyrants: they are "the necessary social cost" of "freedom". It is the sacrifice that the highest god, "the economic laws", demands. I am aware that the logic of this "compressed" argument will not be self-evident to many readers from the affluent world ... May I suggest, however, that a meditation on "the unavoidability of unemployment", "the mystery of inflation", the escalation of programs of defense, and the "need" to cut down on social and assistance programs could be a healthy exercise also for theologians?', José Míguez Bonino, 'For Life and Against Death: A Theology That Takes Sides', *Theologians in Transition*, ed. James Wall (New York: Crossroad, 1981), 171.

63 For an examination of the idolatry behind *both* capitalism and existing socialism, see Franz Hinkelammert, *Crítica a la Razón Utópica* (San José: DEI, 1990).

64 This claim is best presented in Franz Hinkelammert, 'La Crítica de la Religión en Nombre del Cristianismo: Dietrich Bonhoeffer', *Teología Alemana y Teología Latinoamericana de la Liberación: Un Esfuerzo de Diálogo* (San José: DEI, 1990), 45–66.

65 On this cooption see also Helio Gallardo, 'La Teología de la Liberación Como Pensamiento Latinoamericano', *Pasos*, 56 (November–December 1994), 12–22. 'New liberationists', seeking to construct a new liberation theology, serve as another example of this phenomena. See Humberto Belli and Ronald Nash, *Beyond Liberation Theology* (Grand Rapids, Michigan: Baker Book House, 1992).

66 Here I agree with Michael Novak when he writes, 'The option for the poor *is* the correct option. Everything depends, however, upon the next institutional step'. (Michael Novak, *Freedom with Justice: Catholic Social Thought and Liberal Institutions*, San Francisco: Harper and Row, 1984), 192; italics in original.

67 Richard Peet, arguing against modernization theories of development, makes a similar point: 'Modernization can be countered only through alternatives that are more convincing and persuasive, alternatives written from the positions of excluded groups, or alternatives based in criticisms of the very concept of development.' See Peet and Hartwick, *Theories of Development*, 90.

68 José Míguez Bonino, *Doing Theology in a Revolutionary Situation*, ed. William H. Lazareth, Confrontation Books (Philadelphia: Fortress Press, 1975), 38–9.

69 This draws on José Míguez Bonino, *Doing Theology in a Revolutionary Situation*, 39–40. For discussions of liberation theology's historical project see John Pottenger, *The Political Theory of Liberation Theology: Toward a Reconvergence of Social Values and Social Science* (Albany, NY: State University of New York Press, Albany, 1989), 119–21 and Smith, *Emergence of Liberation Theology*, 45–50.

70 Note the differences from Trigo's redefinition of liberation theology.

71 José Míguez Bonino, *Doing Theology in a Revolutionary Situation*, 40.

72 Among Moltmann's many works, see Jürgen Moltmann, *Theology of Hope: On the Ground and the Implications of a Christian Eschatology*, trans. James W. Leitch (New York: Harper Torchbooks/Library-Harper and Row, 1967); Jürgen Moltmann, *The Crucified God: The Cross of Christ as the Foundation and Criticism of Christian Theology*, trans. R.A. Wilson and John Bowden (New York: Harper and Row, 1974) and Jürgen Moltmann, *The Church in the Power of the Spirit: A Contribution to Messianic Ecclesiology* (New York: Harper and Row, 1977). For Bonino on Moltmann, see José Míguez Bonino, *Doing Theology in a Revolutionary Situation*, 137–53 and, more recently, José Míguez Bonino, 'Reading Jürgen Moltmann from Latin America', *The Asbury Theological Journal* 55(1) (Spring 2000), 105–14. For Moltmann's response to Bonino, see Jürgen Moltmann, 'An Open Letter to José Míguez Bonino', *Liberation Theology: A Documentary History*, ed. Alfred Hennelly (Maryknoll, NY: Orbis Books, 1990), 195–204. On German political theology see also Enrique Dussel, *Ethics and the Theology of Liberation* (Maryknoll, NY: Orbis Books, 1978), 159–63.

73 José Míguez Bonino, *Doing Theology in a Revolutionary Situation*, 139.

74 Ibid., 140.

75 Of course, these differences are also related to the different social contexts from which these theologies emerge. Moltmann draws on Karl Barth's Barmen Declaration and seeks to safeguard the Christian message from its political abuse. For Bonino, however, that safeguarding easily slides into a spurious neutrality that ends by upholding the status quo. Whether liberation theology's assessment of political theology is correct, however, is not the point of this discussion. I want to show that the 'historical project' was central to the way liberation theology understood itself as different from political theology.

76 José Míguez Bonino, *Doing Theology in a Revolutionary Situation*, 149.

77 Ibid., 146.

78 Ibid., 147.

79 Ibid., 148.

80 Ibid., 151.

81 Hugo Assmann, *Teología Desde la Praxis de la Liberación* (Salamanca: Ediciones Sigueme, 1973), 104–5; Hugo Assmann, *Theology for a Nomad Church*, Paul Burns (Maryknoll, NY: Orbis Books, 1975), 111–12.

82 Assmann, *Teología Desde la Praxis de la Liberación*, 168. The whole second half of Assmann's foundational text was omitted from the English translation. It is this second half that includes the bulk of Assmann's reflection on 'historical projects'.

83 Assmann, *Teología Desde la Praxis de la Liberación*, 124; Assmann, *Theology for a Nomad Church*, 131.

84 Assmann, *Teología Desde la Praxis de la Liberación*, 111–13; Assmann, *Theology for a Nomad Church*, 117–19.

85 Assmann, *Teología Desde la Praxis de la Liberación*, 166.

86 Gustavo Gutiérrez, *Teología Desde el Reverso de la Historia* (Lima, Peru: Ed. CEP, 1977), 353–4.

87 Gutiérrez, *Teología Desde el Reverso de la Historia*, 354.

88 Ibid., 392.

89 Gustavo Gutiérrez, *A Theology of Liberation: History, Politics and Salvation*, trans. Caridad Inda and John Eagleson (New York: Maryknoll, 1985).

90 Ibid., 36.

91 Ibid., 36–7.

92 Ibid., 37.

93 Ibid.

94 Gutiérrez, *A Theology of Liberation*, 238. I have revised the translation of this text. The original translation mistakenly translates what by now should be clear is an important technical term of early liberation theology – *proyecto histórico* or historical project – as historical task. 'Historical task' fails to convey the fact that Gutiérrez is using a specific term shared by the most influential liberation theologians of that time.

95 Gutiérrez, *A Theology of Liberation*, 238.

96 Gutiérrez does not hesitate to give content to the historical project: 'Only the overcoming of a society divided in classes, only a political power at the service of the great majorities, only the elimination of private appropriation of wealth generated by human labor can give us the bases for a more just society. It is for this reason that the elaboration of the historical project of a new society takes in Latin America the route of socialism. Construction of a socialism that does not ignore the deficiencies of many of its actual historical realizations, a socialism that seeks to escape preconceived schemes and which creatively seeks its own paths' (Gustavo Gutiérrez, *Praxis de Liberación y Fe Cristiana*, Madrid: Zero, 1974), 33.

97 See Gutiérrez, *Teología Desde el Reverso de la Historia*, for an extended discussion of this theme.

98 For these data see *Human Development Report 1998* (United Nations Development Programme, 1998), especially Ch. 1.

99 For perhaps the most popular stoic text, see Marcus Aurelius, *Meditations* (New York: Walter J. Black, 1945).

CHAPTER 2

Liberation Theology as the Construction of Historical Projects

Peter Burns defines liberation theology's situation since the fall of the Berlin Wall in the following fashion: 'It seems to me that liberation theology faces a dilemma, or rather a double dilemma. Baldly stated, it can either forsake socialism for "theology," or it can define socialism, and forsake "theology" for rigorous, empirically grounded sociopolitical analysis and committed political praxis. I have placed "theology" in scare-quotes here because at the heart of this dilemma lies another one, and that is how to define theology itself. This is a dilemma for liberation theology because its original challenge was precisely to raise the question of what theology really is, and how one should pursue it.'[1] This chapter suggests that in order to construct new historical projects liberation theology must first grasp the third prong of the dilemma and ask itself again, 'what theology really is, and how one should pursue it' or, in Gustavo Gutiérrez's words, 'what is meant by making theology?'[2] Indeed, I believe that at stake in the definition of the relationship between theology and sociopolitical analysis lies the capacity to construct historical projects as well as, ultimately, liberation theology's understanding of the theological endeavor itself.[3]

In this chapter I will show that today 'theology' itself is a contested category within liberation theology. The locus of conflict, moreover, lies in liberation theology's innovative incorporation of the social sciences as a mediating tool for doing theology, an issue directly related to the construction of historical projects. My argument develops in two parts. First, I present liberation theology's two main (and conflicting) methodological statements, statements that define how liberation theology is to be done, focusing on how each sets up the relationship between theology and the social sciences.[4] I suggest that none of these positions fully develop the methodological implications of liberation theology's stated goal of liberation, and thus they too abruptly sever or delimit the use of sociopolitical analysis, thereby hindering the development of new historical projects. Second, I develop an alternative position which argues that liberation theologians must use sociopolitical analysis to construct historical projects and that this construction needs to be understood as intrinsically part of what it means to do theology as liberation theology. This is the only way liberation theology can incorporate the argument of the chapters that follow.

Liberation Theology and the Social Sciences

Within the North Atlantic academy, views on liberation theology's relationship to the social sciences subscribe to a simple narrative. On the one hand, as is well known, liberation theologians from the very beginning gave a prominent role to a dialogue with the social sciences, over what they perceived as the more traditional partnership with different philosophical strands.[5] Indeed, for Enrique Dussel, liberation theology's expressed commitment to political and economic change forces the use of 'other analytical, interpretative, tools from those known to previous theological traditions' such as the social sciences which mark 'an epistemological revolution in the world history of Christian theology'.[6] All liberation theologians concur that sociopolitical analysis plays a fundamental and distinctive role in their theology: 'A radical option for, and real commitment to, this [Latin American] exploited class means that liberation theology must embark on a path of reflection that is quite peculiar and distinctive to it. To begin with, it must accept the mediation of a new type of scientific rationality to which it has not been accustomed. This new line of scientific reasoning is a contribution of the human sciences, of the social sciences specifically.'[7]

On the other hand, however, commentators note a shift in the last decade away from the social sciences toward more 'traditional' theological and religious themes.[8] Some celebrate this trend, thankful that liberation theology has outgrown its youthful rebelliousness and settled down to a responsible place in the academy. Some even see the fall of socialism and supposed discrediting of liberation theology's preferred social science, Marxism, as leading directly to liberation theology's demise. For example, according to Joseph Ratzinger: 'The fall of the European governmental systems based on Marxism turned out to be a kind of twilight of the gods for that theology'.[9] Others, instead, bemoan what they see as the abdication of liberation theology's revolutionary promise.[10] Liberation theology's actual relationship to the social sciences, though, is far more complex than this simple narrative. What has been completely ignored in the United States and Europe, and remains downplayed within liberation theology itself, is that there is no consensus among liberation theologians as to the exact role the social sciences must play in their task. Thus the first part of this narrative is accurate: liberation theologians did in fact stress the social sciences as intrinsic to their theology, the second part, liberation theology's supposed abandonment of social science analysis, is less so.

In fact, we will see that there are two different views of the role the social sciences should play within liberation theology leading, in turn, to two different views of how theology is done and what theology is called to do. I call these perspectives the canonical view and the marginal view – in accordance with their current influence within liberation theology itself as well as their degree of visibility within the North Atlantic academy. In both, the goal is the same. As Leonardo and Clodovis Boff state of liberation theology as a whole: 'There is only one goal – the liberation of the oppressed.'[11] In both, however, the lack of a constructive role for the social sciences in the imagination of historical projects hinders the achievement of the goal.

The Canonical View within Liberation Theology: Liberation Theology as the Rereading of Tradition

Clodovis Boff's 'Epistemology and Method of the Theology of Liberation' provides the canonical view of liberation theology's methodology. The piece is canonized in *Mysterium Liberationis*, a two-volume compendium of essays developed with the specific intent of defining liberation theology's central categories. This publication has come to define 'orthodoxy' within liberation theology.

Boff sets up his discussion of liberation theology's methodology by contrasting Latin American theology's understanding of 'liberation' with Vatican theology's understanding of the term. To do so, he draws a distinction between ethico-political liberation and soteriological liberation. The former, he claims, has primacy of urgency while the latter has primacy of value. Yet the two emphases are complementary.[12] So, while the Vatican understands liberation as a notion encompassing the mystery of salvation as a whole, Boff stresses that for liberation theology liberation means social liberation: 'This is the question of our time. And this was the question from which the theology of liberation sprang. This was the reason it arose in the Third World.'[13] The point of departure, therefore, 'has always been the process of oppression-and-liberation of the excluded of history'.[14]

Having set up social liberation as the goal, Boff turns to outlining the actual practice of liberation theology. He sees it as composed of four elements: a living commitment to the cause of the poor, a socioanalytical mediation, a hermeneutical mediation and a practical mediation, the latter three following the pastoral method of 'seeing', 'judging' and 'acting'. Let me present Boff's scheme in more detail.[15]

The Preliminary Stage

The first step for liberation theology is pre-theological and involves faith commitment. The theologian 'must share in some way in the liberative process, be committed to the oppressed'.[16] It is impossible to become a liberation theologian without physical contact with the actual subjects of the theology, whether that contact takes place through sporadic visits to oppressed communities, the alternation of periods of theoretical work with periods of pastoral work in a poor church, or actually living and working full time with the poor. Theology, therefore, is a second act emerging from this contact: 'Before we do theology we have to do liberation.'[17] First comes liberative practice, only afterwards does theology emerge.

Socioanalytical Mediation: Seeing

Liberation theology's second step involves using the social sciences to understand the root causes of oppression. According to Boff, there are three main alternative explanations for the fact of socioeconomic poverty – an empiricist explanation, a functionalist explanation and a dialectical explanation – each providing a different reading of poverty's cause and the means toward its eradication.[18] He rejects the first two and embraces the third. The empiricist explanation, on the one hand, views poverty as a vice and thus sees laziness, ignorance or malice as its root cause. This view fails to take into account the structural and collective dimension of poverty, "that the poor are entire masses and these masses are swelling every day',[19] and thus its prescribed solution ranges from almsgiving to aid campaigns, depending on the perceived gravity of the situation. Here, according to Boff, the poor are mere objects of pity.

The functionalist explanation, on the other hand, views poverty as backwardness. Poverty is the expression of an economy and society that have yet to become fully modern.[20] Within the functionalist perspective economic development, spurred by foreign investment and technology, will eventually eliminate poverty. The solution, therefore, lies in reform; that is, the gradual improvement of the prevailing system. Unlike the empiricist, the functionalist recognizes the collective dimension of poverty. However, like the empiricist, the functionalist fails to recognize the conflictive character of poverty's root: its ultimately class foundation. The functionalist fails to see that poverty 'is not a passing phase ... instead it is the product of economic, social, and political structures, with the result that the rich get richer at the expense of the poor, who get even poorer'.[21] In any case, within this scheme the poor remain the passive objects of governmental top-down reform.

Boff subscribes to the dialectical explanation of poverty as oppression. Poverty, within the dialectical explanation, is the inevitable byproduct of an economic system that either exploits or excludes the great majority of people from the production process. Poverty is a collective phenomenon: the wider masses are poor; a structural phenomena: the workings of the economic system itself produce poverty; and a conflictive phenomenon: reform will not suffice. The way out of poverty, therefore, is 'revolution, understood as the transformation of the bases of the economic and social system'.[22] An alternative system is thus needed. Here, for Boff, the poor emerge as the agents and subjects of change.[23]

Hermeneutic Mediation: Judging

The hermeneutic mediation is the second stage of theological construction and, according to Boff, 'the specific moment by virtue of which a discourse is formally theological discourse'.[24] In this stage the theologian must ask, 'what does the word of God say about this situation?' That is, what does the word of God say about the oppression revealed through the socioanalytical mediation?

To answer this question, the theologian rereads the Bible through a hermeneutic of liberation. This reading prioritizes application over explanation in that it seeks the meaning of the text in order to find its life meaning. The accent falls on the latter: 'in a word, the new/old biblical reading culminates in the experience today of the sense and meaning of yesterday'.[25] The markedly political nature of the Bible, revealed in texts such as Exodus, the various Hebrew prophetic works, the Acts of the Apostles, the Book of Revelation and, of course, the Gospels, is emphasized. The rereading of the Bible through a hermeneutic of liberation, Boff stresses, takes place together with the poor. They are the privileged agents of biblical reflection. Finally, throughout the process as a whole, the hermeneutic of liberation seeks to unleash the Bible's transformative energy to enable the conversion of individuals and history as a whole.

Practical Mediation: Acting

The socioanalytical mediation and the hermeneutic mediation are the tools liberation theologians use to construct a new theology, a new vision of faith geared to face contemporary challenges. Boff stresses, however, that as liberation theology must start with action – the preliminary commitment or antecedent moment – so too must it culminate in action. The practical mediation, the last methodological stage in liberation theology, thus involves the development of new plans of action. The actual shape and definition of these plans will vary according to whether one is a professional, pastoral or popular theologian. According to Boff, professional theologians can only point to broad lines of change, pastoral theologians can be somewhat more determinate, while popular theologians can be quite specific because of their own location in the concrete everyday struggles of the oppressed. In every case, however, the practical mediation involves five levels: the level of conjunctual analysis in which the social forces resisting change are assessed; the level of projects and programs in which short term and long term projects are proposed; the level of strategy and tactics where the more specific means for reaching proposed objectives are determined; the ethical and evangelical level where the means proposed are assessed in terms of the values present in the Christian faith; and, lastly, the performative level, the creation of discourses that inspire people to action.

To recapitulate: according to this explication of liberation theology's method, four stages are required – a preliminary commitment to the oppressed, a socioanalytical mediation in which the social sciences are used to understand the underlying causes of oppression, a hermeneutical mediation in which oppression is understood in light of the Christian tradition and a practical mediation in which actions against oppression are designed. Together, these stages are liberation theology. Reasserting core ideas and revising basic categories – recall liberation theology's three main responses to the fall of the Berlin wall outlined in the previous chapter – fall under the canonical position's methodological umbrella. The general thrust of this methodological statement, however, has come under attack for dissociating liberation theology from its earlier more radical political claims.[26] In this case, in fact, I agree with Marsha Hewitt's claim that 'Liberation theology [I would amend, liberation theologians who espouse this methodological statement] seems to be reorienting itself away from an emancipatory critical religious theory and praxis toward a more traditional type of theological discourse that can only be more acceptable to the official hierarchical church. The price to be paid for this change of direction may be intolerably high.'[27]

The problem with the canonical position is that it implicitly sets up a divide between theology and the social sciences that disables liberation theology from moving from a discourse *about* liberation to the pursuit of liberation as a social reality. This divide emerges for two reasons: first, because the social sciences are only allowed to play the role of reading reality in the socioanalytical stage. For example, Gutiérrez, another exponent of the canonical position, writes that the social sciences 'are simply a means to better understand reality'.[28] Second, and related to the first, is the fact that in the canonical position it is only within the hermeneutical stage that 'the discourse is formally theological'.[29] The social sciences thus are useful 'to understand a situation and not for the study of topics considered strictly more theological'.[30] Even though they are a necessary part of the process of doing liberation theology their use is limited to reading reality, 'they are pre-theological because they simply prepare reality for theological reflection'.[31] The social sciences, relegated to the socioanalytical stage, are therefore of little, if any, intrinsic theological worth.

This strict non-theological delimitation of the social sciences' role in the socioanalytical stage, however, ends up negating liberation theology's supposed focus on liberation. Indeed, when distinguishing liberation theology's and Vatican theology's respective emphases Boff writes that 'Rome takes "ethical–social" liberation for granted, while Latin American liberation theology does the same for soteriological salvation.'[32] So a central difference between liberation theology and Vatican theology lies in that the former seeks to make liberation become social, that is, concretely incarnated in society. The goal, therefore, is not 'the construction of genuinely new syntheses of faith'.[33] The goal, it bears repeating, is *social* liberation. Boff himself recognizes that for liberation theology, liberation, in contradistinction to a document such as *Libertatis conscientiae*, should be understood as 'specifically social and historical ... it was precisely toward this socioliberative aspect that liberation theology, without question, looked'.[34] In this case, however, the focus of liberation theology as theology should therefore fall on the practical rather than the hermeneutical stage, for it is in the former that the goal is formally pursued.

At this point, though, the relegation of the social sciences into the socioanalytical stage and the divide between social science and 'formal' theology come back to haunt the canonical position by leaving the practical stage without the possibility of devising historical projects. There is no possibility of constructing historical projects if the social sciences do not return into the practical mediation and detail the vision of society for which the call to action is heralded. Boff's insistence that the professional theologian can only point to 'broad lines of change' reveals this separation's fatal flaw, for the broadness, and really the vagueness, of liberation theology's practical mediation stems from relegating the social sciences to a mere tool for understanding the causes of oppression. The 'broadness' is the product of a particular way of assigning priority and theological weight to the different stages. The result is that the canonical position comes dangerously close to taking both soteriological and social liberation for granted. At most, the latter remains an afterthought.

The Marginal View within Liberation Theology: Liberation Theology as the Critique of Idolatry

Jung Mo Sung develops the marginal view as an explicit critique of Boff's methodology.[35] This position finds its main institutional locus within the theology and economics school of liberation theology at DEI (Departamento Ecuménico de Investigaciones) in Costa Rica. The position is marginal for three reasons: first, because with the exception of Hugo Assmann none of its main exponents can be counted among liberation theologians' founding figures; second, because as Sung himself documents, DEI's line of work is often not even mentioned in many Latin American surveys of liberation theology (*Mysterium Liberationis*, for example, does not include any essay by a theologian of this approach and emphasis); third, because their work remains untranslated into English and thus outside the North Atlantic academy.[36]

   The kernel of Sung's critique lies in the claim that the hermeneutical mediation is unnecessary; it does not add anything to what is already revealed by the socioanalytical mediation.[37] Sung uses Boff's outline of how to do a theology of land – concretizing the discussion of the canonical view presented above – as an example.[38] Table 2.1 replicates Boff's scheme.[39]

   Sung's first point is that the hermeneutical mediation (step two) does not really interpret or 'judge' the reality read through the socioanalytical mediation. For him, the hermeneutic mediation could only interpret that reality if we assumed that there is no difference between our historical context and that of the Bible and church fathers. Yet this is obviously not the case. In fact, if it were, the turn to the social sciences in order to read reality would be unnecessary. Note that the hermeneutical mediation is supposed to systematize how the people understand the land question in relation to their faith, and what the Bible and Christian tradition say about land in their own time. How the people understand the land question in relation to faith, however, can be placed in the socioanalytical mediation, since there one must also 'see how individuals experience their problems and how they resist oppression', and Christian faith has an impact on these factors. Sung, moreover, contends that the systematization of the Bible and tradition in relation to the land question has little to contribute to the

Table 2.1 Boff's methodological scheme

Step zero: participation in the struggle
Step one: socioanalytical mediation (seeing)
* analyze the land situation for the nation or a particular region;
* encourage workers to stand up for themselves;
* see how individuals experience their problems and how they resist oppression or organize their resistance to it.

Step two: hermeneutical mediation (judging)
* evaluating how the populace faces up to the land question on the basis of its religion and faith;
* evaluating how the Bible views land;
* determining how theological tradition, especially church fathers, see the question of land.

Step three: practical mediation (acting)
* stressing the value of worker unity and organization: unions, cooperatives or other movements;
* publicizing the need for agrarian reform to be brought about by those who work the land;
* making a choice of particular banners under which to fight, linking with other forces, forecasting consequences, allocation of tasks, etc.

---

interpretation of current land problems. The contexts are just too different. In addition, the use of a dialectical social scientific understanding of poverty already supposes the negation of the current system of land tenure in favor of one more suitable to the needs of the wider masses. Reality is already interpreted in accordance with liberation theology's values and goals within the socioanalytic mediation, that is, before the theologian moves to the hermeneutical stage. It is this convergence of interpretation and objectives that brought liberation theology and Marxism together in the first place.[40] In order to highlight the hermeneutical mediation's superfluous nature Sung proposes a revised scheme (Table 2.2) that is exactly the same except for its absence.[41] The table presents the two schemes side by side.[42]

Sung's scheme eliminates the hermeneutical mediation without interrupting the sequence of argument. If one assumes, as does Boff, that Christians are already participating in the struggle (step zero) then one must also suppose that they have already judged reality in light of their faith. If not, why participate? The very choice of a dialectical social theory also implies a judgment on current reality. The hermeneutical stage – its systematization of Bible and tradition – seems merely to serve the function of justifying a prior Christian participation in the struggle at hand. What the canonical position deems the 'formally theological' stage appears to be irrelevant.

Table 2.2   Boff and Sung compared

Boff's methodological scheme	Sung's revised version
Step zero: participation in the struggle Step one: socioanalytical mediation (seeing) • analyze the land situation for the nation or a particular region; • encourage workers to stand up for themselves; • see how individuals experience their problems and how they resist oppression or organize their resistance to it. Step two: hermeneutical mediation (judging) • evaluating how the populace faces up to the land question on the basis of its religion and faith; • evaluating how the Bible views land; • determining how theological tradition, especially church fathers, see the question of land. Step three: practical mediation (acting) • stressing the value of worker unity and organization: unions, cooperatives or other movements; • publicizing the need for agrarian reform to be brought about by those who work the land; • making a choice of particular banners under which to fight, linking with other forces, forecasting consequences, allocation of tasks, etc.	Step zero: participation in the struggle Step one: socioanalytical mediation (seeing) • analyze the land situation for the nation or a particular region; • encourage workers to stand up for themselves; • see how individuals experience their problems and how they resist oppression or organize their resistance to it. Step two (three): practical mediation (acting) • stressing the value of worker unity and organization: unions, cooperatives or other movements; • publicizing the need for agrarian reform to be brought about by those who work the land; • making a choice of particular banners under which to fight, linking with other forces, forecasting consequences, allocation of tasks, etc.

Sung's alternative understanding of liberation theology is based on two moves.[43] In the first move he argues that a closer link between theology and the social sciences is implicit in liberation theology's understanding of God, anthropology and history. For liberation theology God is a God of life.[44] More specifically, however, the life to which God refers is not an abstract ethereal 'life' but material human life, human life in the flesh. Liberation theology thus also espouses a unified anthropology. The marginal position sees a key difference between a Semitic biblical anthropology that focuses on the bodily nature of humans and a Greek anthropology that sees body and soul as two separate entities in conflict with each other. Thus, for the Greeks, escaping the body was a goal, while in Egypt the body is worshipped and preserved after death. Following this distinction, Sung draws on liberationist rereadings of the Pauline epistles to argue that for Paul 'body' and 'soul' do not refer to two separate entities but should be viewed as tendencies within a human being that need to be understood as a whole. The resurrection, therefore, does not replace the body but rather gives it life.[45] Within this conception, body and soul are not two separate entities but two different tendencies in the person. For Paul, all human existence is bodily; Christ resurrects in his body because there is no life without one.[46] The preferential option for the poor is thus based on God's own focus on those who lack the means to sustain bodily life.

Finally, the ideas of a God of life and a unitary anthropology correspond to a unitary vision of history, since to talk of a God of life is also to talk of the concrete conditions for human life within this history. For liberation theology there is no distinction between creation and salvation – history is one.[47] As Gutiérrez himself writes, 'the history of salvation is the very heart of human history'.[48] Granted this theological background, Sung stresses that it is impossible to make a preferential option without also opting for the mechanisms by which the production of goods necessary for life take place. The two cannot be separated. For Sung, therefore, liberation theology's theological categories take the theologian squarely into the economic realm, since 'it is here where the prospects of people's lives are played out and decided'.[49] The social sciences do not just read reality, they are the realm where God's promise of life fails or succeeds.

Having drawn the link between theology and economics, Sung proceeds to argue, against Boff and the canonical position, that the 'formally theological' cannot be reduced to rereading the Bible or tradition. Instead, theology 'above all consists of unmasking the idols that ground the systems of death'.[50] Liberation theology's task lies in revealing the implicit theologies within the social sciences that lead to million of deaths in the Third World. To engage in this task Sung allies himself with social scientists critical of reigning economic orthodoxy. For Sung mainstream economics is idolatrous in that it prioritizes the wellbeing of an abstractly understood market economy over human life.[51] This idolatry, moreover, is based on a fundamentalist faith – faith in the market as a salvific element for all of humankind – that is immune to evidence: 'When they face economic and social problems, the supporters of the current globalization process of the economy, in a neo-liberal perspective, all agree on one point: these problems aren't rooted in the market system, but rather stem from a lack of complete implementation of market rules. Their faith in the market is so strong that they see "more market" as the solution for social problems created by the same.'[52] Such a faith claims that 'the way to go for debt-ridden countries is to pay up interest and principal ... It matters very little if these payments and adjustments bring unemployment to millions of adults and death to countless children. It's the one and only way'.[53]

According to Sung, this argument is based on a blind faith in the market as an institution capable of solving all human problems. The argument is faith based because reality displays the opposite: the policies called for by market proponents plunge the Third World deeper into misery. Yet when those policies are shown to fail more of the same is advocated. Faith dictates that the market is never seen as a problem, it can only be a solution. Economics is revealed as an idolatrous theology whose exclusive faith lies in the market. For this reason 'theologians must step out more often from their theological libraries, full of theologies of the past, and face the new theologies that are conquering society'.[54] The unmasking of idols, therefore, is the critique of this false faith and the human sacrifices it requires. That is liberation theology's main task.

To recapitulate: according to the marginal position there is an intimate link between theology and at least one of the social sciences – economics. That link stems from liberation theology's theological categories. The idea of God as a God of life as well as the belief in a unitary history and a unitary human being leads the theologian into the realm where real bodily life is sustained. For this reason, the preferential option for the poor requires opting for the means through which life is reproduced. Theology and economics are inextricably linked: 'Economics is more than a relevant topic for our theology, it is a "theological" place.'[55] The task of liberation theology, therefore, is to clear the ground of the idols that keep life-sustaining economies from emerging. Underlying this conception of liberation theology's task is the claim that modernity should not be understood as secular; the sacred has not disappeared, it has merely been displaced into the market. Indeed, Sung suggests that at the heart of Boff's attempt to retrieve a formally theological space in the Bible and tradition lies a conception of modernity as secular.[56] In this case, the hermeneutical stage represents the perceived need to find a space for theology in a secularized world.[57]

This marginal position corresponds to the 'critiquing idolatry' response to the fall of the Berlin Wall outlined in the previous chapter. There I argued that critiquing idolatry failed because of its inability to devise an alternative to the idol. Without that alternative, I suggested, the idol rather than unmasked was strengthened. Now we can see more clearly why that position fails. Despite their differences, the problem with Sung is the same as the problem with Boff. He too fails to see the potential theological import the social sciences can play in constructing historical projects. In Sung's case, though, the failure is surprising for three reasons: first, because Sung is highly critical of the economic and political vacuity of liberation theology's discourse on liberation;[58] second, because he argues for an alliance between theologians and social scientists who espouse the same goal of overturning economic orthodoxy. He even suggests that Max Horkheimer's understanding of theology should serve as the backdrop for this alliance: 'Theology is the hope that the injustice that characterizes the world cannot persist, that injustice cannot be considered the last word.'[59] The alliance with some strains of social science, however, is merely to facilitate the critique of other strains, and at no point moves toward designing concrete institutional alternatives to dominant idolatry. Third because he himself is aware that without the devising of alternatives the task remains incomplete: 'we are conscious, at the end of this book, that we have only taken half a step; the other step being the announcement of the historical utopia and its possible roads. We cannot remain satisfied with denouncing, we must also announce. In fact, every denouncement presupposes the existence, even if indefinite, of an alternative'.[60] At times Sung even seems to hint that without an alternative vision the critique of idolatry reaches a standstill: 'if our problem is idolatry, and we denounce idolatry with the instrumental use of the social sciences, then announcing the God of life means also announcing another social system'.[61] Yet his failure to incorporate a role for the social sciences in devising alternatives makes it impossible to make any headway in that direction. To that extent, idolatry and injustice do remain the final word.

An Alternative View: Liberation Theology as the Construction of Historical Projects

Among liberation theology's main figures, Juan Luis Segundo's understanding of the relation between faith and ideology can be seen as providing the closest historical analogy to the position developed in this book.[62] Let me thus set up my position by first reviewing his argument. For Segundo, faith is the value or meaning structure that is an indispensable component of every human life. Every human being structures their life around a set of values. Faith, therefore, is an anthropological component of the person that need not be tied to any religious scheme. Ideology, for Segundo, is also an anthropological component of human beings. Ideology, in his use of the term, is not a pejorative label for the mechanisms which a class uses to sacralize its ruling status.[63] Instead, Segundo defines ideology in a neutral sense, as a system of means that are used to attain an end or goal. One can recognize faith because it is more strongly identified with a goal, while ideology focuses more on the means toward the goal. However, while Segundo separates faith and ideology for analytical purposes, he claims that in reality they are inextricably linked. It is not really possible to separate faith from ideology and ideology from faith.

Take, for example, Jesus' commandment to love your neighbor.[64] Love in this case, especially if one believes that the love commandment is divinely inspired, is the basic meaning structure of the individual. Yet for Segundo 'love' can be expressed in a variety of ways and thus can only be made meaningful through ideologies as the system of means by which values are realized in practice. It is not the same to believe that the love commandment should be expressed solely at an individual personal level as it is to believe that it needs to be expressed through societal structural reform. More deeply, however, Segundo suggests that unless one focuses on the ideological elements of faith the latter cannot even be discussed because it is the means by which faith is made real – of realizing faith in practice – that give content to faith. He notes that in Latin America often it is not faith that separates individuals and groups but faith given different content through different ideological garb.[65] Moreover, such conflict is unavoidable, for there is no non-ideological way to realize the love commandment. For this reason 'Christians cannot evade the necessity of inserting something to fill the void between their faith and their options in history. In short, they cannot avoid the risk of ideologies.'[66] Even Jesus faced that task: 'When Jesus talked about freely proffered love and nonresistance to evil, he was facing the same problem of filling the void between his conception of God and the problems existing in his age. In short, we are dealing here with another ideology, not with the content of faith itself.'[67]

Live faith is always faith related to a particular historical context. Live faith, therefore, is always faith plus ideology. In most cases, we inherit a particular package taken for granted. The question that emerges for Segundo in a time of crisis such as when religion (faith plus ideology) no longer responds adequately to the needs of a historical situation, is how to *consciously* relate faith to ideology.[68] He sees two options. The first option is to turn to scripture and pick and choose what seems most in accord with the current historical situation: 'If, for example, the relationship between the Exodus situation and our own time today seems closer than the situation of the Hebrews in the time of Christ and ours today, then the Exodus rather than the Gospel should serve as our source of inspiration in trying to find a present-day ideology that will dovetail with the faith.'[69] Segundo, though, rejects this option for the same reason that Sung rejects Boff's hermeneutical stage. There just seems to be little sense in looking for similar situations in cultural contexts dating back over 35 centuries ago.[70] He prefers a second option: 'The other possible approach is to invent an ideology that we might regard as the one which would be constructed by a gospel message contemporary with us ... The second approach does call for creativity here and now. But if we must try to imagine what the gospel message would be if it were formulated today, it is becoming more and more obvious to Christians that *secular* inventiveness and creativity is more appropriate and fruitful.'[71]

Segundo's project has been described as one of 'deideologizing – that is, unearthing and exposing the ideologies that are employed both by modern Western societies and by the Christian churches to hide, disguise, or legitimate oppression or social injustice'.[72] Indeed, Segundo is intent on highlighting the inescapably ideological trappings of faith to give him room to critique and revise the content of faith in light of the goal of social liberation. For this reason Segundo suggests that 'a sociology of ideology, a sociology whose object would be the ideology prevailing in social behaviors, is precisely the one starting point that could constitute an *intrinsic* element of the theological task'.[73] This is the element of 'secular inventiveness' that he finds intrinsically necessary to liberation theology. A sociology of ideology would enable liberation theology to peel away the Christian ideological elements that stand in the way of liberation. Within this understanding of Segundo – and this is the understanding he himself espouses – he and Sung engage in similar projects. Sung too seeks to unmask dehumanizing ideologies; the difference is that Sung focuses on economics while Segundo focuses on religion and theology. Both argue that the social sciences can aid in this task yet both fail to see the constructive role the social sciences can play in building historical projects.

Unawares to himself, however, Segundo opens the door to a third understanding of liberation theology's relationship to the social sciences that serves as the cornerstone of my argument throughout this book. In the same way that Segundo posits that faith without ideology is empty, I posit that liberation theology's concepts remain empty without a role for the social sciences in the construction of historical projects.[74] Liberation theology needs to realize that concepts such as the preferential option for the poor and liberation reveal little about the way life chances and social resources may be theoretically approached and institutionally realized. The focus, therefore, needs to fall on the practical political and economic mediations of these ideals and concepts, otherwise the mechanisms by which such abstract goals are to be achieved are handed on a platter to liberation theology's opponents. Thus for liberation theology the construction of historical projects should not be a secondary moment in the theological task, coming after the clarification of our theological concepts, but rather must become a central means by which those concepts are clarified, given analytical rigor and understood. In this case, the construction of historical projects serves the purpose of aiding in the definition of what theological concepts such as the preferential option for the poor and liberation actually mean. The construction of historical projects, therefore, is not merely the application of theological concepts to the social realm but part and parcel of the definition of the concepts themselves.[75]

One cannot really understand liberation theology's theological categories until their implications for the way we relate to each other and the way society is organized are developed. Remember Sung's claim that for liberation theology God is a God of life. One may agree with this conception, yet this agreement may merely serve to hide deeper disagreement. What kind of life does God support? As we saw, for Sung God is not a God of an abstract life of the soul but a God of concrete bodily life, the life that suffers from hunger, from thirst, from lack of shelter, or may not suffer from these lacks. Now, one may still agree with this understanding of God (duly noting that it remains a minority view within the grand history of Christianity), yet Sung claims that such an idea of God is also tied to a unitary anthropology and a unitary history. For him, there is no strict distinction between the body and soul and between an earthly and a heavenly history. The upshot of these ideas is that the body is the true locus of salvation, that salvation has a central this-worldly component and that food, water and shelter are part of God's plan for all.

Now, even if one agrees with all this thus far, this agreement might still hide deeper disagreement. Different people, for example, may agree with a conception of the body as the locus of salvation yet disagree on how this belief is to be translated into the social realm. Some, for example, might claim that the way to realize the idea of the body as locus of salvation is to emphasize charity as a central part of the Christian lifestyle. In this case, the giving of alms expresses and defines the religious idea. Others, however, might claim that making the body the locus of salvation requires more than private acts of charity and should be understood as necessitating a rise in minimum wage and more expansive social welfare entitlements. Still others might disagree with both views and argue that radical structural change such as the replacement of capitalism by socialism is the means to realize the idea in practice. The point is that, while people may espouse a vague but poetic statement of the idea, that idea lacks full development until its shape in practice is worked out. Gutiérrez once noted that in Latin America 'oppressors and oppressed "share" the same faith. But they are separated on the economic, social and political planes; here, in this sphere, one group exploits the other'.[76] Until the ideal is developed institutionally, which necessarily requires using the social sciences in the construction of historical projects, people may seem to share a faith they in reality do not.

To embrace this argument, however, a shift in the locus of 'theology' needs to take place. Both the canonical and the marginal positions retain the theology/sociopolitical analysis dichotomy Peter Burns described in this chapter's opening. In the former the split is explicit and stems from defining the hermeneutical stage and thus the rereading of the Bible and tradition as the specifically theological stage. In the latter the split is less obvious. For the marginal position the critique of market idolatry with the aid of the social sciences is itself theological. The Bible and tradition thus do not serve as the guarantor of the label 'theology'. Yet the social sciences do not aid in the process of developing political and economic alternatives to the reigning global order. Insofar as this is the case, theology stays in the realm of critique while politics takes over the task of construction. In both the canonical and the marginal views this split between theology and the social sciences leads to the vacuity of liberation theology's terminology revealed in Chapter 1. Leonardo Boff once warned: 'What sort of liberation are we talking about? Here we must be careful not to fall into the semantic trap of endowing the same word with several very different meanings. The liberation involved here has to do with economic, social, political and ideological structures. It seeks to operate on structures, not simply on persons. It proposes to change the power relationships existing between social groups by helping to create new structures that will allow for greater participation on the part of those now excluded.'[77] While Boff alludes to the danger inherent in not specifying the concrete meaning of liberation, he too remains vague. At this level of generality there is nothing in his statement that the IMF or some other opponent of liberation theology could not also espouse. Here the oppressor and the oppressed seemingly continue to share the same faith. There is just no way to avoid ambiguity without developing, however tentatively, the institutional content for a term such as liberation.

Instead, my argument denies the theology/sociopolitical analysis split in two ways: first, by collapsing the distinction between the theological and the political and insisting on the development of what could be called the material component of liberation theology's categories. Within my scheme, 'the preferential option for the poor' and 'liberation' are not just values by which the theologian judges society. They are to be developed as alternative social forms; that is, political, economic and social institutions that can be enacted at society's many levels: at the level of the church as well as grass root organizations, at the level of civil society as well as the state, at the level of local economies as well as the national, and eventually global, economy as a whole. The role of the social sciences in liberation theology is not just the uncovering of the causes of oppression. Besides this critical role, there is also a central constructive role in the development of historical projects that help define liberation theology's theological terminology. As I will show in subsequent chapters, disciplines such as law, political economy and social theory are indispensable resources for this task. Such is the 'secular inventiveness' I espouse. Second, the split is refuted by remembering that liberation theology's goal is not to talk about liberation, but concrete social liberation itself: 'the most progressive theology in Latin America is more interested in *being liberative* than in *talking about liberation*'.[78] As I showed in the previous chapter, it was by relating ideals and institutions through the development of historical projects that liberation was truly pursued. Thus, in their denial of a role for the social sciences in the construction of historical projects, neither the canonical nor the marginal position fully takes the goal of liberation to heart.

Conclusion

Today liberation theology possesses two main methodological statements. These statements, which I called the canonical position and the marginal position, make the same mistake. In both, the role the social sciences can play in the construction of historical projects is seen as perfunctory vis-à-vis liberation theology's task as theology. The upshot lies in that the liberation theologian does not see this construction as an intrinsic part of the theological task. Indeed, what is not defined as a priority cannot be asked of liberation theology. As long as the construction of historical projects is written out of liberation theology's methodology, the theologian is relieved of the difficult but necessary task of defining ideals by working out their institutional content. Liberation theology's methodological statements enshrine and thus excuse the incapacity to construct historical projects.

Instead I proposed an understanding of liberation theology in which the construction of historical projects is placed at the forefront. Let me stress that I do not see my position as replacing or superseding the canonical or marginal positions. Rather, these positions should be seen as complementary. The canonical position stresses the rereading of reality in the light of faith and the reconstruction of theological categories (God the Father, Jesus, Christology, Mary, Holy Spirit, and so on) in light of Latin American reality.[79] The marginal position stresses what could be called the 'discernment of gods'; the critique of idolatrous tendencies in the social sciences, tendencies that deify abstract entities such as 'the market' over and against basic human needs. I believe that my position, liberation theology as the construction of historical projects, completes them both for the simple reason that without historical projects liberation theology can never become truly liberative.

The reconstruction of theological categories should be understood as part of the project of liberating theology from its well-documented tendency toward legitimizing social injustice in the Latin American context. Similarly, the critique of idolatry should be understood as the project of liberating the social sciences from their tendency to provide theories that also legitimize injustice. In this sense the canonical and marginal positions work together. In neither case, moreover, is the process a mere academic exercise, in both cases the end goal is liberation understood as social. However, without the construction of historical projects they can never really approximate the goal. At this point my argument comes in; this book will show that making the construction of historical projects a priority remains possible, despite the shift in historical context and liberation theologians' manifest incapacity to think in such terms as described in the previous chapter. Liberation theology must include the revision of Christian concepts, the use of the social sciences to understand the causes of oppression, the critique of idolatry within the social sciences, as well as the construction of historical projects. For the sake of the non-person, liberation theology must not reduce and resign itself to one of the three positions outlined here, liberation theology must be all three at once.

Notes

1 Peter Burns, 'The Problem of Socialism in Liberation Theology', *Theological Studies*, 53(3) (September 1992), 513.

2 Gustavo Gutiérrez, 'Liberation, Theology and Proclamation', in *The Mystical and Political Dimension of the Christian Faith*, ed. Claude Geffre and Gustavo Gutiérrez (New York: Herder and Herder, 1974), 69.

3 For other statements of the theology/sociopolitical analysis dilemma for liberation theology see Edward A. Lynch, 'Beyond Liberation Theology?', *Journal of Interdisciplinary Studies*, 6(1–2) (1994), 147–64; Marsha Hewitt, 'Liberation Theology and the Emancipation of Religion', *The Scottish Journal of Religious Studies* XIII(1) (Spring 1992), 21–38; Paul Sigmund, *Liberation Theology at the Crossroads: Democracy or Revolution?* (New York: Oxford University Press, 1990); the essays in Ricahrd Rubenstein and John Roth (eds), *The Politics of Latin American Liberation Theology: The Challenge to U.S. Public Policy* (Washington DC: Washington Institute Press, 1988) and Michael Novak (ed.), *Liberation Theology and the Liberal Society* (Washington, DC: American Enterprise Institute, 1987).

4 For a recent overview of method in liberation theology generally see Peter Phan, 'Method in Liberation Theologies', *Theological Studies* 61(1) (2000), 40–63.

5 See, for example, Gustavo Gutiérrez's outline of Catholic theology's relationship with Neo-Platonic and Aristotelian philosophies against his definition of theology as 'critical reflection on praxis' (Gustavo Gutiérrez, *A Theology of Liberation: History, Politics and Salvation*, trans. Caridad Inda and John Eagleson, New York: Maryknoll, 1985), 3–15. See also Enrique Dussel, 'Theology of Liberation and Marxism', in *Mysterium Liberationis: Fundamental Concepts of Liberation Theology*, ed. Ignacio Ellacuría and Jon Sobrino (Maryknoll, NY: Orbis, 1993), 85–8.

6 Dussel, 'Theology of Liberation and Marxism', 86 and 87, respectively. This focus on social science was, according to Gustavo Gutiérrez, canonized at Medellin, which marked 'the beginning of a new relationship between theological and pastoral language on the one hand and the social sciences which seek to interpret this reality on the other' (Gutiérrez, *A Theology of Liberation*), 136.

7 Raul Vidales, 'Methodological Issues in Liberation Theology', in *Frontiers of Theology in Latin America*, ed. Rosino Gibellini (Maryknoll, NY: Orbis Books, 1979), 39. Liberation theologians' claim for originality over the the the use of the social sciences as a mediating tool is often overstated (as in Dussel, for example). The North American Social Gospel movement serves as one case of theology embracing the social sciences as a mediating tool. See, most relevantly, Walter Rauschenbusch, *Christianity and the Social Crisis*, ed. Robert D. Cross, American Perspectives (New York: Harper Torchbooks/University Library-Harper and Row, 1967), 1907; Walter Rauschenbusch, *Christianizing the Social Order* (Boston: The Pilgrim Press, 1912) and Walter Rauschenbusch, A *Theology for the Social Gospel* (Nashville: Abingdon Press, 1945). Shailer Mathews was another central figure. On theology and social science, see his *Jesus on Social Institutions*, ed. and introd. Kenneth Cauthen, 'Lives of Jesus' (Philadelphia: Fortress Press, 1971). Paul Tillich's early religious socialism, Ernest Troeltsch's work as well as H.R. Niebuhr all used the social sciences to a degree. For these later three, however, the social sciences were not as central to theology as it was for the social gospelers and as it remains for liberation theology.

8 Within liberation theology Jung Mo Sung develops this argument in Jung Mo Sung, *Economía: Tema Ausente en la Teología de la Liberación* (San José, Costa Rica: DEI, 1994). See also Marcella Althaus-Reid's Latin American feminist/queer theology in Marcella Althaus-Reid, *Indecent Theology: Theological Perversions in Sex, Gender and Politics* (New York: Routledge, 2000). See also Lynch, 'Beyond Liberation Theology?'; Marsha Hewitt, 'Liberation Theology and the Emancipation of Religion' and Sigmund, *Liberation Theology at the Crossroads: Democracy or Revolution?*

9 Joseph Ratzinger, 'Relación Sobre la Situación Actual de la Fe y la Teología', in *Fe y Teología en America Latina* (Santa Fe de Bogota, Colombia: CELAM, 1997), 14. See also Humberto Belli and Ronald Nash, *Beyond Liberation Theology* (Grand Rapids, Michigan: Baker Book House, 1992) and the introduction to the 1991 edition of Michael Novak, *Will It Liberate? Questions About Liberation Theology* (Lanham, Maryland: Madison Books, 1991). For those who do not go so far as to proclaim liberation theology's death but who do raise questions concerning its continued relevance see Christopher Rowland's 'Conclusion' to Christopher Rowland (ed.), *The Cambridge Companion to Liberation Theology* (Cambridge: Cambridge University Press, 1999); Lynch, 'Beyond Liberation Theology?'; Duncan B. Forrester, 'Can Liberation Theology Survive 1989?', *Scottish Journal of Theology*, 47(2) (1994), 245–53; Max Stackhouse, 'Now That the Revolution is Over', *The Reformed Journal*, 40(7) (September 1990), 16–20; and Sigmund, *Liberation Theology at the Crossroads: Democracy or Revolution?*

10 See Althaus-Reid, *Indecent Theology*; Sung, *Economía: Tema Ausente en la Teología de la Liberación*; and Marsha Hewitt, 'Liberation Theology and the Emancipation of Religion'.

11 Clodovis Boff and Leonardo Boff, *Salvation and Liberation: In Search of a Balance Between Faith and Politics* (Maryknoll, NY: Orbis Books, 1984), 24.

12 José Comblin would not provide so generous an interpretation of the Vatican's use of 'liberation'. For him, 'The words are there, but always in a context that avoids all possibility of conflict: this is a poor and a liberation with which all social classes can identify themselves. No one feels denounced. In this way liberation theology's themes acquire a level of generality, abstraction and also of insignificance so that they become valid for all continents, for all peoples' (José Comblin, 'La Iglesia Latinoamericana

Desde Puebla a Santo Domingo', in *Cambio Social y Pensamiento Cristiano en América Latina*, ed. by José Comblin, José I. Gonzalez Faus and Jon Sobrino, Madrid: Editorial Trotta, 1993), 51.

13 Clodovis Boff, 'Epistemology and Method of the Theology of Liberation', in *Mysterium Liberationis: Fundamental Concepts of Liberation Theology*, ed. Ignacio Ellacuría and Jon Sobrino (Maryknoll, NY: Orbis Books, 1993), 62.

14 Clodovis Boff, 'Epistemology and Method of the Theology of Liberation', 62.

15 See also Boff and Boff, *Salvation and Liberation*; Clodovis Boff and Leonardo Boff, *Introducing Liberation Theology* (Maryknoll, NY: Orbis Books, 1987) and Clodovis Boff, *Theology and Praxis* (Maryknoll, NY: Orbis Books, 1987).

16 Clodovis Boff, 'Epistemology and Method of the Theology of Liberation', 73.

17 Ibid.

18 Boff stresses that oppression takes many shapes (class, gender, race, culture) yet he stresses the primacy of class oppression as a determining factor: 'it is important to observe that the socioeconomically oppressed (the poor) do not simply exist alongside the other oppressed, like the black, the Indian, or the woman (to restrict ourselves to the most significant categories of the oppressed in the Third World). No, the oppression of a class – socioeconomic poverty – is precisely the infrastructural expression of the process of oppression. The other types represent mere superstructural expressions of oppression. As such, they are profoundly conditioned by the infrastructural. A black taxi driver and a black soccer star are not the same thing. Similarly, a female domestic servant and the first lady of the land are not the same. An Indian whose land is stolen and an Indian in possession of it are not the same' (Clodovis Boff, 'Epistemology and Method of the Theology of Liberation'), 77.

19 Clodovis Boff, 'Epistemology and Method of the Theology of Liberation', 75.

20 I describe what Boff calls 'functionalism' as modernization theory in Chapter 4. See Walter Rostow, *The Stages of Economic Growth: A Non-Communist Manifesto* (Cambridge: Cambridge University Press, 1960) for a classic statement. For a critique of modernization theory see Arturo Escobar, *Encountering Development: The Making and Unmaking of the Third World* (Princeton, NJ: Princeton University Press, 1995).

21 Clodovis Boff, 'Epistemology and Method of the Theology of Liberation', 76.

22 Ibid.

23 Included within the socioanalytical mediation is a historical mediation that takes into account the history of oppressed peoples to achieve better conditions, thus highlighting their role as acting subjects within history (see ibid.).

24 Ibid., 79.

25 Ibid., 80.

26 See Marcella Althaus-Reid: 'Apologetics still exists in Liberation Theology, and in recent years it has seen a surprising revival in the writings of influential Roman Catholic theologians from the Catholic University of Central America in El Salvador. Their main intention for several years has been to demonstrate in a quasi-scientific (Stalinist) way how 'proper' (dogmatic) Liberation Theology really is. Their recently published works have been collected into a volume entitled *Mysterium Liberationis*. As Latin is not spoken in Latin America except amongst certain Roman Catholic priests, we wonder what readership they had in mind for this publication. The book is organized thematically, dealing with classical topics such as 'The Trinity', 'God the Father', 'The Virgin Mary'. Liberation Theology, far from liberating itself from systematic Western patterns, has become domesticated, a decent construction without the transgressive elements one might have expected' (Althaus-Reid, *Indecent Theology*), 31.

27 Marsha Hewitt, 'Liberation Theology and the Emancipation of Religion', 35.

28 Gustavo Gutiérrez, 'Teología y Ciencias Sociales', in *La Verdad los Hara Libres* (Lima: CEP, 1986), 87.

29 Clodovis Boff, 'Epistemology and Method of the Theology of Liberation', 79.

30 Gutiérrez, 'Teología y Ciencias Sociales', 83.

31 João Batista Libanio, *Teología de la Liberación: Guía Didáctica para Su Estudio* (Santander: Sal Terrae, 1989), 216.

32 Clodovis Boff, 'Epistemologia y Metodo de la Teología de la Liberación', in *Mysterium Liberationis: Conceptos Fundamentales de la Teología de la Liberación*, ed. Ignacio Ellacuría and Jon Sobrino (Madrid: Editorial Trotta, 1990), 86. I cite from the Spanish (with my own translation) because the English version mistranslates 'descontada' (takes for granted) for 'arrives at'. See Clodovis Boff, 'Epistemology and Method of the Theology of Liberation', 62.

33 Clodovis Boff, 'Epistemology and Method of the Theology of Liberation', 83.

34 Clodovis Boff, 'Como Veo Yo la Teología Latinoamericana Treinta Años Despues', in *El Mar Se Abrio: Treinta Años de Teología en America Latina*, ed. Luis Carlos Susin (Santander: Sal Terrae, 2000), 85.

35 The critique is developed in Sung, *Economía: Tema Ausente en la Teología de la Liberación*.

36 The only book length exception is Franz Hinkelammert, *The Ideological Weapons of Death: A Theological Critique of Capitalism* (Maryknoll, NY: Orbis Books, 1986). In addition to Sung and Hinkelammert see Hugo Assmann, *La Idolatría del Mercado* (San José, Costa Rica: DEI, 1997) and the collection Richard Pablo *et al.*, *The Idols of Death and the God of Life* (Mayknoll, New York: Orbis Books, 1983).

37 In the following I draw on Sung, *Economía: Tema Ausente en la Teología de la Liberación*, 111–18.

38 See Boff and Boff, *Introducing Liberation Theology*, 41–2. This example comes at the end of Chapter 3, a chapter that outlines what I have called the canonical view. The essay I draw on is almost exactly the same, but does not include this 'theology of land' example.

39 See Boff and Boff, *Introducing Liberation Theology*, 41–2.

40 See José Míguez Bonino, *Christians and Marxists: The Mutual Challenge to Revolution* (Grand Rapids: William B. Eerdmans, 1976).

41 Sung, *Economía: Tema Ausente en la Teología de la Liberación*, 113.

42 See Sung, *Economía: Tema Ausente en la Teología de la Liberación,* 112–13, for his presentation of the two diagrams.

43 Only one article of Sung's is available in English. See Jung Mo Sung, 'Economics and Theology: Reflections on the Market, Globalization and the Kingdom of God', in *Global Capitalism, Liberation Theology and the Social Sciences*, ed. Andreas Muller, Arno Tausch and Paul Zulehner (New York: Nova Science Publishers, Inc., 2000), 47–60. For the Spanish version see Jung Mo Sung, 'Economía y Teología: Reflexiones Sobre Mercado, Globalización y Reino de Dios', *Alternativas*, 5(9) (1998), 97–118. In addition, see Jung Mo Sung, 'Idolatría: Una Clave de Lectura de la Economía Contemporanea', *Alternativas*, 5(10) (1998), 19–38; Jung Mo Sung, *Neoliberalismo y Pobreza* (San José, Costa Rica: DEI, 1993); Jung Mo Sung, *La Idolatría del Capital y la Muerte de los Pobres* (San José, Costa Rica: DEI, 1991).

44 See Sung, *La Idolatría del Capital y la Muerte de los Pobres*, 31–2.

45 See Romans 8:23

46 This anthropology is found most developed in Enrique Dussel, *El Humanismo Semita* (Buenos Aires: Eudeba, 1969). Sung's discussion takes place in Sung, *La Idolatría del Capital y la Muerte de los Pobres*, 32.

47 Sung cites the following from Gutiérrez: 'Creation is presented in the Bible, not as a stage previous to salvation, but as part of the salvific process' (Gustavo Gutiérrez, *A Theology of Liberation: History, Politics and Salvation*, trans. and ed. Sister Caridad Inda and John Eagleson, Maryknoll, New York: Orbis, 1973), 154.

48 Gutiérrez, *A Theology of Liberation: History, Politics and Salvation*, 153.

49 Sung, *La Idolatría del Capital y la Muerte de los Pobres*, 33.

50 Sung, *Neoliberalismo y Pobreza*, 33.

51 Sung thus subscribes to the 'critiquing idolatry' response to the fall of the Berlin Wall. See my analysis in Chapter 1.

52 Sung, 'Economics and Theology', 52.

53 Ibid., 53.

54 Sung, *Neoliberalismo y Pobreza*, 56.

55 Sung, *La Idolatría del Capital y la Muerte de los Pobres*, 35.

56 Sung, *Economía: Tema Ausente en la Teología de la Liberación*, 116.

57 Boff practically admits as much in an essay reviewing his theological development. He writes: 'It was clear to me that any social reflection that wanted to claim to be theology had to be constitutively related to faith, had to be able to measure itself in relation to faith, unless it were to risk losing its identity. Thus my preocupation with theology's "hermeneutic mediation" ... But how to define more concretely the "formality" of theology, or its "theologicalness"? Then appeared the expression "in the light of faith". This was the definitive and defining clause of all truly theological discourse. And in case one might want to make the concept "in light of faith", constitutive of theology, more concrete, it is then necessary to speak "in light of God's word" or also "from the perspective of Scripture"' (Clodovis Boff, 'Como Veo Yo la Teología Latinoamericana Treinta Años Despues'), 77.

58 Sung's *Economía: Tema Ausente en la Teología de la Liberación* is an investigation of the causes of this problem.

59 Max Horkheimer, cited in Sung, 'Idolatría', 37.

60 Sung, *La Idolatría del Capital y la Muerte de los Pobres*, 117.

61 Ibid., 118.

62 Segundo develops his views on the matter most completely in Juan Luis Segundo, *Liberation of Theology*, trans. John Drury, reprint, 1975 (Maryknoll, New York: Orbis, 1979) and Juan Luis Segundo, *Faith and Ideologies* (Maryknoll, NY: Orbis Books, 1982). Also helpful is Juan Luis Segundo, 'Fe e Ideologia', *Perspectivas de Dialogo*, November 1974, 227–33. On Segundo, see Alfred Hennelly, *Theologies in Conflict: The Challenge of Juan Luis Segundo* (Maryknoll, NY: Orbis Books, 1979) and Marsha Hewitt, *From Theology to Social Theory: Juan Luis Segundo and the Theology of Liberation* (New York: Peter Lang, 1990).

63 Hennelly, *Theologies in Conflict*, 123.

64 See Segundo, *Faith and Ideologies*, 129–30. See also Hewitt, *From Theology to Social Theory*, 48–9.

65 Segundo, 'Fe e Ideologia', 229.

66 Segundo, *Liberation of Theology*, 109.

67 Ibid., 116.

68 Here I see some affinity between Segundo's project and some strands of liberal North American theology. Shailer Mathews, *The Growth of the Idea of God* (New York: The Macmillan Company, 1931), for example, can be seen as providing concrete examples of how the ideologies that concretize faith change in different contexts. In addition, the notion that we must consciously relate faith to ideology is similar to the idea of theology as 'imaginative construction' developed in Gordon Kaufman, *In Face of Mystery: A Constructive Theology* (Cambridge: Harvard University Press, 1993).

69 Segundo, *Liberation of Theology*, 117.

70 Ibid.

71 Ibid., 117–18.

72 Juan Luis Segundo, *Signs of the Times:Theological Reflections*, ed. Alfred Hennelly (Maryknoll, NY: Orbis Books, 1993), 3.

73 Ibid., 8.

74 See Ivan Petrella, 'Latin American Liberation Theology, Globalization, and Historical Projects: From Critique to Construction', in *Latin American Perspectives on Globalization: Ethics, Politics, and Alternative Visions*, ed. Mario Saenz (Lanham, MD: Rowman and Littlefield Publishers, 2002) and Ivan Petrella, 'Liberation Theology and Democracy: Toward a New Historical Project', *Journal of Hispanic/Latino Theology*, 7(4) (May 2000), 50–67, for two articles where I develop this claim.

75 Note that I use Segundo's understanding of faith and ideology to draw an analogy with my understanding of the relation between liberation theology's concepts and historical projects. I am not drawing on Segundo's hermeneutical circle which has been (I believe correctly) criticized for an uncritical espousal of scripture as liberative. Neither am I arguing that one can move directly from

religious ideals – whether found in scripture or in tradition – and the construction of institutions as if scripture and tradition were not themselves ambiguous and open to interpretation and contestation. I am merely pointing out the vacuity of liberation theology's terminology in the absence of the construction of historical projects. For the classic critique of Segundo and liberation theology generally on the issue of biblical interpretation, see Elisabeth Schüssler Fiorenza, *Bread not Stone: The Challenge of Feminist Biblical Interpretation* (Boston: Beacon Press, 1984), 43–64.

76 Gustavo Gutiérrez, *Teología Desde el Reverso de la Historia* (Lima, Peru: Ed. CEP, 1977), 353–4; emphasis added.

77 Leonardo Boff, *Jesus Christ Liberator: A Critical Christology for Our Time* (Maryknoll: Orbis Books, 1981), 275.

78 Segundo, *Liberation of Theology*, 9.

79 See the two volume Ignacio Ellacuría and Jon Sobrino (ed.), *Mysterium Liberationis: Fundamental Concepts of Liberation Theology* (Maryknoll, NY: Orbis Books, 1993).

CHAPTER 3

Liberation Theology, Democracy and Historical Projects

Chapter 1 offered a new interpretation of liberation theology's current situation. There I suggested that the main obstacle to liberation theology's continued relevance lies in the abandonment of the notion of a historical project, a concept once central to its thought and practice. Chapter 2 took a key step in its recovery by showing that the concept has been written out of liberation theology's methodological statements and by proposing an alternative way of thinking about liberation theology as theology. The previous two chapters thus set the context – liberation theology's responses to the shift in their historical context and the debate around liberation theology's methodology – within which this book seeks to recover the notion of a historical project. Now we take a further step in that direction. Today any such project must be couched in the language of democracy. For this reason, an examination of how this concept is currently understood in relation to Latin America, and has been understood by liberation theology, is the next step in clearing the space for the reconstruction and reimagination of new historical projects.

This chapter is divided into two parts. First, I examine and critique the dominant theoretical lens with which Latin American democracy is analyzed in the North American academy. Second, I present and evaluate liberation theology's changing relationship with democracy. More specifically, I will argue that new historical projects should take the shape of an alternative to the Latin American formal democracies legitimized by influential modes of thinking in the North American academy. I will show that the dominant social science approach to democracy in Latin America subscribes to a minimalist procedural definition of democracy, a form of government in which citizens choose candidates frequently and fairly, grounded in a truncated understanding of Joseph Schumpeter's political theory. In this understanding, criteria of efficiency, stability and even mere electoral mandate are the sole prerequisites that confer legitimacy on a democratic regime. This hegemonic definition of democracy serves the apologetic function of separating the understanding of democracy from the foundation of poverty, marginalization and exclusion upon which it rests. It forgets that the right to vote allows for a change in masters while a nation remains in slavery. It thus stands in the way of the imagination of new historical projects. In the second case, I show that there are three distinct but related phases in liberation theology's understanding of democracy: democracy via revolutionary socialism, participatory democracy via the base communities and the current analysis of stagnant democracy. At the center of all three phases is the refusal to separate democracy as a political mechanism from the social, political–participatory and economic basis upon which it rests.

Schumpeter and Democracy

In relation to Latin America, the dominant understanding of democracy within the North American academy derives from Joseph Schumpeter's classic work, *Capitalism, Socialism and Democracy*. This section begins, therefore, by outlining this text's main ideas as they apply to my argument. Schumpeter's take on democracy, as is the case with any such understanding, is conditioned by the time period in which it was formulated and has its roots most particularly in the European experience with war, fascism and communism. A central concern was thus the need to achieve stability in Europe after the experience of two 'great' wars. Schumpeter, rather than describing an idealized version of democracy, presents himself as describing and explaining the way democracies actually work in modern society. He begins by setting his position apart from the 'classical doctrine of democracy' in which 'the democratic method is that institutional arrangement for arriving at political decisions which realizes the common good by making the people itself decide issues through the election of individuals who are to assemble in order to carry out its will'.[1] Instead, Schumpeter argues that democracy is a political method, an institutional mechanism to arrive at decisions. Democracy, therefore, is the realization of neither a common good nor a popular will, nor the rule of the people. Modern societies are too diverse and heterogeneous to give way to a unified common good; instead, multiple understandings of the common good are bound to emerge.

For Schumpeter this was true at an individual level as well: since values differed from one person to another there was no such thing as a common good to be realized.[2] In addition, Schumpeter argued that the idea of an independent popular will was a fiction. The reality of political life was that the masses were so susceptible to manipulation that the popular will was in fact manufactured: 'the product and not the motive power for the political process'.[3] The purpose of a democracy, therefore, was not to select representatives that would carry out the will of the people but to choose individuals who could govern: 'democracy does not mean and cannot mean that the people actually rule in any obvious sense of the terms "people" and "rule". Democracy means only that the people have the opportunity of accepting or refusing the men who are to rule them ... Now one aspect of this may be expressed by saying that democracy is the rule of the politician'.[4] In a nutshell, Schumpeter defined democracy as 'that institutional arrangement for arriving at political decisions in which individuals acquire the power to decide by means of a competitive struggle for the people's vote'.[5] Democracy, in other words, is a system in which the people choose their rulers in periodic and competitive elections.

It is important to note that Schumpeter was writing about democracy in the modern industrial nations. He did not explicitly consider the question whether democracy could exist in the developing world and it is clear that Schumpeter did not think that democracies could function properly, or even survive, in all nations and conditions.[6] Quite the contrary, he believed that democracies could only survive when a number of strict conditions are given.[7] Those conditions are:

1   The caliber of the politicians must be high.
2   The effective range of political decisions should not be extended too far.
3   Government must count with a well-trained and independent bureaucracy to aid in the formulation and administration of policy.
4   Government and society must exhibit 'democratic self-control'. So, for example, there must be agreement around the undesirability of violent behavior, excessive criticism and voters and politicians confusing their respective roles.
5   There must be a culture tolerant of differences of opinion.

Schumpeter sums up his section on the preconditions for democracy by adding the final and, I will suggest later, most important condition: 'the reader need only review our conditions to satisfy himself that *democratic government will work to full advantage only if all the interests that matter are practically unanimous not only in their allegiance to the country but also in their allegiance to the structural principles of existing society*. Whenever these principles are called into question and issues arise that rend a nation into two hostile camps, democracy works at a disadvantage. And it may cease to work at all as soon as interests and ideals are involved on which people refuse to compromise'.[8]

Today Schumpeter's understanding of democracy is the consensus in North American social science work on democracy in Latin America. Witness Samuel Huntington: 'For some while after World War II a debate went on between those who were determined in the classical vein to define democracy in terms of source or purpose, and the growing number of theorists who adhered to an institutionalist concept of democracy in the Schumpeterian mode. That debate is now over. Schumpeter has won. His concept of democracy is the established and the Establishment concept of democracy.'[9]

North American Social Science and Latin American Democracy

The transition to democracy in Southern Europe and Latin American in the 1970s and 1980s inaugurated the so-called 'Third Wave' of democratization.[10] This process gave birth to an ample literature whose focus was the transition from military regimes to civilian governments and the latter's subsequent consolidation.[11]

The three studies that set the tone for this burst of scholarly activity are the four-volume work, *Transitions from Authoritarian Rule: Prospects for Democracy*, particularly the fourth volume, *Tentative Conclusions about Uncertain Democracies* by O'Donnell and Schmitter, *Democracy in Developing Countries*, edited by Diamond, Linz and Lipset, and finally, because it condenses and summarizes the scholarly consensus on democracy, Huntington's *The Third Wave: Democratization in the Late Twentieth Century*. Central to these works is the endorsement of Schumpeter's procedural model of democracy. For O'Donnell and Schmitter, democracy is a system that 'places the burden of consent upon party elites and professional politicians (sporadically subject to electoral approval) who agree among themselves, not on ethical or substantive grounds, but on the procedural norm of contingency'.[12] Diamond, Linz and Lipset define democracy as 'a system of government that meets three essential conditions: meaningful and extensive competition among individuals and organized groups (especially political parties) for all effective positions of government power, at regular intervals and excluding the use of force; a highly inclusive level of political participation in the selection of leaders and policies, at least through regular and fair elections, such that no major (adult) social group is excluded; and a level of civil and political liberties – freedom of expression, freedom of the press, freedom to form and join organizations – sufficient to ensure the integrity of political competition and participation'.[13] In the same vein, for Samuel Huntington, 'a political system is defined as democratic to the extent that its most powerful collective decision-makers are selected through periodic elections in which all candidates freely compete for votes and in which virtually all the adult population is eligible to vote'.[14] So 'the key institution in a democracy is the selection of leaders through competitive elections'.[15]

These works, and the work they inspired, emphasize the role of elite action in the installation and conservation of emerging democracies. For Huntington, to give one example, democratic institutions best emerge from the top down, 'through negotiations and compromises among political elites calculating their own interests and desires'.[16] All three also stress the separation of democracy as a political mechanism from civil society and the economic foundation of society. One is not related to the other. For O'Donnell and Schmitter, the democratization of the economy, the workplace, schools, parties and other institutions falls under the heading of 'socialization' and are excluded from what they understand as political democracy.[17] Diamond, Linz and Lipset assert that democracy is 'a political system, separate and apart from the economic system to which it is joined'.[18] Finally, for Huntington, 'defining democracy in terms of goals such as economic well-being, social justice, and overall socio-economic equity is not very useful'.[19]

Mainstream social science literature on democracy in Latin America, therefore, endorses Schumpeter's procedural definition in which democracy is equivalent to free and frequent elections to select leaders. This literature, however, only remembers one part of Schumpeter's understanding of democracy. It remembers the definition but forgets the strict preconditions Schumpeter set for the proper functioning of democracy. It forgets that Schumpeter had in mind the advanced industrial nations as the proper – and only – place where his understanding of democracy could thrive. Most importantly, this literature forgets that Schumpeter explicitly states that democracy requires the creation of a number of habits and conditions that the 'democratic method itself cannot be relied on to produce'.[20] Those habits, remember, included an aversion to violence and tolerance of different opinions. Remember, moreover, that for Schumpeter the emergence of such a culture, as the precondition for the success of his democratic method, requires a practical unanimous allegiance to 'the structural principles of the existing society'.[21] It is for this reason that Schumpeter limits his analysis to the advanced industrial nations that had the resources and material capability to enact social programs that would ensure allegiance to society's structural principles.[22]

Historically, the Western European nations that Schumpeter had in mind consolidated their democracies through the emergence of various systems of social welfare – in short, the creation of the welfare state.[23] In the context of the rise of the Soviet Union and the economic disaster of World War II, this was the main mechanism through which the preconditions for the success of the democratic method were established.[24] In every case, the consolidation of democracy was tied to the expansion of social programs designed to fight inequality and avoid the polarization of the population into antagonistic camps. And these programs proved successful. Here, thus, lies the paradox of Latin American democracy: while the European democracies emerged and were consolidated in the context of a successful attempt to lower inequality, poverty and polarization, in Latin America the exact opposite is occurring.[25] In Latin America, democracy runs beside a substantial increase in these variables, an increase that is glossed over and ignored by current scholars' truncated use of Schumpeter. In a case of partial amnesia, the current use of this definition completely severs democracy from the social conditions that Schumpeter himself argued were needed for its consolidation.

When Schumpeter's understanding is applied to Latin America, the conditions he sets out for its success are left behind. Never before has the notion of democracy been so severed from all conception of socioeconomic equality.[26] Thus O'Donnell and Schmitter claim that there is no room in the new Latin American democracies for providing the population with equal benefits in terms of wealth, income, education, health and housing.[27] This process of 'socialization' – as we saw they termed it – is excluded from political democracy and remains a 'persistent (if remote) goal'.[28] The key issue, though, is that while Schumpeter too drew a distinction between democracy as a political mechanism and its preconditions he saw that the preconditions were crucial for democracy's survival. Without those preconditions, he thought, democracy would not be able to maintain itself and would be overrun by the masses who had decided, tired of waiting, to take matters into their own hands and pursue a communist alternative. This point is forgotten by the most influential scholars in the field.[29]

This minimal definition also blurs the fact the outcome of the 'third wave' of democratization in Latin America was really less than liberal democracy in that it often did not include, in addition to elections, the rule of law, government accountability, a proper balance between branches of government and civilian control over the military.[30] In reality, neither Schumpeter's social conditions nor his political conditions are met. O'Donnell's notion of 'delegative democracy' exemplifies the extent to which scholars are willing to go to defend such a truncated understanding of democracy.[31] O'Donnell argues that, while democratic theory concentrates its attention on the different species of representative democracy, in Latin America a new type of democratic regime, delegative democracy, is emerging He explains: 'Delegative democracies rest on the premise that whoever wins the election to presidency is thereby entitled to govern as he or she sees fit, constrained only by the hard facts of existing power relations and by a constitutionally limited term of office. The president is taken to be the embodiment of the nation and the main custodian and definer of its interests. The policies of his government need bear no resemblance to the promises of his campaign – has not the president been authorized to govern as he (or she) thinks best?'[32] While for O'Donnell delegative democracy represents a new type of democratic regime, it seems more plausible to claim that such democracies are in reality part of a disturbing trend toward authoritarian solutions for problems of governability stemming from the massive exclusion caused by rapid economic liberalization in conjunction with the reduction of state capacity to meet social needs. O'Donnell, however, justifies the honorific label of 'democracy' with the assertion that these regimes display few constraints on contestation and participation by citizenry during the electoral period. Indeed, here social science literature on democracy finds itself unable to get beyond analysis of what is, gives an academic gloss to the real process of transition, and ends up presenting as a virtue what is at best a product of necessity and, at worst, a vice.[33]

The bottom line is that even a democratic theorist as sympathetic to political elites and as hostile to popular participation as Schumpeter recognized that the installation and consolidation of democracy could not succeed in a context of extreme inequality.[34] Unlike current theorists, Schumpeter recognized that every political system is by necessity grounded upon an economic foundation. The hegemony of an understanding of democracy that pays no account to this fact owes its ascendancy to a momentous shift in the historical context in which thinking about democracy takes place. Remember that Western European democracies sought consolidation in the face of a communist threat. Allegiance to democracy, and thus a version of capitalism, had to be bought through an improvement in the population's standard of living. Today, however, the demise of socialism and the lowering of people's expectations about the role of government in alleviating inequality lead to a situation in which such a truncated understanding of democracy smacks of realism. The current social, economic and political context – in a nutshell, the crisis of leftist activism and thought worldwide – is what lends this model of democracy credibility. Such a democracy no longer needs legitimization through material improvement or social inclusion; its very definition can dispense with these elements. Its legitimization lies, in fact, in the negative claim that there is no alternative.[35] No wonder, then, that in Latin America the triumph of democracy runs beside the increasing political apathy of the majority of the population.[36]

Liberation Theology and Democracy

The development of new historical projects must begin by rejecting the mainstream definition of democracy as a political method for choosing leaders. In its present variant, this understanding of democracy completely severs the link between political democracy and the economic foundation of society, a link present even, as we saw, in Schumpeter. The following section examines liberation theology's understanding of democracy in an attempt to glean possible contributions to new historical projects.

Since its inception, liberation theology has consistently opposed the reduction of democracy to a political method for choosing leaders independent of society's social condition. There are three distinct, yet related, phases in liberation theology's understanding of democracy: democracy via revolutionary socialism, participatory democracy via the base communities, and the current analysis of stagnant democracy. Central to all three phases is the refusal to separate democracy as a political mechanism from the social, political–participatory and economic basis upon which it rests.

Democracy via Revolutionary Socialism

Contrary to what some interpreters believe, early liberation theology's espousal of socialism is best read as an attempt to deepen democratic forms of political and economic organization.[37] When Bonino called for the exposure of 'the hoax of democracy' and allied himself with a 'socialist project of liberation';[38] when Gutiérrez claimed that 'the movement toward modern liberties, democracy and rational thought in Europe and the United States, meant for Latin America a new oppression and the more virulent exploitation of the underclass',[39] they were not rejecting democracy itself but a conception of democracy deemed disparagely as 'formal'. Such a democracy allowed for elections but paid no attention to helping the large disenfranchised masses to acquire the tools that would actually enable them to exercise citizenship. Latin American democracy, liberation theologians argued, served to mask capitalist exploitation of the vast underclass; it was a democracy that was allowed to function as long as the privilege of entrenched elites remained unthreatened. It was a democracy for the few. As Bonino states:

> It is true that all the forms of democracy were incorporated into our constitutions, but they remained as external to the life of the people as the Spanish 'laws of the Indies' had once been. The leaders of the emancipation and modernization had their faces turned toward Europe and the USA and their backs to the interior of the countries. There, Indians and peasants were simply

incorporated as cheap labor for production. Their condition, was, if anything, worse than it had been before under a sometimes more or less lenient paternalistic system. A free press, free trade, education, politics – all the 'achievements' of liberalism – were the privilege of the elite. For the growing Latin American masses, undernourishment, slavery, illiteracy, and later on forced migration, unemployment, exploitation, crowding and finally repression when they claim their rights – these are the harvest of one century of 'liberal democracy.'[40]

The point, however, was to break through this facade of democracy to inaugurate a real democracy. Thus Gutiérrez could write, while referring to the Bonino–Moltmann debate around the notion of a historical project, that 'our historical experience is different, and this difference makes us aware of bourgeois society's lies and the paths that the popular classes must take to conquer *an authentic democracy* and real freedom. This process is a part of what we call liberation'.[41] For him, 'the search for a socialist road and a *real democracy* will not be stopped with blows and repression'.[42] The task, therefore, was to make democracy real for the population as a whole.

Liberation theology's belief that only socialism could guarantee a real democracy stems from the local sociopolitical context of the time, particularly the failure of Christian Democracy and the rise of national security states. As a movement, Christian Democracy drew its inspiration from Catholic social teaching, Catholic Action and the work of Jacques Maritain.[43] Its kernel included four main ideas. First, Maritain attempted to devise a communitarian framework that would avoid the excesses of liberal individualism and communist collectivism. Second, democracy was to be understood not just as electoral democracy but also included an egalitarian component. Third, the notion of 'socialization' was used instead of and against the notion of socialism.[44] Finally, for Christian Democracy, societal transformation should occur by means of gradual reform.

Liberation theologians agree that between 1930 and 1960 the rise of Christian Democracy in Latin America provided for a reforming project over and against the traditionally oligarchic tendency of Latin American Catholicism.[45] At that time, Christian Democracy was a movement that drew mostly from middle sectors (but also from some popular sectors of the population) in contrast to the oligarchy whose roots were in the upper echelons of society. Christian Democracy also possessed a reformist and developmentalist ideology that lent itself to addressing social problems that the traditional liberal and conservative parties refused to address. Thus, Christian Democracy opened a new political, economic and religious option in Latin America. The political option, to take the banner under which Eduardo Frei was elected in Chile, consisted of a 'revolution in freedom,' the economic option avoided both socialism and capitalism advocating 'communitarian ownership' and the religious option brought together religious ideals and politics, refusing thus the strict separation between the gospel and politics advocated by conservative Latin American Catholicism.[46] The first two options, however, would fail to deliver what they promised, while the third would be radically transformed into liberation theology.

According to liberation theologians, after 1960 Christian Democracy's limitations become evident. They claimed that the actual practice of Latin American Christian Democracy in power revealed irresolvable contradictions in its program. Liberation theologians argued that Christian Democracy lacked an adequate social–economic analysis of capitalism, lacked a concrete political program, and mistakenly believed in harmony between social classes, failing to realize that social reality was in fact conflictive. A 'revolution in freedom', for example, was an evangelical ideal that would only be possible through the conversion of those who held privilege.[47] Otherwise the oligarchy would fight back and conflict was then unavoidable, proving revolution in freedom impossible. The notion of 'communitarian ownership' showed itself as too vague: neither capitalism nor socialism, it inevitably ended in a tepid reformism that changed nothing. These failures led to an inescapable conflict in Christian Democratic politics: on the one hand, the left finds the movement not really revolutionary or transformative, while the right, on the other hand, finds it endangering entrenched privilege when it actually succeeds in its transformative quest.[48] The end result is that Christian Democracy is deprived of a social base, unable as it is to please either workers or employers, it settles for a pragmatic politics of accommodation which, according to liberation theologians, becomes a bulwark for continued capitalist exploitation. At best, therefore, the Christian Democratic third way dissolves into a weak dependent capitalism; at worst, it becomes a veil for military regimes.[49]

The failure of Christian Democracy led to the radicalization of Latin American politics in a process that is the exact opposite of the path that the European nations followed to consolidate their democracies. In Europe, as we saw, the liberal democratic state legitimized itself in the face of a socialist threat through successful social reform. In Latin America, however, the failure of such reform led to a demand to go beyond reform, a demand centered on a radical break from the liberal democratic state and the capitalism that state is perceived as upholding. Witness Bonino: 'The liberal modernization project, as incorporated in the liberal democratic state built on the base of free-enterprise capitalism, seems to have run its course and proven unable to respond to the needs of humanity at the present stage of human development.'[50] While in Europe reform served to disarm and dissolve revolutionary socialist movements, in Latin America it is the failure of reform that gives birth to and feeds such movements.[51]

The emergence of revolutionary socialist movements, however, led to the installation of national security states to safeguard elite and capitalist privilege.[52] Already in the 1950s and 1960s Brazil, Peru and Bolivia suffered military coups to keep democratically elected leftist alliances from assuming power.[53] For liberation theologians, though, Chile remains the case that most fully demonstrates the alliance between liberal democracy and capitalism, an alliance designed to preserve the privilege of the rich and further the exploitation of the poor. The Chilean story is familiar. The founder of the Christian Democratic party, Eduardo Frei, was elected president from 1964 to 1970 with 55.7 per cent of the vote. The failure of most of his reforms – agrarian reform was the main accomplishment but proved only 20 per cent effective in terms of peasant families helped[54] – led to increased support for more radical alternatives within segments of the Chilean population.[55] In a subsequent splintered election a Marxist, Salvador Allende of the Popular Unity party, won the presidency with a minority vote. Initially, Allende worked with full support from Congress. He proceeded to double the rate of land expropriation and agrarian reform and nationalized the copper and automotive industry. But increasing domestic problems (spiraling inflation and a shortage of consumer goods) led to dwindling support. In addition, a drop in copper prices, Chile's main export, hurt the economy while the United States blocked loans from the International Development Bank and the World Bank.[56] Finally, the military, in September 1973, in the midst of civil strife and conservative, Christian Democrat and covert North American support, staged a coup that ended in Allende's death and the detention, expulsion and execution of thousands of people.

These national security states claim to suspend democracy for the sake of democracy.[57] They present themselves as the guarantee that democracy will not fall prey to socialism and anarchy; although they oust a democratically elected government they are the true guarantors of the democratic order. In this line of reasoning, popular movements, rather than deepening democracy, are a threat to democracy.[58] The governability of democracies, from this perspective, depends on the capacity to control social movements and the organizations that express them, whatever the cost. The national security states were heavily imbued with a pseudo-Christian ideology that justified their actions in the name of defending Western civilization from atheistic communism and, in the process, according to liberation theologians, serve as 'a cover for and in the service of the economic hegemony of multinational capitalism'.[59] In practice, they adopt the following policies: (a) legal mechanisms of oppression to enact emergency legislation that suspends constitutional guarantees; (b) new governmental institutions such as boards of national security with authority extending into all areas of civilian life; (c) suspension of the electoral process and the election of the chief executive by military juntas; (d) dissolution of legislative bodies and prohibition of all political activity; (e) limits on the organization of labor and the right of association; (f) control of means of communication; (g) prohibition of cultural activities that may be deemed threatening; (h) creation of military courts with jurisdiction over civilians and the suppression of habeas corpus.[60]

This dismantling of democracy is done in the name of preparing the nation for a responsible return to democracy. Given this twist, it is not surprising that liberation theologians saw Latin American democracy as a sham, valid insofar as its operation did not threaten society's underlying structure of privilege. But they did not oppose democracy per se, rather they opposed a democracy based on the forceful exclusion of the great majority of Latin Americans. When they advocated socialism they were calling for an end to an oligarchic model of democracy, a democracy that served the interests of a small minority. For liberation theologians, democracy could not be separated from a process of incorporation for excluded segments of the population. This, in turn, required attacking structural inequality at both the political and economic levels to give people the tools to exercise citizenship. Given their historical context they believed that revolutionary socialism was the only way to break the alliance between military, local and foreign elites, and inaugurate a truly democratic order. Third-way reformism failed when Christian Democracy failed; there was no other path to democracy but socialism. Even in its earliest phase, therefore, Latin American liberation theology should not be read as opposed to democracy but rather as geared toward deepening democratic forms of political and economic organization.

Participatory Democracy via the Base Communities

While the first approach to democracy – democracy via revolutionary socialism – is contextualized through the failure of Christian Democracy and the rise of national security states, the second approach, the attempt to make of the base communities a stepping stone for the creation of a new 'participatory democracy', is contextualized through the heady days of democratization in Latin America.[61]

The timing of the democratic transitions varied considerably.[62] Argentina's transition to democracy, for example, was spurred by general discontent over human rights violations and economic crises, and was sealed by a military defeat in a war with Great Britain over the Malvinas/Falkand Islands in 1982. After that defeat, the military junta announced elections and in October of 1983 Raul Alfonsin was elected president, thus inaugurating Argentina's return to democracy. Brazil's transition to democracy was more gradual, starting with a policy of *abertura* or political relaxation in the 1970s, following with indirect presidential elections in 1985 and finally completed with presidential elections in 1990. Peru held presidential elections in 1980, 1985 and 1990, although there was a general disenchantment with the political class that fed into Fujimori's *autogolpe* – the suspension of the constitution and dissolution of congress in 1992 – that received considerable public support. In Chile, the constitution called for a 1988 plebiscite on General Pinochet's continuity as president. Despite receiving 44 per cent of the vote Pinochet lost the plebiscite opening up the way for presidential elections in 1989 and a formal transfer of power in 1990.

The authoritarian withdrawal changed the face of the continent and forced liberation theologians to bring to the forefront the question of what kind of democracy they deemed appropriate for Latin America. In the first place, they voiced their support for the process of redemocratization, fundamentally the reinstallation of the liberties (elections, freedom of the press, freedom of association, constitutional guarantees) that had previously been denounced as purely formal. In the second place, however, liberation theologians sought to link the process of political redemocratization with social and economic democratization. As Dussel states: 'Formal democracy, of which we must applaud many positive aspects, covers up also a great injustice.'[63] For this reason, while they supported the new political democracies they refused to abandon the quest for a more radical social democracy, hoping even that democracy could lead to the socialist organization of the economy. In the process, they embraced democracy, rather than socialism, as the central concept that best expressed their aspirations. The 1986 'Document of Latin American Theologians for the Second General Assembly of Third World Theologians' places the question of democracy first on its list of challenges and deserves to be quoted at length:

> In the first place, we need to focus on the type of democratic organization that Latin America wants to give itself. There was a period (the sixties and early seventies) when popular sectors associated democracy with a bourgeois institutional order. It was thus necessary to overcome this democracy and break the mould of liberalism and bourgeois representation. Unfortunately, the dominant classes succeeded in imposing the national security state administered by the military against popular pressure that sought transformation. This brought repression, much suffering and death for the popular sectors ... In spite of the power these national security dictatorships managed to accumulate they have suffered a process of erosion that led to their fall in Argentina, Brazil, Uruguay, Bolivia, Peru, Guatemala, etc ... These processes resulted from the tenacious resistance of popular organizations and the administrative incapacity of the military in power itself. The military, as a consequence of the action of the popular movements and their own incapacity, returned to the barracks.
>   In this context emerged the question: Which democracy? If before this question was asked by the dominant classes, today it is formulated by the popular sectors. Now that the night of dictatorship is gone, how is the people to articulate a political order that would allow it to open paths toward a better standard of living? New models of democratic organization have not been designed nor proposed, even though this seemed to be the intention when the military returned to their normal role. Thus a bourgeois liberal and representative order dominates once again. Nevertheless, the popular sectors want to participate decisively in the history in which it is their right to participate. This means that they have reached a new understanding of democracy's value, seen more and more as a space where different political projects can meet.
>   The popular sectors want to create something new. In this sense their action has a prophetic character and their thought carries the positive sign of utopia ... The challenge, in these circumstances, is how can we forge a new democracy in which the majority participate? And related to this question, how can we build a popular unity that will give strength to the people's movement to guarantee the birth and permanence of this new democracy.[64]

Note the following: first, the document tells the story told in the previous section of this chapter. In the 1960s and 1970s, popular movements read democracy as bourgeois and formal, a cover for capitalist exploitation. National security states emerged in reaction to the increasingly radical nature of those movements. Second, the end of military authoritarianism and subsequent redemocratization emerges hand in hand with a new respect for the rights guaranteed under political democracy. Liberation theologians and popular movements alike now see political democracy as an arena where they can strive for an alternative model of democratic organization in which the majority would be able to participate. Third, this model must be created by the popular classes themselves. In the meantime, a limited political democracy remains as the default option.

Liberation theologians thus abandoned revolution and embraced political democracy while remaining unwilling to grant it the last word. Instead, they suffused the concept of democracy with an ideal content of far greater participation and equality than allowed for in existing democratic regimes. For Assmann, for example, 'democracy is a radical issue, not in terms of revolution, but in terms of participation. Democracy with a social content is a very radical issue'.[65] Leonardo Boff develops most the ideal content of democracy:

> From now on we must try that which is opposed to all forms of domination and oppression: democracy ... I do not mean, however, bourgeois democracy but democracy *tout court*. More than a social form, democracy supposes an attitude that must be lived in all spheres of life, in our intersubjectivity and society itself. Democratic ideals are profoundly revolutionary; they subvert all forms of domination. Democracy is also one of the West's most ancient aspirations. It possesses a utopian dimension that illuminates every aspect of life and cannot be exhausted in any particular historical form.[66]

We can begin to intuit the answer to one commentator's question: 'If liberation theologians fully embrace the liberal democratic process in Latin America, will not their theology, de facto, increasingly resemble the progressive reformist theology which they repudiated in the late 1960s?'[67] The answer, of course, is no. Liberation theologians embraced liberal or political or formal democracy but as a first step toward a more radical democratic model. Their acceptance of liberal democracy, moreover, did not carry over into an acceptance of capitalism. Capitalism was still to be overcome. For Boff, real democracy and capitalism are fundamentally incompatible. The former aspires toward equality while the latter 'enthrones accumulation on the one hand and poverty on the other hand'.[68] He builds his conception of democracy upon four pillars.[69] First, the greatest possible participation by all those concerned. This participation, moreover, should start from below to assure that no one remain marginalized from the democratic process. Second, the equality of all stemming from this global participation. Participation, for Boff, keeps difference from becoming inequality. Third, an espousal and celebration of difference. Difference should not be seen as a menace to equality, difference – unlike poverty and inequality – is an expression of equality. Finally, communion as the person's capacity to relate to others as brother or sister as well as entering in communion with God. These four pillars stand together and the attempt to make them real in society is the means to overcome mechanisms of oppression. Boff thus connects democracy to the notion of liberation, not just for the Third

World but for the wealthy nations as well. Latin Americans and Europeans are both challenged to create this 'social, popular, participatory and transcultural' democracy. It requires an alliance between the third and first worlds: 'Democracy is the concrete carrier of liberation for those who historically have been on opposite sides, the oppressors on one side, the oppressed on the other side. Democracy operates a revolution for both of them, allowing them to build together, now, forms of relating without domination.'[70]

For Boff and other liberation theologians, the key to managing the tension between the espousal of political democracy and the attempt to create a social and participatory democracy lay in the *comunidades eclesiales de base* (CEB) or Christian base communities. Base communities are lay led grassroots groups composed of individuals from the lower strata of society that meet in homes, community centers or church facilities to reflect on scripture and discuss its relevance to their lives and the social and political conditions of society.[71] The development of CEBs in Latin America, starting in the late 1960s and reaching a peak in the early 1980s, was spurred by the repressive political climate of the national security state. At that time, after the military coups, the Catholic church emerged as the only organization that could operate with some measure of independence from the state. In this context, base communities became havens from political persecution and surrogates for other institutions.[72] In the absence of any other locus for opposition to the government, CEBs assumed this role as well.

Social science literature on CEBs stresses their potential to promote conditions necessary for democracy.[73] CEBs, for example, contribute to the associational fabric necessary for a vibrant civil society.[74] They foster an attitude of engaged criticism that helps to overcome passivity and fatalism among the poor. Here Paulo Freire's notion of *conscientisization* was implemented by many CEBs. Through a process of *conscientisization*, CEB members begin to see their, and society's, problems as human products that can be altered through collective action, rather than an unchangeable fate.[75] This attitude, in turn, strengthens civil society's vigilance over government forcing the latter to become accountable for its actions. CEBs also develop their members' communication, organizational and leadership skills and thus function as micro-democracies that prepare members for participation in politics at the macro level. They cultivate a sense of responsibility for the condition of society and even directly mobilize political participation. Finally, CEBs serve as a power base for organized influence over political parties.

Liberation theologians held high hopes for the democratic potential of CEBs. As Frei Betto put it: 'In the practice of the CEBs within the popular movements, utopia becomes *topia* ... The process of constructing the popular political project results in a society where political power will be exercised by the people in the service of the people and the means of production will be socialized.'[76] In a historical context where revolution is ruled out, 'the path is the slow, long process of popular *conscientisization* and of successive conquests through legal means ... The parliamentary way is given as the place for the inevitable historical passage'.[77]

CEBs would serve as the popular foundation to push political democracy toward social democracy. This was now a two-stage process. Political democracy came first but as a stepping stone for popular or participatory democracy. For Boff, this participatory democracy should

> transcend the limits of bourgeois representative democracy which in Latin America functions in an elitist and anti-popular way, frequently introducing a military dictatorship in order to prevent the advancement of the people and to safeguard the interests of capital. Participatory democracy is based on the organized people; it can and must have representation, but this is continually controlled by the popular organizations themselves, the true subjects of social power. This participatory democracy is not just a project. The seed of it is alive in the popular movements, in the Christian communities on the ground and other movements ... Participatory democracy represents the new and the alternative to the capitalist social mould which up to now has not succeeded, in any country in the world, in resolving the basic problems of the people in terms of work, shelter, health and education.[78]

Here the base communities are the tool to work towards a parliamentary democracy and, at a later stage, popular or participatory democracy.[79] This would then lead to economic democracy or socialism, this time reached by an open political process rather than revolution; socialism built from the ground up rather than imposed from the top down.

Stagnant Democracy

This hope, the hope that in the process of redemocratization CEBs would emerge as the vehicles for a new social and participatory democracy, has vanished. The case of Brazil serves as an example.[80] In the previous section the high hopes placed by liberation theologians on the CEBs were illustrated. CEBs, remember, were to be the seed of a new democracy. This project, however, failed for many reasons, among which are a changed political context and the ambivalent nature of politics and the CEBs themselves. So, for example, in Brazil liberation theologians such as Boff and Betto argued that CEBs should support the Brazilian Worker's Party (PT) since this party, they claimed, drew its membership from the same social classes as CEBs and because its program paralleled that of CEBs. At the fourth CEB *Intereclesial* (1981), however, the CEBs disagreed with liberation theologians and decided that they were neither a party, part of a party, nor supporters of any one political party. Boff's and Betto's hope that CEBs could offer a unified political front was thus shattered. In addition, with the process of democratization the CEBs and the church lost their monopoly over political life. Now other avenues of expression were open. This process also led to splintering within the church itself as the Brazilian hierarchy, in the face of Vatican criticism of liberation theology, pulled back on its support of CEBs. Further studies on CEBs showed that the claim that they represent the poor is not entirely accurate.[81] Their membership comes from the working class but not from the poorest of the poor. Literacy expectations, for example, ruled out illiterates. The need for a high level of commitment drove away those who could not find the time to attend owing to work needs. CEBs, furthermore, found it difficult to translate their local activism onto a national scale. Their tendency to absolutize the working class hindered alliances with multi-class parties and their suspicion of politicians made members hesitant to engage in national politics.

Currently, liberation theologians display a general sense of unease with Latin American democracies. José Comblin summarizes the position of the Latin American church since Puebla: 'The bishops had expressed their commitment to the struggle for human rights and for them this meant the end of the military regimes and the return to democracy. From democracy the bishops hoped for an end to Latin America's problems. But democracy came and the problems are even worse than 13 years ago. What does the church think today, 13 years after Puebla? The answer: It is perplexed by the new democracy.'[82]

Present-day democratic regimes are described as 'low intensity democracies' and 'restricted democracies', which require limiting the scope for economic and participatory demands to avoid chaos; 'facade democracies', in which democratic rights embodied in the constitution are incapable of being met; and 'democracies under tutelage', in which an outside agent such as the United States or the IMF is needed to ensure a regime's stability.[83] Essentially, the liberationist critique of Latin American democracy is the same as in the late 1960s and 1970s, tempered this time by an acceptance of political democracy. Liberation theologians are well aware that political democracy 'means the end of torture, arbitrary arrest, secret police, being underground'.[84] Still, the critique boils down to the same claim that 'without economic democracy, political democracy becomes appearance – as has been the case throughout history. This is the biggest obstacle to the unfolding of a true democracy'.[85] The possibility that national security states would give way to limited political democracies was anticipated by liberation theologians before the process of democratization. As long ago as 1979, Gutiérrez warned that 'the church would fall into a trap if it easily and naively accepts a restricted democracy; that is, a formal restitution of some liberties and individual rights that leave untouched the existing profound social and economic inequality'.[86]

Liberation theologians argue that despite the demise of the national security state, national security ideology continues to drive Latin American democracy. Democracy is allowed insofar as it does not touch elite privilege and question the underlying capitalist order: 'The fact that the armed forces have returned to their barracks does not mean that they have given up the role that they have always played of being the ultimate backup ... As in the past, when the ruling classes have perceived that the democratic system might grant a modicum of real power to the workers, they will ask the army to step in to maintain their traditional control. They have always done so in the past, and there is no reason for them not to do so in the future.'[87] They claim that while in the past democracy was conceived of as both a process of social inclusion and a political mechanism, today's Latin American democracies (following the truncated understanding of Schumpeter described in the first section of this chapter) present themselves as mere mechanisms for organizing government.

What emerges, therefore, is a democracy from above that installs itself over popular movements that have been destroyed in the name of democracy.[88] The return to democracy, in fact, is premised on the destruction of those movements. Only then can elites ensure that democracy would not threaten their social standing. These new democracies, liberation theologians claim, begin by controlling popular movements to keep them from resurfacing and thus continue the same line as the national security states. Rather than being premised on an improvement in the population's general standard of living, their governability is instead based on disarticulating the means by which grievances can be expressed. A strong and vigorous civil society is thus not, as Tocqueville thought, a condition of democracy but an obstacle to democratic governability; the exact opposite of Tocqueville becomes true: the more disengaged civil society becomes, the greater the stability of the democracy.[89] Liberation theologians go so far as to suggest that current democracies are grounded not just on the squashing of popular movements, but more fundamentally on the destruction of all hope in an alternative to the limited democracies now enshrined in history and in social science. As Hinkelammert states: 'The negation of any and all alternatives – the total lack of hope – convinces. And the national security democracies are legitimized upon that ground.'[90]

Conclusion

Liberation theology's complex relationship to democracy takes three different shapes: democracy via revolutionary socialism, democracy via the base communities and a focus on democracy as stagnant. Democracy is never rejected in any of these shapes, but neither is democracy fully accepted as it stands in history. Note that the first two approaches to democracy – democracy via revolutionary socialism and participatory democracy via the base communities – contain elements critical of their context and constructive in relation to the future. The third and last approach, the analysis of stagnant democracy, is emblematic of our time in remaining purely critical in its inability to envision a more positive future.

Liberation theology's description of stagnant democracy parallels the democracy legitimized by current social science work on Latin America. Although they see the same thing – a focus on democracy as a political mechanism, the exclusion of economics as a legitimizing factor, a focus on elites and low popular political mobilization, all supposedly grounded on realism and 'common sense' – one criticizes while the other endorses. In reality, however, they operate with different understandings of democracy. The mainstream social science position defines democracy purely in procedural terms, while liberation theology advocates what could be termed a substantive conception of democracy. Huntington, for example, would likely argue that liberation theologians define democracy in terms of a purpose or goal, 'such as social justice, equality, or individual fulfillment', and that such attempts suffer from 'ambiguity and imprecision'.[91] He is only partly right. Democracy, as a historical project, is often described in the symbolic and elusive language found in Boff's four pillars. There certain ideal goals, such as communion, are expressed. Yet there is a basic way in which liberation theology's substantive understanding of democracy is more firmly grounded in reality than the seemingly realistic procedural model. In the Latin American context, to forget Schumpeter's preconditions for democracy is to forget the conditions for the reproduction of life for a vast majority. And life is not a purpose or a goal, it is the very possibility of possessing a goal.[92] This is the fundamental blindness of the procedural model: new historical projects are not part of a utopian or romantic or messianic quest, on the contrary, they are based on the tragic recognition that an alternative to the present is required to give most people a chance to survive. With this recognition, liberation theology is more realistic than the procedural model espoused by North American social science work on Latin American democracy.

Liberation theology needs to be able to think in terms of new historical projects. This chapter traced the failure of democracy via revolutionary socialism and democracy via the base communities, and thus, in reality, the failure of two such projects. The focus on stagnant democracy speaks forcefully to the current void of options. Before we fully tackle this void, though, we must examine the second part of the equation – liberation theology's approach to, and understanding of, capitalism. It is to this task that we turn in the next chapter.

Notes

1 Joseph Schumpeter, *Capitalism, Socialism and Democracy* (New York: Harper and Row, 1950), 250. The book was first published in 1942. A good summary of Schumpeter and other democratic theorists can be found in David Held, *Models of Democracy* (Stanford, CA: Stanford University Press, 1987). This section of the chapter is heavily indebted to the superb analysis of Schumpeter and his heirs in relation to contemporary North American social science in Paul Cammack, *Capitalism and Democracy in the Third World: The Doctrine for Political Development* (London: Leicester University Press, 1997).

2 Schumpeter, *Capitalism, Socialism and Democracy*, 251.

3 Here Schumpeter draws on theories of crowd psychology and studies on the success of advertising in creating new needs. In these theories the individual stands almost helpless as outside forces manipulate their desires. The success of Nazi propaganda in mobilizing the German people also influenced his position on this matter, Schumpeter, *Capitalism, Socialism and Democracy*, 263.

4 Schumpeter, *Capitalism, Socialism and Democracy*, 284–5. While Athens, of course, provides an image of the classical understanding of democracy as realizing the common good or the popular will, Esparta, on the other hand, provides an early picture of Schumpeter's rule of the politician. In Esparta, members of the city council were selected by a process that resembles, in a rudimentary fashion, the election process of today's representative democracies. Candidates paraded before an assembly of gathered citizens who in turn voiced their approval or disapproval while impartial observers registered the 'voters' reaction to determine the outcome (José Nun, *Democracia: Gobierno del Pueblo o Gobierno de los Políticos?*, Buenos Aires: Fondo de Cultura Económica, 2000), 21–2.

5 Schumpeter, *Capitalism, Socialism and Democracy*, 269.

6 Remember that Schumpeter published his text in 1942. In 1920 there existed 35 representative democracies, in 1938 that number had been cut by half; and by 1942 there were 12 left (Nun, *Democracia*, 24).

7 See Schumpeter, *Capitalism, Socialism and Democracy*, 289–96.

8 Schumpeter, *Capitalism, Socialism and Democracy*, 295–6; emphasis added. Cited in Cammack, *Capitalism and Democracy in the Third World*, 18–19.

9 Samuel Huntington, 'The Modest Meaning of Democracy', in *Democracy in the Americas: Stopping the Pendulum*, ed. Robert A. Pastor (New York: Holmes & Meier, 1989), 15. Or as put by a critic with some irony; 'For the self-declared mainstream tradition that dates itself from Schumpeter, democracy in mass society can be no more than a means for selecting leaders through competitive elections.' See Kurt von Mettenheim and James Malloy (eds), *Deepening Democracy in Latin America* (Pittsburgh: The University of Pittsburgh Press, 1998), 173.

10 See Samuel Huntington, *The Third Wave: Democratization in the Late Twentieth Century* (Norman: University of Oklahoma Press, 1991).

11 See, in addition to those works here presented, Juan Linz and Arturo Valenzuela, *The Failure of Presidential Democracy* (Baltimore: Johns Hopkins University Press, 1994); Juan Linz, *Problems of Democratic Transition and Consolidation: Southern Europe, South America, and Postcommunist Europe* (Baltimore: Johns Hopkins University Press, 1996); Larry Diamond, Marc Plattner, Yun-han Chu and Tien-Hung-Mao (eds), *Consolidating the Third Wave Democracies: Themes and Perspectives* (Baltimore: Johns Hopkins University Press, 1997) and Scott Mainwaring and Arturo Valenzuela (eds), *Politics, Society and Democracy* (Boulder, Colorado: Westview Press, 1998). For a good overview of this literature, see John Peeler, *Building Democracy in Latin America* (London: Lynne Rienner Publishers, 1998). For literature critical (to different degrees) of Huntington's 'Establishment' concept of democracy, see Atilio Boron, *State, Capitalism, and Democracy in Latin America* (London: Lynne Rienner Publishers, 1995); Douglas Chalmers *et al.*, *The New Politics of Inequality in Latin America: Rethinking Participation and Representation* (Oxford: Oxford University Press, 1997); Graciela Ducatenzeiler and Philip Oxhorn (eds), *What Kind of Democracy? What Kind of Market? Latin America in the Age of Neoliberalism* (Pennsylvania: The Pennsylvania State University Press, 1998); von Mettenheim and Malloy, *Deepening Democracy in Latin America*; Felipe Aguero and Jeffrey Stark (eds), *Fault Lines of Democracy in Post-Transition Latin America* (Miami: North–South Center Press, University of Miami, 1998); Philip Oxhorn and Pamela Starr (eds), *Markets and Democracy in Latin America: Conflict or Convergence?* (London: Lynne Rienner Publishers, 1999).

12 Guillermo O'Donnell and Peter Schmitter, *Transitions from Authoritarian Rule: Tentative Conclusions about Uncertain Democracies* (Baltimore: Johns Hopkins University Press, 1986), 59; cited in Cammack, *Capitalism and Democracy in the Third World*, 218.

13 Larry Diamond, Juan Linz and Seymour Lipset (eds), *Democracy in Developing Countries,* Vol. 2 (London: Adamantine Press, 1988), xvi; Cammack, *Capitalism and Democracy in the Third World*, 219.

14 Samuel Huntington, 'Will More Countries Become Democratic?', *Political Science Quarterly*, 99(2) (1984), 195; Cammack, *Capitalism and Democracy in the Third World*, 224.

15 Huntington, 'The Modest Meaning of Democracy', 15.

16 Huntington, 'Will More Countries Become Democratic?', 212; Cammack, *Capitalism and Democracy in the Third World*, 225.

17 O'Donnell and Schmitter, *Transitions from Authoritarian Rule*, 14; Cammack, *Capitalism and Democracy in the Third World*, 221.

18 Diamond, Linz, and Lipset, *Democracy in Developing Countries,* Vol. 2, 16; Cammack, *Capitalism and Democracy in the Third World*, 221.

19 Huntington, 'The Modest Meaning of Democracy', 19.

20 Schumpeter, *Capitalism, Socialism and Democracy*, 295.

21 Ibid., 296.

22 Nun, *Democracia*, 69.

23 The best work on the development and varied manifestations of the welfare state remains Gosta-Espig Anderson, *The Three Worlds of Welfare Capitalism* (Princeton, NJ: Princeton University Press, 1990).

24 For examples one can take the post World War II economic history of Germany, Austria, Italy, Greece, Portugal, Spain, France and, in Asia, Japan. For a brief review see Nun, *Democracia*, 77–83.

25 Nun, *Democracia*, 127.

26 Schumpeter himself is taken to task by critics for developing a view of democracy that leaves out the egalitarian component found in authors as varied as Aristotle, Plato, Machiavelli, Marx and Tocqueville. For this view of Schumpeter, see Boron, *State, Capitalism, and Democracy in Latin America*. While Schumpeter was no radical democrat, he did understand that a measure of socioeconomic equality was the only sure basis upon which democracy could rest. While equality was not part of the definition of democracy, or part of its purpose, it was a fundamental precondition for its well functioning and its preservation. The link between equality and democracy is still present. Current social science scholarship on democracy in Latin America, however, for the first time, severs this link completely.

27 O'Donnell and Schmitter, *Transitions from Authoritarian Rule*, 11–14, Fig. 2.1; Cammack, *Capitalism and Democracy in the Third World*, 221.

28 O'Donnell and Schmitter, *Transitions from Authoritarian Rule*, 12.

29 This mainstream position is propagated by the *Journal of Democracy* and a number of important (and wealthy) institutions such as US National Endowment for Democracy, the Hoover Institution and the Woodrow Wilson International Center for Scholars. On this, see Cammack, *Capitalism and Democracy in the Third World*, 232.

30 Chalmers *et al*, *The New Politics of Inequality in Latin America*, 9.

31 This argument against O'Donnell draws on Ducatenzeiler and Oxhorn, *What Kind of Democracy? What Kind of Market?*, 234–9.

32 Guillermo O'Donnell, 'Delegative Democracy', *Journal of Democracy* 5(1) (January 1994), 59–60; cited in Ducatenzeiler and Oxhorn, *What Kind of Democracy? What Kind of Market?*, 236.

33 Chalmers, et al., *The New Politics of Inequality in Latin America*, 9.

34 For a classic example of the argument that too much popular mobilization is a threat to democracy – the 'overburdening of political institutions' – see Samuel Huntington, *Political Order in Changing Societies* (New Haven: Yale University Press, 1968).

35 For this argument see Cammack, *Capitalism and Democracy in the Third World*, 250–51.

36 See Patricio Silva, 'The New Political Order in Latin America: Towards Technocratic Democracies?', in *Latin America Transformed: Globalization and Modernity*, ed. Robert N. Gwynne and Cristobal Kay (London: Arnold, 1999), 62.

37 These interpreters include, most significantly, Paul Sigmund, *Liberation Theology at the Crossroads: Democracy or Revolution?* (New York: Oxford University Press, 1990) and Michael Novak, *Will It Liberate? Questions About Liberation Theology* (Lanham, Maryland: Madison Books, 1991).

38 José Míguez Bonino, *Doing Theology in a Revolutionary Situation*, ed. William H. Lazareth, Confrontation Books (Philadelphia: Fortress Press, 1975), 15 and 39, respectively.

39 Gustavo Gutiérrez, *La Fuerza Histórica de los Pobres* (Lima: Centro de Estudios y Publicaciones, 1979), 341.

40 José Míguez Bonino, *Doing Theology in a Revolutionary Situation*, 15.

41 Gutiérrez, *La Fuerza Histórica de los Pobres*, 341.

42 Ibid., 138.

43 Maritain's most important work is Jacques Maritain, *Integral Humanism: Temporal and Spiritual Problems of a New Christendom* (New York: Charles Scribner's Sons, 1968). This section draws on the excellent overview of Christian Democracy in Frank Sawyer, *The Poor Are Many: Political Ethics in the Social Encyclicals, Christian Democracy and Liberation Theology in Latin America* (Kampen, the Netherlands: Uitgeversmaatschappij J.H. Kok, 1992), 60–90.

44 Sawyer notes that this term had three meanings. In economics, it meant the nationalization and government takeover of industries or services. A sociological meaning referred to the diversification of

social relationships and a psychopedagogical meaning meant the fuller integration of the individual with others as well as societal institutions generally. Its use in Catholic Encyclicals and in Christian Democratic writings 'is often to point out the need for social responsibility, especially the social–ethical aspect of economics, while avoiding the appearance of a socialism which it feared errs on the side of collectivism and party dominance' (Sawyer, *The Poor Are Many*, 36).

45 For the liberationist take on Christian Democracy see, for example, Hugo Assmann, 'Prologue', in *Habla Fidel Castro Sobre los Cristianos Revolucionarios*, ed. Hugo Assmann (Montevideo: Nueva Tierra, 1972); Rolando Ames Cobian, 'Factores Económicos y Fuerzas Políticas en el Proceso de Liberación', in *Fe Cristiana y Cambio Social en América Latina* (Salamanca: Ediciones Sigueme, 1973), 33–55; Enrique Dussel, 'A Specious Alternative: The Third Way', in *The Church at the Crossroads* (Rome: IDOC, 1978); Franz Hinkelammert, 'Socialdemocracia y Democracia Cristiana: Las Reformas y las Limitaciones', in *El Juego de los Reformismos Frente a la Revolución en Centroamerica*, ed. Hugo Assmann (San José: DEI, 1981); Juan Luis Segundo, *El Hombre de Hoy Ante Jesus de Nazaret: Fe y Ideología* (Madrid: Cristiandad, 1982); Juan Luis Segundo, *The Liberation of Theology* (Maryknoll: Orbis Books, 1985); Pablo Richard, 'The Political Organization of Christians in Latin America', *Concilium*, 5 (1987); Otto Maduro, 'Christian Democracy and the Choice in Latin American Catholicism of Liberating the Oppressed', *Concilium*, 5 (1987); Franz Hinkelammert, *Democracia y Totalitarismo* (San José: DEI, 1990). See also the analysis in Sawyer, *The Poor Are Many*.

46 The case of Chile is paradigmatic for liberation theologians. See Segundo, *The Liberation of Theology*, 90–95, for an analysis.

47 Segundo analyzes the evangelical – and thus utopian – nature of Christian Democracy's platform. See Segundo, *The Liberation of Theology*, 90–95.

48 Sawyer, *The Poor Are Many*, 174.

49 Ibid., 175.

50 José Míguez Bonino, *Toward a Christian Political Ethics* (Philadelphia: Fortress Press, 1983), 76.

51 See Segundo, *The Liberation of Theology*, 94; Hinkelammert, *Democracia y Totalitarismo*, 224–5.

52 'We sowed modern democracy and reaped the national security state. What went wrong?' (José Míguez Bonino, *Toward a Christian Political Ethics*, 65).

53 Paz Estenssoro in Bolivia (1951), Haya de la Torre in Peru (1962) and Goulart in Brazil (1964).

54 Sawyer, *The Poor Are Many*, 71.

55 Segundo, *The Liberation of Theology*, 94.

56 Sawyer, *The Poor Are Many*, 72.

57 A justification for this move can be found in Schumpeter. For Schumpeter, when democracy encountered trouble because its preconditions were not met, it was appropriate 'to abandon competitive and adopt monopolistic leadership' as long as it be for a period definitely limited in time. See Schumpeter, *Capitalism, Socialism and Democracy*, 296.

58 For another example of this perspective, see Huntington, *Political Order in Changing Societies*.

59 José Míguez Bonino, *Toward a Christian Political Ethics*, 70.

60 Ibid., 71. The best study of the emergence of the national security state from a liberationist perspective remains José Comblin, *The Church and the National Security State* (Maryknoll NY: Orbis Books, 1979).

61 The best analysis of this period and approach is Iain Maclean, *Opting for Democracy: Liberation Theology and the Struggle for Democracy in Brazil* (New York: Peter Lang, 1999); see also Iain Maclean, 'Participatory Democracy – the Case of the Brazilian Ecclesial Base Communities: 1981–1991', *Religion and Theology*, 5(1) (1998). I remain indebted to his groundbreaking work in this section.

62 Here I draw on Alejandro Moreno Menendez, *Political Cleavages: Issues, Parties, and the Consolidation of Democracy* (Boulder, Colorado: Westview Press, 1999), 108–10. Even though the timing and process of transition varied, a common core can be gleaned. Generally, four demands were presented by the departing regime for the re-establishment of political liberties and democratic institutions: (a) an amnesty for offences committed by members of the departing authoritarian regime; (b) the exclusion of radical parties from future governments; (c) continued repression against disloyal

forces; (d) postponement of social and economic reforms and acceptance of the liberal capitalist model. See Diane Ethier (ed.), *Democratic Transition and Consolidation in Southern Europe, Latin America and Southeast Asia* (London: The Macmillan Press Ltd, 1990), 11.

63 Enrique Dussel, *The Underside of Modernity: Apel, Ricouer, Rorty, Taylor, and the Philosophy of Liberation*, Eduardo Mendieta (New York: Humanity Books, 1998), 230.

64 'Documento de los Teólogos Latinoamericanos: Segunda Asamblea General de la Asociación Ecuménica de Teólogos del Tercer Mundo', *Revista Latinoamericana de Teología*, 3 (September–December 1986), 303–25.

65 Michael Novak (ed.), *Liberation Theology and the Liberal Society* (Washington, DC: American Enterprise Institute, 1987), 59–60.

66 Leonardo Boff, 'Libertad y Liberación. Puntos de Contacto y de Fricción en el Primer y Tercer Mundo', *Revista Latinoamericana de Teología*, 14 (May–August 1988), 201–2.

67 Christian Smith, *The Emergence of Liberation Theology: Radical Religion and Social Movement Theory* (Chicago: University of Chicago Press, 1991), 232.

68 Leonardo Boff, 'Libertad y Liberación', 201.

69 Ibid., 202.

70 Ibid.

71 William Swatos, *Religion and Democracy in Latin America* (New Brunswick: Transaction Publishers, 1995), 76. On base communities see also Maclean, *Opting for Democracy*; Maclean, 'Participatory Democracy'; M. Adriance, 'Base Communities and Rural Mobilization in Northern Brazil', *Sociology of Religion* 55 (1994), 163–78; P.J. Krischke, 'Church Base Communities and Democratic Change in Brazilian Society', *Comparative Political Studies* 24 (1991), 186–210; W.E. Hewitt, *Base Christian Communities and Social Change in Brazil* (Lincoln: University of Nebraska Press, 1991); G. Valdivieso, *Comunidades de Base* (Santiago: CISOC, 1989); S. Mainwaring and A. Wilde (eds), *The Progressive Church in Latin America* (Notre Dame, IN: University of Notre Dame Press, 1989); Scott Mainwaring, *The Catholic Church and Politics in Brazil: 1916–1985* (Stanford: Stanford University Press, 1986); Daniel Levine (ed.), *Religion and Political Conflict in Latin America* (Chapel Hill: University of North Carolina Press, 1986); Daniel Levine, *Religion and Politics in Latin America* (Princeton, NJ: Princeton University Press, 1981); B.H. Smith, *The Church and Politics in Chile* (Princeton, NJ: Princeton University Press, 1982).

72 Swatos, *Religion and Democracy in Latin America*, 77.

73 Here I draw on Christian Smith, 'The Spirit of Democracy: Base Communities, Protestantism, and Democratization in Latin America', in *Religion and Democracy in Latin America*, ed. William Swatos (New Brunswick: Transaction Publishers, 1995), 4–7.

74 For a now classic study that focuses on the relationship between the density of a society's associational life and the quality of its democracy, see Robert Putnam, *Making Democracy Work: Civic Traditions in Modern Italy* (Princeton: Princeton University Press, 1993).

75 Paulo Freire, *Pedagogy of the Oppressed*, trans. Myra Bergman Ramos (New York: Seabury Press, Continuum, 1970).

76 Frei Betto, 'As CEBs e o Projeto Político Popular', *Revista Eclesiástica Brasileira*, 41(162) (December 1986), 579, 583; cited in Maclean, *Opting for Democracy*, 191.

77 Clodovis Boff, 'Comunidades Cristas e Política Partidaria', *Revista Eclesiástica Brasileira*, 38 (September 1978), 387; cited in Maclean, *Opting for Democracy*, 184.

78 Leonardo Boff, 'Liberation Theology: A Political Expression of Biblical Faith', *Christian Jewish Relations*, 21(1) (Spring 1988), 20–21.

79 In 1981, the Brazilian bishops also advocated the move from political to social democracy: 'Democracy, today a reference of national consensus, in countries like Brazil, marked by such unacceptable forms of social inequity, doesn't consist only in the preservation of political liberties. It consists also in a process of incorporation of the large masses into higher forms of education and capacitation, a better level of living and full participation in public decision making. Political democracy is a form and prerequisite, whose very definition and destination is social democracy'. (CNBB, *Reflexão*

Cristã Sobre a Conjuntura Política, Ediçoes Paulinas, 1981, 10); cited in Michael Novak, *Liberation Theology and the Liberal Society*, 47.

80 Here I rely on Maclean, *Opting for Democracy*, especially Ch. 5.

81 Maclean, *Opting for Democracy*, 190–93. See also José Comblin, 'La Iglesia Latinoamericana Desde Puebla a Santo Domingo', in *Cambio Social y Pensamiento Cristiano en América Latina*, ed. José Comblin, José I. González Faus and Jon Sobrino (Madrid: Editorial Trotta, 1993), 37–40.

82 Comblin, 'La Iglesia Latinoamericana Desde Puebla a Santo Domingo', 35–6.

83 Xavier Gorostiaga, 'La Mediación de las Ciencias Sociales', in *Cambio Social y Pensamiento Cristiano en América Latina*, ed. José Comblin, José I. González Faus and Jon Sobrino (Madrid: Editorial Trotta, 1993), 132.

84 José Comblin, *Called for Freedom: The Changing Context of Liberation Theology*, trans. Phillip Berryman (Maryknoll, New York: Orbis Books, 1998), 128.

85 Comblin, *Called for Freedom: The Changing Context of Liberation Theology*, 132.

86 Gutiérrez, *La Fuerza Histórica de los Pobres*, 151.

87 Comblin, *Called for Freedom: The Changing Context of Liberation Theology*, 131.

88 Here I draw on Franz Hinkelammert, 'Democracia y Nueva Derecha en América Latina', in *Ecuador: Coyuntura Política* (Quito: CEDEP, 1990), 72–5.

89 See Alexis de Tocqueville, *Democracy in America*, rev. edn, vol. 1, ed. Francis Bowen and Phillips Bradley, reprint, 1945 (New York: Vintage, 1954) and Alexis de Tocqueville, *Democracy in America*, rev. edn, vol. 2, ed. Francis Bowen and Phillips Bradley, reprint, 1941 (New York: Vintage, 1956).

90 Franz Hinkelammert, *Cultura de la Esperanza y Sociedad Sin Exclusión* (San José, Costa Rica: DEI, 1995), 123.

91 Huntington, 'The Modest Meaning of Democracy', 14–15.

92 Dussel's ethics of liberation is built around this premise. See Enrique Dussel, *Ética de la Liberación en la Edad de la Globalización y de la Exclusión* (Madrid: Editorial Trotta, 1998).

CHAPTER 4

Liberation Theology, Capitalism and Historical Projects

The previous chapter offered an evaluation of liberation theology's understanding of democracy. I believe that liberation theology is correct to insist, against mainstream North American social science, that democracy as a political mechanism cannot be severed from the economic foundation of society. An important step in opening up a space for the imagination of new historical projects is to realize that in the midst of widespread misery formal political liberty sooner or later succumbs to hunger. A democracy that fails to incorporate into its self-understanding the pursuit of the economic conditions required for the reproduction of life of its citizens condemns itself to civil unrest and police repression. For this reason, the next step in my analysis is the examination of liberation theology's understanding of capitalism. There is no dearth of literature on liberation theology and capitalism.[1] What I do here is new in two respects. First, analyses of liberation theology and capitalism typically argue that liberation theologians initially espoused dependency theory and then later moved away from dependency theory as they shifted from politics to more traditional theological concerns. I, however, show that in reality liberation theology has approached capitalism in three main ways: capitalism as understood through the lens of dependency theory, capitalism as seen through the framework of world systems theory and capitalism as 'undertheorized'.

Second, and more importantly, I seek to examine the discursive effects of liberation theologians' understanding of capitalism on their aspirations for social change. Here I take into account the 'performativity of social representations – in other words, the ways they are implicated in the worlds they ostensibly represent'.[2] I thus examine how the definition and description of capitalism used by liberation theologians shape their perception of the struggle they face to achieve liberation and the best means to confront the challenges its pursuit poses.[3]

More specifically, I will argue that the very way liberation theology conceptualizes capitalism proves itself a hindrance to the development of new historical projects. I will show that throughout its history liberation theology has theorized capitalism as an abstractly defined, hegemonic, unified and indivisible totality, and while this approach highlights the economic woes of an entire continent, it remains devoid of constructive power. It is this particular understanding of capitalism that is also responsible for liberation theology's Achilles heel – its inability to construct historical projects. Within such an understanding there is either no escape outside a radical revolutionary overcoming of existing society or, given the present impossibility of revolution, only a willful and defiant resistance is possible from within hegemonic capitalism. In both cases, the imagination of new historical projects remains paralyzed. The image of capitalism that liberation theologians work with actively participates in creating an intellectual framework in which a deepening of political and economic democracy seems an impossibility.

Liberation Theology and Capitalism

Liberation theology has approached the concept of capitalism in three different ways. First, in the early formative stages of its development, liberation theology used dependency theory as its theoretical framework. This stage, the use of dependency theory, is the most important thing to understand in liberation theology's encounter with capitalism. The influence of dependency theory endures long after liberation theology has ceased openly to espouse such a framework. The next two stages merely take up and further develop the underlying understanding of capitalism found in dependency analysis. Consequently, a good deal of the discussion will focus on this first stage. After dependency theory, liberation theology has undertheorized capitalism: that is, failed to give capitalism concrete content owing to the lack of a developed social theory, or used world system theory. While the same theologian may make more than one move in the same work or even statement, for example undertheorizing with world systems theory as the tacit background, the differences (and as we shall see the commonalities) remain pertinent enough to separate analytically each position.

The Initial Context: the Failure of Modernization Theory

Modernization theory emerged as the product of three events in the post-World War II scenario: the rise of the United States as the world's main superpower, the spread of a worldwide communist movement and the disintegration of European colonial power in Africa, Asia and Latin America.[4] In such a context, North American political science and economics sought to provide emerging nation states with a model of society and development in order to avoid losing them to the communist bloc.[5] In a nutshell, modernization theory views underdevelopment as a condition which all nations have experienced at one time. Progress, therefore, comes through the spread of North American and European values and institutions to backward and traditional areas. In this view, the transition from a traditional to a modern society should be regarded as the process of traditional societies catching up with the modern world. Latin America faces the same problems the industrial world did before its economic take-off: scarcity of capital, undeveloped technology and a lack of budding capitalists seeking to make profits via more efficient production. Latin America thus needs to abandon traditional value schemes and focus on raising efficiency and productivity levels. Contact between advanced industrial countries and developing nations aids and accelerates the modernization process. Advanced countries are in a position to supply the missing links required for economic take-off through foreign aid and direct investment, as well as the transfer of technology and managerial skills.

Latin America followed this model of development during the first decades after World War II. An important aspect of this model, however, came under attack from Raul Prebisch and the Economic Commission on Latin America (ECLA).[6] Prebisch criticized the view that each country should merely specialize in its comparative advantage.[7] According to modernization theory, Latin America should focus on producing primary goods and trade for manufactured and industrial goods. Instead, Prebisch argued that reliance on primary products rendered developing countries vulnerable to short-term price fluctuations as well as a long-term deteriorations of their terms of trade in relation to imported industrial goods. ECLA thus advocated state promotion of Latin American industrialization through the production of industrial goods. Import substitution industrialization (ISI) emerged as the development model. Capitalist national development would be brought about by limiting imports and establishing an industrial base for the production of the corresponding goods within the nation. Through this process, it was thought that a new industrial and commercial bourgeoisie would eventually emerge. While Prebisch and ECLA kept much of modernization theory's analytical framework, they introduced a central distinction between core countries and peripheral countries that would be taken up by dependency theory: global capitalism was no longer a simple positive sum game in which everyone automatically benefited.

ECLA's program did not succeed. ISI merely transferred import dependency from consumption goods to capital goods, purchasing power remained limited to the upper classes, and domestic markets refused to expand. Greater income concentration emerged as a result of the transfer of resources from rural areas to the cities and agriculture to industry in the effort to industrialize. At the same time that the import substitution model reached its end Latin America's wider political context shifted as well. In 1959, the Cuban Revolution presented Latin America with the viability of socialism as an alternative to capitalist development. Military coups in Brazil and Argentina (1964 and 1965) installed conservative authoritarian governments in response to a perceived growing communist threat. In addition, the United States' diminished interest in the Alliance for Progress and the 1965 invasion of the Dominican Republic seemed to deny Latin America the possibility of development outside terms set by the United States. Worldwide opposition to the Vietnam War only served to reinforce this sentiment. It is in the shadow of modernization theory and ECLA's failure in addressing Latin America's social woes and an increasingly radical political context that dependency theory was born.

Liberation Theology and Dependency Theory

Liberation theology emerged at a time when dependency theory controlled the imagination of Latin American intellectuals. Indeed, the importance of dependency theory for liberation theology's understanding of society and the economy is impossible to overestimate. Dependency theory provided the framework within which Latin American reality was analyzed, the picture of the enemy to be fought in pursuit of liberation and the choice of weapons by which to fight best. As José Míguez Bonino states: 'The major historical shift was the rise of dependency theory. It was a dividing of the waters. When people influenced by the Catholic renewal were confronted with the dependency theory crisis, there was a parting of the ways. Some remained in the modern European renewal and others left to pursue liberation.'[8] Juan Luis Segundo also claims: 'As is well known by now, liberation theology arose as a reaction against the developmentalist theories and models formulated by the United States for Latin America in the decade of the sixties. The developmentalist model was characterized by the fact that it covered over and tried to hide the critical and decisive relationship of dependence versus liberation.'[9] Dependency theory, however, was not a monolithic movement.[10] A key issue, I will show, lies in exactly which version of dependency theory liberation theologians actually espoused.

Dependency theory can be divided into a Marxist and a reformist camp.[11] Andre Gunder Frank is the main exponent of the former. According to Frank, countries are not found underdeveloped (as modernization theory would have it) but made underdeveloped by the workings of a global capitalist system that incorporated the Third World through colonialism: 'Underdevelopment is not original or traditional ... The now developed countries were never *under*developed, though they may have been *un*developed.'[12] He thus rejects the modernization idea of development in which there are no external constraints developing countries suffer in their attempt to develop. Frank opens his *Capitalism and Underdevelopment in Latin America*, the classic Marxist dependency text, by stating:

> underdevelopment [in Chile] is the *necessary product* of four centuries of capitalist development and of the internal contradictions of capitalism itself. These contradictions are the expropriation of economic surplus from the many and its appropriation by the few, the polarization of the capitalist system into metropolitan center and peripheral satellites, and the continuity of the fundamental structure of the capitalist system throughout the history of its expansion and transformation, due to the *persistence or re-creation* of these contradictions *everywhere and at all times.* (emphasis added)[13]

For him 'economic development and underdevelopment are the opposite faces of the same coin ... One and the same historical process of the expansion and development throughout the world has simultaneously generated – and continues to generate – both economic development and structural underdevelopment'.[14] In Frank's scheme capitalism necessarily produces underdevelopment in the Third World; there is no escaping this system which encompasses the whole globe. Capitalism's contradictions, as well as their ability to persist and recreate themselves, seem spatially omnipresent and untouched by time or history; capitalism is depicted as a totality encompassing the whole globe and a unity that stands or falls in one piece. Its essence is understood as a hegemonic totality that is necessarily exploitative. Such a capitalism is by definition a beast immune to step-by-step reform: 'Therefore, short of liberation from this capitalist structure or the dissolution of the world capitalist system as a whole, the capitalist satellite countries, regions, localities, and sectors are condemned to underdevelopment.'[15] Latin America thus needs to decide between two poles: 'capitalist underdevelopment or socialist revolution'.[16] There are no other options.

Frank's version of dependency, however, was not the only available option at the time of liberation theology's emergence. Fernando Henrique Cardoso represents the main figure within the reformist dependency fold. While he agrees with Frank that global capitalism imposes severe constraints on developing countries, two main differences set them apart. The first difference lies in the scope of his analysis. Unlike Frank, who paints on a broader canvas, Cardoso focuses on more local, concrete and changing situations of dependency. Cardoso, in fact, avoids writing of dependency 'theory' and prefers to speak of the basic 'fact' of dependency. He thus avoids Frank's sweeping analyses and focuses instead on concrete situations or expressions of dependency. Second, according to Cardoso, the dichotomy between dependence and development that Frank sets up is too stark. Cardoso's specific analysis of particular situations of dependency leads him to postulate a third option, 'associated-dependent development'. For him, 'the present situation of dependent development goes beyond the traditional dichotomy between the terms "development" and "dependence", because it permits an increase in development while maintaining and redefining the links of dependency'.[17]

For Cardoso, dependency does not necessarily lie in opposition to the economic development of dependent countries; the revolutionary overcoming of capitalism is not an immediately necessary option. Latin America does have room to grow within dependent capitalism. Even for Cardoso, however, 'it is not realistic to imagine that capitalist development will solve basic problems for the majority of the population. In the end, what has to be discussed as an alternative is not the consolidation of the state and the fulfillment of "autonomous capitalism", but how to supersede them. The important question, then, is how to construct paths toward socialism'.[18] On the one hand, he rejects Frank's claim that capitalism is synonymous with underdevelopment. Capitalism can lead to economic growth in Latin America. On the other hand, he does not believe that fully autonomous development is possible from within capitalism. Capitalism must be, and can be through the right combination of policy and struggle, reworked into socialism.

Liberation theology's central statement regarding dependency theory is Gonzalo Arroyo's 'Pensamiento latinoamericano sobre subdesarrollo y dependencia externa'.[19] This article was published in a volume containing a collection of conferences, presentations and seminars delivered at the 1972 Escorial conference that counted among its participants Gustavo Gutiérrez, José Míguez Bonino, Enrique Dussel, Juan Carlos Scannone, Hugo Assmann, Juan Luis Segundo, José

Comblin, and Segundo Galilea among others – one of liberation theology's defining moments.[20] Arroyo outlines two main positions. The first he calls developmentalist, essentially the modernization–ECLA perspective. Remember that this position argued that state planning coupled with private initiative could lead to development within a capitalist system. Arroyo rejects this stance and outlines the understanding of dependency theory that shaped liberation theology's initial formulation and subsequent development.[21] The liberationist incorporation of dependency included three main ideas. First, the belief that Latin America's social and economic problems need to be understood within the context of a global capitalist system. Underdevelopment is not merely a local problem such as a lack of capital or technology. Rejected are theories that claim that underdeveloped nations need to follow the path of economic take-off taken by the industrial nations. Also rejected are theories that envision development as the process of moving from a traditional to a modern social structure. Second, underdevelopment was not a natural state; the now advanced countries were never underdeveloped: underdevelopment is the product of the workings of capitalism itself. Global capitalism's dynamic is understood as one in which countries in the center exploit countries in the periphery. This leads to the enrichment of the former and the pauperization of the latter. Finally, given this analysis, autonomous economic and social development is impossible within capitalism, the only solution being liberation from dependence through liberation from capitalism itself.[22]

Liberation theology, therefore, embraced Frank's extreme version of dependency theory.[23] His vision of dependency – the focus on global constraints toward development, the belief that underdevelopment was caused by capitalism itself, and the claim that only a socialist revolution can lead to development – can be traced throughout liberation theology's foundational authors and texts. This point cannot be overstated; allow me to cite a number of examples from liberation theology's founding fathers to drive it home. For example, in *Doing Theology in a Revolutionary Situation*, José Míguez Bonino argues: 'As the process of modernization developed, the darker aspects of the whole "modern enterprise" have begun to loom larger and larger. Latin America suddenly realized that it had been incorporated into the modern world indeed, but not as a junior partner with increasing participation in the total enterprise but as a dependant, serving the further development of the owner's profit ... Latin America has discovered the basic fact of its dependence.'[24]

Bonino rejects modernization theories of development that understand and describe 'the rise to power and wealth of the North Atlantic countries as a moral achievement due to certain conditions of character and the principles of democracy, free enterprise, and education. Any country, therefore, which would adopt these principles and acquire these qualities would naturally develop in the same way'.[25] Instead, the currently rich countries built their prosperity by pillaging the resources of the now underdeveloped world.[26] Bonino thus follows Frank in asserting: 'Latin American underdevelopment is the dark side of Northern development; Northern development is built on third-world underdevelopment. The basic categories for understanding our history are not development and underdevelopment but domination and dependence. This is the crux of the matter.'[27] Capitalist exploitation is not the product of particular individuals; exploitation is the product of the system as such. Capitalism and exploitation go hand in hand, they cannot be separated: 'we are not dealing with particularly wicked people or with cancerous outgrowths of a system which has to be cleansed and restored to health. We are simply facing the normal and unavoidable consequences of the basic principles of capitalist production as they work themselves out in our global, technological time'.[28] For this reason Bonino speaks of 'a Latin American socialist project of liberation' and the need to find 'an authentic Latin American socialism'.[29] Reforming capitalism is not a viable option.

Hugo Assmann's *Theology for a Nomad Church* argues in the same vein. He too asserts that underdevelopment is not a natural state prior to development: 'We are beginning to realize what we are in history: not merely underdeveloped peoples in the sense of "not yet sufficiently developed", but peoples "kept in a state of underdevelopment": dominated and oppressed peoples – which is a very different thing.'[30] For Assmann dependency theory shows that capitalism is a necessarily oppressive system shaping the internal workings of individual nations as well as the global economy as a whole: 'Dependence is not simply an "external factor" affecting international relations; it is a situation that has molded the internal structures of our countries. This means that development and underdevelopment must be placed within the same world historical system.'[31] Liberation must stem from 'the revelation of the workings of domination that keep us in an underdeveloped state. Underlying them is the major event of an historical experience raised to a conscious level'.[32] For Assmann, a central figure in the Christians for Socialism movement, overcoming capitalism was the means to overcome dependence.[33]

In his early works, including the classic *A Theology of Liberation*, Gustavo Gutiérrez sees the situation in the same light. For him 'the poor countries are becoming ever more clearly aware that their underdevelopment is only the by-product of the development of other countries, because of the kind of relationship which exists between the rich and poor countries'.[34] Once again capitalism is defined as intrinsically exploitative: 'It has become ever clearer that underdevelopment is the end result of a process ... The underdevelopment of the poor countries, as an overall social fact, appears in its true light: as the historical byproduct of the development of other countries. The dynamics of the capitalist economy lead to the establishment of a center and a periphery, simultaneously generating progress and growing wealth for the few and social imbalances, political tensions, and poverty for the many.'[35] Given this reality, Gutiérrez follows Frank and claims that 'autonomous Latin American development is not viable within the framework of the international capitalist system'.[36] He remains decisively opposed to reformist measures: 'Hence we speak of social revolution, not reform, of liberation, not development, of socialism; not the modernization of the existing system.'[37] And he thus concludes: 'It is a matter of opting for revolution and for socialism ... Only the overcoming of a society divided into classes, only a political power at the service of the great majorities, only the elimination of private appropriation of wealth generated by human labor can give us the bases for a more just society. It is for this reason that the elaboration of the historical project of a new society takes in Latin America the route of socialism, construction of a socialism that does not ignore the deficiencies of many of its actual historical realizations, a socialism that seeks to escape preconceived schemes and which creatively seeks its own paths.'[38]

Leonardo Boff provides a final example. He writes that 'underdevelopment is the reverse side of the same coin. It is the opposite of development and a consequence of it. It is a product of development as conceived in capitalistic terms. If the developed nations of the center are to keep up their pace of development and their level of goods, they must keep the peripheral nations in a state of dependence in order to extract what they need for their own affluence'.[39] Capitalism is again pictured as an entity that functions by exploiting the (under)developing world in benefit of the developed nations. Interestingly, however, Boff, unlike Bonino, Assmann and Gutiérrez, at times seems to follow Cardoso and consider the reform of capitalism a viable option: 'The overall state of affairs obliges us to seek changes *in* the system in order to get to a change *of* system. This does not mean that we give up our option for a liberation project and for a different sort of society. It is simply a strategy for achieving that goal in terms of the historical and conjectural factors imposed on us by an overall situation of repression and bondage.'[40] He suggests, in a critique of revolutionary fervor and expectation, that 'proposed revolutionary approaches seem to be too utopian and not viable politically. Revolutionary transformations within the existing system would seem to offer us a way to arrive gradually at a more just and equitable system'.[41]

At other times, however, he stresses the need for the radical rupture only revolution can provide: 'The acute understanding of the mechanisms that keep Latin America in an underdeveloped state – dependence and domination – led to the notion of liberation. Liberation, which as a category is correlative to another, dependency, articulates a new way of facing the problem of development ... The category of liberation implies a global rejection of the developmentalist system and a denunciation of its oppressive structure.'[42] Following this latter line of thought in their popular introductory text *Introducing Liberation Theology*, Clodovis and Leonardo Boff distinguish three ways of explaining poverty: first, an empirical explanation that sees poverty as vice and the appropriate response as aid; second, a functional explanation that sees poverty as backwardness and the appropriate response as reform; finally, a dialectical explanation that sees poverty as oppression. This position, the one they espouse, 'sees poverty as a collective and also conflictive phenomenon, which can be overcome only by replacing the present social system with an alternative system. The way out of this situation is revolution, understood as the transformation of the bases of the economic and social system'.[43] Once again, reform will not do the trick. Capitalism must be overcome as a whole.

These figures' understanding of capitalism echo and mimic Frank's analysis. The kernel of Frank's thought is found in each one: the notion that development and underdevelopment are part of the same process, the understanding of capitalism as a necessarily exploitative system, and the conviction that only socialism – the complete overcoming of capitalism – can save Latin America. Liberation theology thus appropriates dependency theory in such a way that liberation becomes synonymous with a radical rupture from capitalism as the cause of dependence. Such a break is required because of the way that liberation theology, through dependency theory, thinks about capitalism. For liberation theologians, capitalism is a global system that fosters development for the few and underdevelopment for the many. It is a total system that encompasses the whole globe, both developed and underdeveloped countries falling into its grasp. Capitalism necessarily produces underdevelopment, this necessity is part of capitalism's very definition. Reform will not do the trick, capitalism must be superseded and replaced; a revolution is required to liberate Latin America from dependency. Even in the cases when Boff speaks of gradual reform, this reform is still geared toward overcoming a capitalism that stands as a total system. As I show below, this vision of capitalism as a necessarily exploitative monolithic entity continues to haunt liberation theology today, suffocating the imagination of new historical projects.

Liberation Theology and World System Theory

World system theory provides the second lens through which liberation theology has viewed capitalism. World system theory and dependency theory are siblings and thus it is not surprising that liberation theologians would also incorporate the former into their socioanalytical framework. They share a common heritage that includes Marxism, Lenin's theory of imperialism and Latin American structuralism; indeed, dependency theory itself is the major influence in world system theory's development. Currently, in fact, Andre Gunder Frank is a major contributor to the development of world systems theory. Reflecting on his intellectual journey, he offers the following critique of dependency theory and his movement toward a world systems framework:

> First, real dependence exists, of course, and more than ever, despite arguments to the contrary. However, dependency 'theory' and policy have never answered the question of how to eliminate it and how to pursue the chimera of nondependent or independent growth. Second, dependence heterodoxy has nonetheless maintained the orthodoxy that (under)development must refer to and be organized by and through (nation-state) societies, countries, or regions. This orthodox tenet turns out to be wrong. Third, although I turned orthodoxy on its head, I maintained the essence of the thesis that economic growth through capital accumulation equals development. Thereby, the socialist and dependence

heterodoxies were caught in the same trap as development orthodoxy, and any
real alternative definitions, policy, and praxis of 'development' were precluded.
Fourth, in particular, this orthodoxy incorporated the patriarchal gender structure
of society as a matter of course.[44]

While Frank highlights four main differences with dependency theory, here I will
focus on numbers two and three, the demotion of the nation state and regional
economies in favor of the capitalist world system as the unit of analysis, and the
rejection of national socialism as an alternative mode of economic and social
organization. For the purposes of my argument, these two moves mark the break
between dependency and world system theory. They have the effect of discursively
strengthening the capitalism that liberation theology struggles against by expanding
the scope of capitalist dominance beyond that postulated by Frank's earlier
dependency theory. Within dependency theory, socialism was the solution; within
world system theory, socialism as conceived by dependency theory remains part of
the problem. Within dependency theory, a national solution to underdevelopment
was deemed possible; within world system theory, national solutions are rendered
ineffectual by capitalism's global scope. For dependency theory, national projects of
socialist liberation were the path to take. For world system theory, only a worldwide
alternative will do.

The expansion of capitalist dominance is evident in world system theory's
founding father and most influential proponent, Immanuel Wallerstein.[45]
Wallerstein defines a world system as an intersocietal system that is shaped by a
self-contained division of labor.[46] For him, the world system, not the nation state as
with dependency theory, is the fundamental unit of analysis. As he puts it: 'If there
is one thing which distinguishes a world-system perspective from any other, it is its
insistence that the unit of analysis is a *world*-system defined in terms of economic
processes and links, and not any units defined in terms of juridical, political,
cultural, geological, or other criteria.'[47] According to Wallerstein, the current
capitalist world system dates from the 16th century and possesses four main traits.
First, the capitalist world economy is a distinctive reality in world history with its
own laws and dynamics, its fundamental law being the need for capital
accumulation.[48] Second, capitalism necessarily increases inequality: 'the so called
"widening gap" is not an anomaly but a continuing basic mechanism of the
operation of the world economy'.[49] Capitalism, as was the case in dependency
theory, possesses laws and dynamics that make it necessarily exploitative. Third,
Wallerstein argues that all facets of the social and political organization of territorial
units, even states, derive from their position in the world system.[50] So, for example,
'the development of the capitalist world-economy has involved the creation of all
the major institutions of the modern world: classes, ethnic/national groups,
households – and the "states". All of these structures postdate, not antedate
capitalism; all are consequence, not cause'.[51] Capitalism, within this conception,
defines all of global society since the birth of the modern era. It is all-encompassing;

nothing lies beyond its scope. Finally, for Wallerstein capitalism and socialism as they have existed in history are really opposite sides of the same coin. Both are the product of a soon to be defunct Western civilization obsessed with economic growth.[52]

World system theory exacerbates the problems found in liberation theology's use of dependency theory. Both view capitalism as a unified, monolithic system. In both, capitalism is a total system that encompasses the whole globe; capitalism is defined by laws internal – never external – to its being, and capitalism is seen as the real subject of history to the point that all other structures are its creation. Yet within world system theory capitalism is even more daunting than dependency theory's version of the beast. Dependency theory at least had a model – socialism, however flawed – that it viewed as a possible alternative. Its link to the state as a unit of analysis allowed for envisioning a national solution to the problem posed by dependency. Here countries could escape the periphery and achieve autonomy through a socialist revolution. World system theory, instead, collapses the dichotomy capitalism/socialism into an absolute rejection of Western culture that, however, remains abstractly defined as capitalist through and through. It represents the most extreme version of an understanding of capitalism as an all-encompassing, monolithic totality. Nothing lies beyond its grasp. So, for example, Franz Hinkelammert claims that in the current global context:

> we face not only a crisis of capitalism but a crisis of the foundational basis of modernity ... The crisis of capitalism has been transformed into a crisis of Western civilization itself ... Now, instead of the polarization capitalism/socialism, there emerges another, which is capitalism/life, capitalism/survival of humankind. Only now capitalism has a wider meaning ... It means Western civilization, modernity and the belief in universal institutional systems that can homogenize all human relations. For this reason, the crisis includes socialism as well, as it emerged in the socialist societies of the Soviet tradition.[53]

For Hinkelammert, therefore, liberation theology must overcome not just an economic system but Western civilization as a whole. Under the influence of world system theory, the enemy to be struggled against becomes even more daunting than it was during the heyday of dependency theory. Not even the revolutionary overcoming of society's economic structure suffices. Collapsing capitalism into Western civilization as a whole has the further effect of giving capitalism power over our very being. Capitalism begins to define our ontology. According to Ignacio Ellacuría capitalism displays:

> an almost irresistible pull toward a profound dehumanization as an intrinsic part of the real dynamics of the capitalist system: abusive and/or superficial and alienating ways of seeking one's own security and happiness by means of private accumulation, of consumption, and of entertainment; submission to the laws of the consumer market promoted by advertising in every kind of activity, including

the cultural; and a manifest lack of solidarity in the individual, the family, and the state with other individuals, families, or states.[54]

Capitalism's ability to possess our very being is taken to the extreme in the following statement from Boff:

> the dominant system today, which is the capitalist system ... has developed its own ways of collectively designing and constructing human subjectivity ... The capitalist and mercantile systems have succeeded in penetrating into every part of the personal and collective human mind. They have managed to decide the individual's way of life, the development of the emotions, the way in which an individual relates to his or her neighbors or strangers, a particular mode of love or friendship, and, indeed, the whole gamut of life and death.[55]

This is the final straw. Capitalism is everywhere and is responsible for everything. Within this conception it is practically impossible to find a place to anchor the construction of new historical projects, even envisioning a means of negative resistance is a close to impossible task.

Liberation Theology and the Undertheorizing of Capitalism

The third way liberation theology thinks about capitalism can be called, perhaps unelegantly, the undertheorizing of capitalism. So far I have argued that in its inception liberation theology approached capitalism via dependency theory leading thus to the dichotomy dependence/capitalism versus liberation/socialism. I have also argued that world system theory serves as a second socioanalytical framework through which liberation theologians have understood capitalism. Undertheorizing capitalism, however, emerges when capitalism is critiqued from a perspective that lacks grounding in a developed social theory. To undertheorize capitalism is to use the concept without developing the social theoretic background that specifies its meaning and implications.

This section will show that the lack of a social theory and subsequent failure fully to theorize capitalism reproduces by default the same picture of capitalism as a unified, all-encompassing and necessarily exploitative system found in dependency theory and world system theory. If capitalism is not consciously theorized differently and thus positively rewritten in an alternative form, it will implicitly contain the same traits – monolithic, necessarily exploitative and all-encompassing – as long as liberation theology lacks another way to approach the concept.[56]

Today many liberation theologians have distanced themselves from dependency theory in particular, and the use of social and political theories such as Marxism in general. This distancing from social theory is often linked to a trend away from a focus on sociopolitical critique and towards more traditional theological concerns such as ecclesiology, spirituality and faith.[57] Gustavo Gutiérrez serves as a notable example of this trend. Marsha Hewitt points out that Gutiérrez's understanding of liberation theology has changed. Initially, in his classic *A Theology of Liberation*, Gutiérrez described such theology as 'reflection born of the experience of shared efforts to abolish the current unjust situation and to build a different society, freer and more human'.[58] Theology was critical reflection on Christian praxis.[59] Theology thus follows practice and comes as a second step.[60] As should be clear from the section on liberation theology and dependency theory, this practice in Gutiérrez's case was the open espousal of socialism to overcome the dependence brought about by capitalism. For Gutiérrez, socialism was the historical project that pertained to liberation; liberation had a specific political and economic content that could be envisioned and enacted within history.[61] I am not saying, however, that for Gutiérrez liberation was completely equivalent to socialism; I am not accusing him of collapsing God's reign into a particular human project. Yet it remains true that in *A Theology of Liberation* and other works of the period socialism played the role of being the worldly political embodiment of a liberation that could be fully completed only by God.

In the early 1980s, however, Gutiérrez started to describe theology differently. Theology became '"a discourse about God" which must always proceed from within the church, and by church, he means the official ecclesial structures'.[62] Paralleling the shift in his understanding of theology, Gutiérrez has also played down his previous use of dependency theory and Marxism as well as his espousal of socialism as the means toward liberation.[63] The end result is that when he does address economic issues his analysis, owing to the lack of a social theory, is far less sophisticated than it used to be. Jung Mo Sung notes, for example, that Gutiérrez has abandoned his once incisive take on socioeconomic issues for a much vaguer discourse.[64] He cites a passage from Gutiérrez's *The God of Life* as an example:

> Jesus goes to the root of the matter: all dependence on money must be rooted out. It is not enough to throw off foreign political domination; one must also break away from the oppression that arises from attachment to money and the possibilities it creates of exploiting others. Return the money to Caesar, Jesus is telling them, and you yourselves will be free of the power exercised by wealth, by mammon; then you will be able to worship the true God and give God what belongs to God.[65]

Sung, however, counters:

> to say that money universally victimizes the dispossessed ... to propose freedom from money as an evangelical solution for our social problems may sound poetic but it remains nonetheless ineffective. If 'to be a Christian today means to worry about where the poor will sleep', as Gutiérrez states, that requires, for example, the need to build new houses. There is, therefore, a need for investments and thus for money. It is not enough to simply say 'freedom from money', it is necessary to articulate that subjective liberty with the objective need we have for money, for social investment and as a means of exchange.[66]

Back in the late 1960s and 1970s, in the days that he embraced dependency theory, Gutiérrez would have agreed with Sung's critique. Gutiérrez seems to have forgotten his claim that 'the lyrical and vague calls for the defense of human dignity that do not take into account the real causes of the present social order and the concrete conditions for the construction of a just society are totally useless, and in the long run subtle ways to delude and be deluded'.[67] According to Sung it was the discrediting of Marxism as a social science and the demise of socialism as a historical project, initially with the coup against Allende, the rise of national security states and today with the fall of the Berlin Wall, that pushed liberation theology to a vague critique of capitalism and an understanding of liberation that remains detached from any social theory.[68]

Hewitt, on the other hand, thinks this situation stems from the two Vatican *Instructions* on liberation theology, the 1984 *Instruction on Certain Aspects of the 'Theology of Liberation'* and the 1986 *Instruction on Christian Freedom and Liberation*. For her, 'both *Instructions* appear to have succeeded to some extent in co-opting liberation theology in terms of re-orienting it more in the direction of discourses about liberation, thereby weakening its critical, practical force'.[69] Whatever the reasons for this shift, insofar as Gutiérrez exhibits a more vague and undertheorized approach to capitalism in particular and economic issues in general, he may have abandoned dependency theory, but he has not abandoned a notion of capitalism as something that needs to be rejected completely. Even without dependency theory as the explicit theoretical lens, the same underlying understanding of capitalism remains.

The end result, therefore, is that liberation theology's abandonment of dependency theory has not been followed by the abandonment of a notion of capitalism as a monolithic totality. As long as capitalism is undertheorized and thus not consciously rethought in a different mode it retains its systemic, necessarily exploitative, all-encompassing quality. In this undertheorizing, capitalism is invoked rather than analyzed and often serves as a placeholder for radical evil. The following instances may seem trivial, but they represent undertheorized modes of thinking that reproduce by default an image of capitalism that paralyzes the imagination of historical projects. For example, Iain Maclean relates how Leonardo Boff, in a short commentary on the Lord's Prayer, declared that the petition to deliver us from evil should be translated as 'deliver us from the evil one'. Boff then went on to state, 'He has a name; he is the capitalism of private property and the capitalism of the state.'[70]

Another example is Hinkelammert's claim that 'the world which now appears and announces itself is a world where there is only "one lord" and "master", where there is only one system ... There is no place of asylum ... The empire is everywhere. It has total power and knows it.'[71] Capitalism appears metaphorically as an all encompassing and absolute empire that cannot be escaped. Take also Hinkelammert's claim that 'today we are before a system of domination which includes even our souls, and which tries to suffocate even the very capacity for critical thinking'.[72] Here capitalism becomes the devil itself; nothing, not even our souls, lies beyond its scope. Today, in addition, the terms 'market' or 'globalization' are also catch phrases, capitalism's alter egos, depicting entities marching toward world domination or already triumphant.

So Pablo Richard can write that 'it is not possible to live *outside* the system, since globalization integrates everything, but it is possible to live *against* the spirit of the system'.[73] In this case, the main trait of this opponent is that it remains vaguely defined as a 'system' which it is impossible to escape. Capitalism, moreover, seems to completely control the deployment of political power itself: 'For *el pueblo* [the people] (the popular sectors, social movements at the base) political power has become impossible (the system does not allow for the orientation of political power in benefit of popular interest), political power becomes *irrelevant* (since everything is determined by market logic and it is impossible to govern against that logic').[74] Given the enemy's awesome scope and power, it is not surprising that the only possible resistance becomes a vague shift in attitude that leaves the actual structures of oppression untouched.

Conclusion

Dependency theory was foundational for liberation theology to the point that Bonino can remark that 'it was the social scientists' reflection on "dependence and liberation" that awakened us to a basic *biblical* motif'.[75] I believe, however, that liberation theology took a fateful turn when it embraced Frank's dependency theory, a turn that continues to haunt it today by drastically limiting the space within which historical projects can be imagined. The turn is fateful for two reasons. First, the picture of capitalism inherited leads to drastically limiting the scope of political action (only revolution will do) while dramatically increasing the size and ferocity of the opponent to be combated. No wonder there is a general perception that liberation theologians are disoriented in the current global, decidedly non-revolutionary, context. Second, liberation theology inherits a style of political and economic analysis that is provocative and sweeping in scope, but relies on generalizations and remains devoid of the concrete analysis required to actually envision paths of change. Here much could have been learnt from Cardoso's more subtle and empirical approach to the fact, rather than the theory of dependency. The two elements, of course, are related. The following chapter will show that an analysis that focuses on the particularities of capitalist systems problematizes the claim that there is one necessarily exploitative system and serves as the starting point for developing new historical projects.

In this chapter I demonstrated that liberation theology theorizes capitalism as a necessarily exploitative, all encompassing, indivisible entity that can be overcome only by a socialist revolution. As such, capitalism must be rejected as a whole. This basic framework was inherited from dependency theory and remains in place today even when capitalism is invoked and undertheorized or viewed from world system theory. Yet my discursive approach to the examination of liberation theology and capitalism operates under the assumption that social theories are not neutral mirrors of reality; they shape and thus also facilitate and constrain modes of acting in society. Because there is no neutral theory, no God's eye view from which to analyze society, social theories do not just represent reality, they also construct reality. Every construction necessarily closes off some perspectives as it opens up others. An approach that focuses on social representations and the way they shape, facilitate and constrain modes of acting thus pays careful attention to the metaphors used to describe phenomena.[76] It realizes that the adoption of a social theory – the selection of metaphors one chooses to use as a roadmap to our environment – is inevitably a political act in that they are constitutive of the worlds we inhabit. What really matters, therefore, is how different theories make sense of the world and move people to act in different ways and in different directions.[77] In the final analysis, at stake in the choice and development of our social theories is a fateful and urgent prize: the degree of freedom individuals and societies have in shaping their political and economic institutions.[78] To develop an alternative approach to capitalism and society that facilitates the construction of historical projects, liberation theology will have to become more attentive to the fact that, as William James put it, our descriptions add to the world.

From this standpoint, liberation theology's approach to capitalism reveals itself as a straitjacket that must be escaped. The very way liberation theology theorizes capitalism makes radical structural change a virtual impossibility; liberation theology's approach to capitalism blocks rather than opens avenues for change. In this framework there seems to be no middle space between revolution and local activism; yet to aspire to revolution is to hope for too much, while to rest satisfied with community building is to not hope enough. Indeed, in the movement from dependency theory to world system theory and undertheorizing, capitalism takes up more and more space, becomes more and more all-encompassing, ever more powerful. What makes the need for an alternative understanding of capitalism urgent is that liberation theology often depicts capitalism not just as an economic system but also as the defining element of all of society, Western civilization as a whole, and life itself. Combating such a capitalism is a gargantuan task, no avenue of escape comes into sight. The idea of capitalism as an all-pervasive indivisible totality, encompassing the nation, the globe and even the inner recesses of the human heart, cannot but suffocate the emergence of new historical projects.

There is no small irony in this end result of liberation theology's approach to and critique of capitalism. If I am correct, the socioanalytic tools that were to further liberation have become the shackles that bind the theologian. This irony, however, is lost on liberation theologians. Take Jon Sobrino:

> The experience of God and witness to a just life becomes ever clearer in Latin America because structural injustice is there given explicit or implicit theological sanction. The presently prevailing structures – a capitalism of

dependence and national security, whatever their forms – function as real deities with divine characteristics and their own cult. They are deities because they claim attributes that belong to God alone: ultimacy, definitiveness, and inviolability. They have their own cult because they demand the daily sacrifices of the masses and the violent sacrifice of any who resist them.[79]

The irony lies in the fact that liberation theologians' own analysis of capitalism reinforces the latter's idolatrous tendencies; instead of unmasking idolatry, liberation theology inadvertently ends up reinforcing idolatry. Sobrino *et al* are blind to the fact that their own discourse on capitalism, an economic system of Western civilization of awesome force, that shapes all other aspects of our lives, and that can only be resisted but not changed unless it were to collapse of its own accord, further infuses capitalism with the very same aura of ultimacy, definitiveness and inviolability they bemoan. The best way to combat the idolatrous nature of capitalism, therefore, is to rid it of its systemic, all powerful, all encompassing, quasi-divine quality. The task is to show that the idol is an idol; that it is made of clay. Only then can room be made for the development of new historical projects.

Gustavo Gutiérrez once warned that 'the lyrical and vague calls for the defense of human dignity that do not take into account the real causes of the present social order and the concrete conditions for the construction of a just society are totally useless, and in the long run subtle ways to delude and be deluded'.[80] When he wrote these words in 1974, socialism as a historical project was Gutiérrez's answer to the mistake of vagueness. Today, however, the mistake – and perhaps even the delusion – lies in remaining tied to the modes of thought that made liberation theology's abstract conception of socialism a viable alternative. Marx's dictum that 'the tradition of all dead generations weigh like a nightmare on the brains of the living' applies to the kinship between dependency theory and liberation theology.[82] It is time, however, to repudiate that kinship, for the sake of the very liberation for which it was first related.

Notes

1 By far the best source on liberation theology and dependency theory, as well as capitalism more generally, is Jung Mo Sung, *Economía: Tema Ausente en la Teología de la Liberación* (San José, Costa Rica: DEI, 1994), 34–48. For more on liberation theology and dependency theory, see Thomas Kochuthara, *Theology of Liberation and Ideology Critique: A Study on the Praxis of Liberation in the Light of Critical Theory* (New Delhi: Intercultural Publications, 1993), esp. 111–22; Robert Andelson and James Dawsey, *From Wasteland to Promised Land: Liberation Theology for a Post-Marxist World* (Maryknoll, NY: Orbis Books, 1992), esp. 42–7; Christian Smith, *The Emergence of Liberation Theology: Radical Religion and Social Movement Theory* (Chicago: University of Chicago Press, 1991), esp. 145–9; Arthur McGovern, *Liberation Theology and Its Critics: Toward an Assessment* (Maryknoll, NY: Orbis Books, 1989), esp. 156–76; Arthur McGovern, 'Dependency Theory, Marxist Analysis, and Liberation Theology', in *Expanding the View: Gustavo Gutiérrez and the Future of Liberation Theology*, ed. Marc Ellis and Otto Maduro (Maryknoll, NY: Orbis Books, 1988), 77–93; Arthur McGovern, 'Latin America and Dependency Theory', in *Liberation Theology and the Liberal Society* (Washington, DC:

American Enterprise Institute, 1987), 106–32; David Lehmann, *Democracy and Development in Latin America: Economics, Politics and Religion in the Post-War Period* (Philadelphia: Temple University Press, 1990), 88–148; John Pottenger, *The Political Theory of Liberation Theology: Toward a Reconvergence of Social Values and Social Science* (Albany, NY: State University of New York Press, 1989), 99–130; Roberto Goizueta, *Liberation, Method, and Dialogue – Enrique Dussel and North American Philosophical Discourse* (Atlanta: American Academy of Religion, Scholars Press, 1988), esp. 3–30; Roland Robertson, 'Liberation Theology, Latin America, and Third World Underdevelopment', in *The Politics of Latin American Liberation Theology: The Challenge to U.S. Public Policy*, ed. Richard Rubenstein and John Roth (Washington, DC: Washington Institute Press, 1988), 117–34; William Garrett, 'Liberation Theology and Dependency Theory', in *The Politics of Latin American Liberation Theology: The Challenge to U.S. Public Policy*, ed. Richard Rubenstein and John Roth (Washington, DC: Washington Institute Press, 1988), 174–98; John Roth, 'The Great Enemy? How Latin American Liberation Theology Sees the United States and the USSR', in *The Politics of Latin American Liberation Theology: The Challenge to U.S. Public Policy*, ed. Richard Rubenstein and John Roth (Washington, DC: Washington Institute Press, 1988), 225–46.

2 J.K. Gibson-Graham, *The End of Capitalism (as We Knew It): A Feminist Critique of Political Economy* (Cambridge: Blackwell Publishers, 1996), ix.

3 See Ivan Petrella, 'Liberation Theology and Democracy: Toward a New Historical Project', *Journal of Hispanic/Latino Theology*, 7(4) (May 2000), 50–67, for a brief account of this argument.

4 On modernization or diffusionist theories of development I have found helpful Richard Peet and Elaine Hartwick, *Theories of Development* (New York: The Guilford Press, 1999); Arturo Escobar, *Encountering Development: The Making and Unmaking of the Third World* (Princeton, NJ: Princeton University Press, 1995); Ray Kiely, *Sociology and Development: The Impasse and Beyond* (London: UCL Press Limited, 1995); Alvin So, *Social Change and Development: Modernization, Dependency, and World-System Theories* (London: Sage Publications, 1990) and Ronald Chilcote and Joel Edelstein (ed.), *Latin America: The Struggle with Dependency and Beyond* (New York: Halsted Press, 1974). For an example of a classic text in the modernization school, see Walter Rostow, *The Stages of Economic Growth: A Non-Communist Manifesto* (Cambridge: Cambridge University Press, 1960).

5 As Kiely notes: 'The theory of modernization was an attempt by mainly First World scholars to explain the social reality of the "new states" of the Third World' (Kiely, *Sociology and Development*, 37).

6 Most books on development theory include a section on ECLA and Prebisch or Latin American structuralism. In addition to books cited, see Joseph Love, 'Raul Prebisch and the Origins of the Doctrine of Unequal Exchange', *Latin American Research Review*, 15(3) (1980), 45–72.

7 For Dos Santos this hypothesis strikes 'directly at the heart of classical and neoclassical economic theories to the effect that comparative advantage should cause each country to specialize in the products in which it shows the greatest productivity or the best endowment of factors of production. Many concluded from this that the best road to well-being and modernization for a nation was specialization in those products in which it could best compete on world markets. These arguments were used ad nauseam to deny the necessity of industrialization for countries on the periphery in the world economic system' (Theotonio Dos Santos, 'The Theoretical Foundations of the Cardoso Government', *Latin American Perspectives*, 25(1), January 1998, 54).

8 Cited in Smith, *The Emergence of Liberation Theology*, 258, from the text of an interview with Bonino in 1987.

9 Juan Luis Segundo, *Liberation of Theology*, trans. John Drury, reprint, 1975 (Maryknoll, New York: Orbis, 1979), 37. Cited in Garrett, 'Liberation Theology and Dependency Theory', 183.

10 For dependency theory, see Cristobal Kay, *Latin American Theories of Development and Underdevelopment* (New York: Routledge, 1989); Cristobal Kay, 'For a Renewal of Development Studies: Latin American Theories and Neoliberalism in the Era of Structural Adjustment', *Third World Quarterly*, 14(4) (1993), 691–702; and Cristobal Kay, 'Reflections on the Latin American Contribution to Development Theory', CDS occasional paper no.7 (Centre for Development Studies: University of Glasgow, 1990). On Frank, Will Hout, *Capitalism and the Third World: Development, Dependence and*

the World System (Aldershot: Edward Elgar Publishing Limited, 1993) is helpful. See also, Frans Schuurman, 'Introduction: Development Theory in the 1990s', in *Beyond the Impasse: New Directions in Development Theory* (New Jersey: Zed Books, 1993), 1–48; Charles Oman and Ganeshan Wignaraja, *The Postwar Evolution of Development Thinking* (London: Macmillan Academic and Professional LTD, 1991); Joseph Love, 'The Origins of Dependency Analysis', *Journal of Latin American Studies*, 22(1) (1990), 143–68; So, *Social Change and Development*, Jorge Larrain, *Theories of Development: Capitalism, Colonialism and Dependency* (Cambridge: Polity Press, 1989); Ronald Chilcote, *Theories of Development and Underdevelopment* (Boulder, Colorado: Westview Press, 1984); Magnus Blomstrom and Bjorn Hettne, *Development Theory in Transition: The Dependency Debate and Beyond – Third World Responses* (London: Zed, 1984) and Gabriel Palma, 'Dependency: A Formal Theory of Underdevelopment or a Methodology for the Analysis of Concrete Situations of Underdevelopment?', *World Development*, 6 (1978), 881–924. For the debate between Marxism and dependency theory see Ronald Chilcote (ed.), *Dependency and Marxism: Toward a Resolution of the Debate* (Boulder, Colorado: Westview Press, 1982); for an examination of what Latin American dependency theory can learn from East Asian development see Peter Evans, 'Class, State, and Dependence in East Asia: Lessons for Latin Americanists', in *The Political Economy of the New Asian Industrialism*, ed. Frederic Deyo (Ithaca: Cornell University Press, 1987), 203–26; for an account of the resurgence of neoclassical economics in development theory, see John Toye, *Dilemmas of Development* (Oxford: Blackwell Publishers, 1993).

11 Here I will use Cristobal Kay's often cited *Latin American Theories of Development and Underdevelopment*, which draws a divide between Marxist *dependistas*, who believe that development is impossible within capitalism and thus argue for a socialist revolution as the only way to break the ties of dependency, and reformist *dependistas*, who believe that it is possible to resolve the problem of dependence by reforming the capitalist system in the direction of socialism. The former would include Andre Gunder Frank, Ruy Mauro Marini, Theotonio Dos Santos and others. The latter would include, among others, Fernando Henrique Cardoso and Enzo Faletto, Osvaldo Sunkel, Celso Furtado and Helio Jaguaribe. Sung, from within liberation theology, draws a similar division. For him, the division stems from whether the options for Latin America are merely dependence or revolution (which would be Kay's Marxist *dependista*) or whether the options fall between dependency, revolution or dependent development (which would be Kay's reformist *dependista*). See Sung, *Economía: Tema Ausente en la Teología de la Liberación*, 36. Gabriel Palma, instead, chooses to draw a three way division that has also proved influential. First, there are those theorists who seek to construct a general theory of underdevelopment. According to Palma the main points of this group are that underdevelopment is the direct result of dependency on central economies and capitalism's inability to spur any development (Frank, Dos Santos). Second, there is a group that seeks to reformulate ECLA's analyses and stress obstacles to national development stemming from external conditionings (Sunkel and Furtado). Finally, he identifies a tendency that seeks to study concrete situations of dependency and rejects the attempt to come up with a formal theory (Cardoso and Faletto). See Palma, 'Dependency'; Larrain, *Theories of Development*; Oman and Wignaraja, *The Postwar Evolution of Development Thinking*.

12 Andre Gunder Frank, 'The Development of Underdevelopment', *Monthly Review*, 18 (September 1966), 17, 18.

13 Andre Gunder Frank, *Capitalism and Underdevelopment in Latin America: Historical Studies of Chile and Brazil* (New York: Monthly Review Press, 1967), 3, emphasis added.

14 Frank, *Capitalism and Underdevelopment*, 3.

15 Ibid., 11.

16 Cited in Kay, *Latin American Theories of Development and Underdevelopment*, 162.

17 Fernando Henrique Cardoso and Enzo Faletto, *Dependency and Development in Latin America* (Berkeley and Los Angeles: University of California Press, 1979), 174; see also Fernando Henrique Cardoso, 'Associated-Dependent Development: Theoretical and Practical Implications', in *Authoritarian Brazil: Origins, Policies, and Future*, ed. Alfred Stepan (New Haven: Yale University Press, 1973), 142–78; Fernando Henrique Cardoso, 'Dependent Capitalist Development in Latin America', *New Left Review*, 74 (July–August 1972), 83–95.

18 Cardoso and Faletto, *Dependency and Development in Latin America*, xxiv.

19 Gonzalo Arroyo, 'Pensamiento Latinoamericano Sobre Subdesarollo y Dependencia Externa', in *Fe Cristiana y Cambio Social en América Latina* (Salamanca: Ediciones Sigueme, 1973), 305–22. Bonino cites the article as an important reference in José Míguez Bonino, *Doing Theology in a Revolutionary Situation*, ed. William H. Lazareth, Confrontation Books (Philadelphia: Fortress Press, 1975), 36. Sung also begins his discussion of liberation theology and dependency theory by referring to an earlier article by Arroyo that served as the basis for the later expanded text. See Gonzalo Arroyo, 'Pensamiento Latinoamericano Sobre Subdesarrollo y Dependencia,' *Mensaje*, 17 (1968), 516–20 and Sung, *Economía: Tema Ausente en la Teología de la Liberación*, 34.

20 On the significance of this Congress for liberation theology's self-definition, see Horacio Cerutti Guldberg, *Filosofía de la Liberación Latinoamericana* (Mexico: Tierra Firme, 1983), 134.

21 Sung, *Economía: Tema Ausente en la Teología de la Liberación*, 35.

22 This statement is qualified in another essay, but it is this formulation that would influence liberation theology. See Gonzalo Arroyo, 'Consideraciones Sobre el Subdesarrollo de América Latina', in *Fe Cristiana y Cambio Social en América Latina* (Salamanca: Ediciones Sigueme, 1972), 325.

23 For statements on Frank's importance to liberation theology see Enrique Dussel, *Teología de la Liberación: Un Panorama de Su Desarrollo* (Ciudad de Mexico: Potrerillos Editores, 1995), 92; Iain Maclean, *Opting for Democracy: Liberation Theology and the Struggle for Democracy in Brazil* (New York: Peter Lang, 1999), 134. Frank himself states: 'Dependence theory writing, including mine, also made a notable impact on and through the "theology of liberation", which was and still is spread through Catholic Church groups in Latin America. Although we have never met, the Peruvian "founder" of liberation theology, Gustavo Gutiérrez, acknowledged this influence in writing. The Chilean Jesuit Gonzalo Arroyo baptized my sister in law's children and took the occasion to invite me to participate in his seminar at the Catholic University of Chile. We have been friends ever since' (Andre Gunder Frank, *The Underdevelopment of Development*, ed. Franklin Vivekananda, Series in International Political Economy, vol. 2, Stockholm, Sweden: Bethany Books, 1991, 35).

24 José Míguez Bonino, *Doing Theology in a Revolutionary Situation*, 13–14, 15.

25 Ibid., 15–16.

26 Ibid., 16.

27 Ibid.

28 Ibid., 29.

29 Ibid., 39, 40.

30 Hugo Assmann, *Theology for a Nomad Church*, ed. Paul Burns (Maryknoll, NY: Orbis Books, 1975), 48–9; emphasis added.

31 Assmann, *Theology for a Nomad Church*, 130; Hugo Assmann, *Teología Desde la Praxis de la Liberación* (Salamanca: Ediciones Sígueme, 1973), 123. I have added the last sentence of this quotation from the Spanish edition. This sentence was not included in the English translation of the text.

32 Assmann, *Theology for a Nomad Church*, 130; Assmann, *Teología Desde la Praxis de la Liberación*, 123. I have added the last sentence of the quotation from the Spanish edition. This sentence was not included in the English translation of the text.

33 On the movement, see John Eagleson (ed.), *Christians and Socialism: The Christians for Socialism Movement in Latin America* (Maryknoll, NY: Orbis Books, 1975).

34 Gustavo Gutiérrez, *A Theology of Liberation: History, Politics and Salvation*, trans. Caridad Inda and John Eagleson (New York: Maryknoll, 1985), 26.

35 Gutiérrez, *A Theology of Liberation*, 84.

36 Gutiérrez, *A Theology of Liberation*, 88.

37 Gustavo Gutiérrez, *Praxis de Liberación y Fe Cristiana* (Madrid: Zero, 1974), 32.

38 Ibid., 20, 33; translation is my own.

39 Leonardo Boff, *Jesus Christ Liberator: A Critical Christology for Our Time* (Maryknoll: Orbis Books, 1981), 276.

40 Boff, *Jesus Christ Liberator*, 277.

41 Leonardo Boff, *Liberating Grace* (Maryknoll, NY: Orbis Books, 1979), 80.

42 Cited in Sung, *Economía: Tema Ausente en la Teología de la Liberación*, 47.

43 Clodovis Boff and Leonardo Boff, *Introducing Liberation Theology* (Maryknoll, NY: Orbis Books, 1987), 26–7. See also Sung, *Economía: Tema Ausente en la Teología de la Liberación*, 48. What William Garrett states of Gutiérrez can be stated of Boff: 'The source from which Gutiérrez derived a goodly portion of his original dependency theory was the work of such moderates as Fernando Henrique Cardoso, Raul Prebisch, and their colleagues who explicitly rejected a neocolonial Marxist reading of the Latin American situation. In the same connection, however, Gutiérrez also integrated Frank's notion of the development of underdevelopment. The lack of conceptual symmetry between the moderate presuppositions of Cardoso and the neo-Marxist assumptions of Frank unfortunately passed by the board without ever being addressed in Gutiérrez's diligent effort to conflate these two perspectives' (Garrett, 'Liberation Theology and Dependency Theory', 183–4).

44 Andre Gunder Frank, 'Latin American Development Theories Revisited: A Participant Review', *Latin American Perspectives*, 19(73) (Spring 1992), 136. Kay calls Frank a 'reluctant *dependista*', and states that 'in retrospect Frank's writings can best be considered belonging to the world-system perspective to which he, together with Samir Amin and Immanuel Wallerstein, has made such a vital contribution' (Kay, *Latin American Theories of Development and Underdevelopment*, 155 and 156).

45 For a representative sampling of his work see, Immanuel Wallerstein, *The Modern-World System: Capitalist Agriculture and the Origins of the European World-Economy in the Sixteenth Century*, Studies in Social Discontinuity (New York: Academic Press, 1974); Immanuel Wallerstein, *The Modern World System II: Mercantilism and the Consolidation of the European World-Economy, 1600–1750*, Social Studies in Discontinuity (New York: Academic Press, 1980); Immanuel Wallerstein, *Historical Capitalism and Capitalist Civilization* (New York: Verso, 1983); Immanuel Wallerstein, *Unthinking Social Science: The Limits of Nineteenth-Century Paradigms* (Cambridge: Polity Press, 1991); Immanuel Wallerstein, *After Liberalism* (New York: The New Press, 1995); Immanuel Wallerstein, *The End of the World as We Know It* (Minneapolis: University of Minnesota Press, 1999). Two influential critiques of Wallerstein are Theda Skocpol, 'Wallerstein's World Capitalist System: A Theoretical and Historical Critique', *American Journal of Sociology*, 82(5) (1977), 1075–90, and John Agnew, 'Sociologizing the Geographical Imagination: Spatial Concepts in the World-System Perspective', *Political Geography Quarterly*, 1(2) (April 1982), 159–66. Good introductions to world system theory can be found in Thomas Shannon, *An Introduction to the World-System Perspective* (Boulder, Colorado: Westview Press, 1992) and So, *Social Change and Development*. For recent review essays see Thomas Hall, 'The World System Perspective: A Small Sample from a Large Universe', *Sociological Inquiry*, 66(4) (November 1996), 440–54; Colin Flint, 'Structure, Agency, and Context: The Contributions of Geography to World Systems Analysis', *Sociological Inquiry*, 66(4) (November 1996), 496–508; Christopher Chase-Dunn and Peter Grimes, 'World Systems Analysis', *Annual Review of Sociology*, 21 (1995), 387–417. Finally, for the debate around the dating of the world system, see Andre Gunder Frank and Barry Gills (eds), *The World System: Five Hundred Years or Five Thousand?* (New York: Routledge, 1993) and James Blaut, *1492: The Debate on Colonialism, Eurocentrism and History* (Trenton, NJ: Africa World Press, Inc., 1992). For the differences between Frank and Wallerstein, see Frank and Gills, *The World System*.

46 My discussion of Wallerstein is indebted to Hout's excellent exposition in *Capitalism and the Third World*, see esp. 112–21, from which elements one, two and three are taken.

47 Immanuel Wallerstein, T.K. Hopkins *et al.*, *World Systems Analysis: Theory and Methodology* (Beverly Hills: Sage, 1982), 72; cited in Hout, *Capitalism and the Third World*, 114.

48 Hout, *Capitalism and the Third World*, 114.

49 Immanuel Wallerstein, *The Capitalist World Economy: Essays* (Cambridge: Cambridge University Press, 1979), 73; cited in Hout, *Capitalism and the Third World*, 115.

50 Hout, *Capitalism and the Third World*, 114–15.

51 Immanuel Wallerstein, *The Politics of the World-Economy: The States, the Movements, and the Civilizations* (Cambridge: Cambridge University Press, 1984), 29; cited in Hout, *Capitalism and the Third World*, 115.

52 On this, see especially Wallerstein, *After Liberalism*. For the main liberationist work developing this idea, see Franz Hinkelammert, *Crítica a la Razón Utópica* (San José: DEI, 1990).

53 Franz Hinkelammert, 'Capitalismo y Socialismo: La Posibilidad de Alternativas', *Pasos*, 48 (July–August 1993), 14.

54 Ignacio Ellacuría, 'Utopia and Prophecy in Latin America', in *Mysterium Liberationis: Fundamental Concepts of Liberation Theology*, ed. Ignacio Ellacuría and Jon Sobrino (Maryknoll, NY: Orbis Books, 1993), 298.

55 Leonardo Boff, *Ecology and Liberation: A New Paradigm* (New York: Orbis Books, 1995), 33–4.

56 I owe this insight to J.K. Gibson-Graham: 'But the "failure" to theorize the economy is inevitably associated with certain problematic effects ... Unless the economy is explicitly written out, or until it is deconstructively or positively rewritten, it will write itself into every text of social theory [or liberation theology], in familiar and powerful ways. When it is not overtly theorized, it defines itself as capitalism because it lack another name' (Gibson-Graham, *The End of Capitalism*, 39).

57 On this trend, see Sung, *Economía: Tema Ausente en la Teología de la Liberación*; Marsha Hewitt, 'Liberation Theology and the Emancipation of Religion', *The Scottish Journal of Religious Studies*, XIII(1) (Spring 1992), 21–38; Paul Sigmund, *Liberation Theology at the Crossroads: Democracy or Revolution?* (New York: Oxford University Press, 1990) and McGovern, *Liberation Theology and Its Critics*.

58 Gutiérrez, *A Theology of Liberation*, ix; cited in Marsha Hewitt, 'Liberation Theology and the Emancipation of Religion', 26. Hewitt also cites Leonardo and Clodovis Boff: 'there is one, and only one theology of liberation. There is only one point of departure – a reality of social misery – and one goal – the liberation of the oppressed'. From Clodovis Boff and Leonardo Boff, *Salvation and Liberation: In Search of a Balance Between Faith and Politics* (Maryknoll, NY: Orbis Books, 1984), 24; cited in Marsha Hewitt, 'Liberation Theology and the Emancipation of Religion', 26. For Hewitt's own constructive project see Marsha Hewitt, *Critical Theory of Religion: A Feminist Analysis* (Minneapolis: Fortress Press, 1995).

59 Gutiérrez, *A Theology of Liberation*, 6.

60 Ibid., 11.

61 See Marsha Hewitt, 'Liberation Theology and the Emancipation of Religion', 26, for more on this.

62 Marsha Hewitt, 'Liberation Theology and the Emancipation of Religion', 27. Hewitt is quoting from the 1984 essay 'Theology and the Social Sciences' in Gustavo Gutiérrez, *The Truth Shall Make You Free* (Maryknoll, NY: Orbis Books, 1990), 223. See also Gustavo Gutiérrez, 'La Teología: Una Función Eclesial', *Paginas* XIX(130) (December 1994), 10–17.

63 Gustavo Gutiérrez, 'Expanding the View', in *Expanding the View: Gustavo Gutiérrez and the Future of Liberation Theology*, ed. Marc Ellis and Otto Maduro (Maryknoll, NY: Orbis Books, 1988), 3–38. This essay appeared as the new introduction to the 15th anniversary edition of *A Theology of Liberation*.

64 Sung, *Economía: Tema Ausente en la Teología de la Liberación*, 97.

65 Gustavo Gutiérrez, *The God of Life* (Maryknoll, NY: Orbis Books, 1991), 60; cited in Sung, *Economía: Tema Ausente en la Teología de la Liberación*, 98.

66 Sung, *Economía: Tema Ausente en la Teología de la Liberación*, 98; translation my own.

67 Gutiérrez, *Praxis de Liberación y Fe Cristiana*, 21; translation my own.

68 Sung, *Economía: Tema Ausente en la Teología de la Liberación*, 98–9.

69 Marsha Hewitt, 'Liberation Theology and the Emancipation of Religion', 23.

70 Cited in Maclean, *Opting for Democracy*, 142.

71 Franz Hinkelammert, 'Changes in the Relationships Between Third World and First World Countries', in *Spirituality of the Third World*, ed. K.C. Abraham and Bernadette Mbuy-Beya (Maryknoll, NY: Orbis, 1994), 10–11; cited in Daniel M. Bell Jr, *Liberation Theology After the End of History: The Refusal to Cease Suffering* (London: Routledge, 2001), 67.

72 Franz Hinkelammert, 'Determinación y Autoconstitución del Sujeto: Las Leyes Que Se Imponen a Espaldas de los Actores y el Orden por el Desorden', *Pasos* 64 (March–April 1993), 18.

73 Pablo Richard, 'Teología de la Solidaridad en el Contexto Actual de Economía Neoliberal de Mercado', in *El Huracan de la Globalización*, ed. Franz Hinkelammert (San José, Costa Rica: DEI, 1999), 228, original emphasis.

74 Richard, 'Teología de la Solidaridad en el Contexto Actual de Economía Neoliberal de Mercado', 233, original emphasis.

75 José Míguez Bonino, 'For Life and Against Death: A Theology That Takes Sides', in *Theologians in Transition*, ed. James Wall (New York: Crossroad, 1981), 175; original emphasis.

76 Trevor Barnes offers a description of the approach: 'In brief, the argument developed over the past three decades, particularly in history, sociology and philosophy of science, is that objectivism, the idea that our theories mirror reality, is not sustainable. Both the Duhem–Quine thesis, which claims that by necessity the validity of a theory is always underdetermined by the facts used to verify it, and Kuhn's conclusions about the value-ladenness of empirical inquiry, make the task of hooking theory to the 'real world', whether it be theories of quantum physics or accumulation and regulation, inherently problematic. With this realization, attention has switched increasingly to how theories are formulated and developed, and away from issues of strict empirical validation. In undertaking that former task a number of people have turned to metaphor' (Trevor Barnes, 'Theories of Accumulation and Regulation: Bringing Life Back Into Economic Geography', in *Geographies of Economies*, ed. Roger Lee and Jane Wills, London: Arnold, 1997, 231–47).

77 I owe these last two points to Bojan Bugaric, 'From Plan to Market: One Way or Alternative Paths – a Critique of Institutional Reforms in Central and Eastern Europe' (University of Wisconsin, Madison, 1996), 23.

78 This approach to social theory has its roots in the pragmatist critique of the mirror of nature. For this view, the conception of the knowing mind and of knowledge as representation was overcome by three events: the continual failure of those candidates selected to serve as absolute foundations for knowledge (whether clear and distinct ideas, sense-data, categories of pure understanding, structures of pre-linguistic consciousness, etc), the historicist dismantling of the image of the mind as a separate inner space in which processes produce knowledge of the outside world, and by the understanding of knowledge that emerged with the scientific revolution. In the pragmatist conception the world is not static, ready to be understood as a whole, there is no clear-cut distinction between mind and body, nor between the human subject and the world. Here ideas and theories are rules for action that need to be put to the test experimentally and truths, rather than the Truth, are both the temporary resting places found after a successful intervention in the world as well as the starting point for new avenues of inquiry. For the early pragmatist view, see John Dewey, *The Quest for Certainty: A Study of the Relation of Knowledge and Action* (New York: Putnam's, Capricorn, 1960) and John Dewey, *Reconstruction in Philosophy*, enlarged edn, reprint, 1948 (Boston: Beacon Press, 1957). The essays collected in John Dewey, *The Influence of Darwin on Philosophy* (New York: Henry Holt and Company, 1910) are also helpful. The most influential recent pragmatist work is Richard Rorty, *Philosophy and the Mirror of Nature* (Princeton, New Jersey: Princeton University Press, 1979). See also Richard Rorty, *Consequences of Pragmatism (Essays: 1972–1980)* (Minneapolis: University of Minnesota Press, 1982); Richard Rorty, *Objectivity, Relativism, and Truth* (Cambridge: Cambridge University Press, 1991); Richard Rorty, *Essays on Heidegger and Others* (Cambridge: Cambridge University Press, 1991) and Richard Rorty, *Truth and Progress* (Cambridge: Cambridge University Press, 1998). This perspective is also developed by recent strands of poststructuralist Marxism. See, for example, Ernesto Laclau and Chantal Mouffe, *Hegemony and Socialist Strategy: Towards a Radical Democratic Politics* (New York: Verso, 1985); Stephen Resnick and Richard Wolff, *Knowledge and Class: A Marxian Critique of Political Economy* (Chicago: University of Chicago Press, 1987) and Gibson-Graham, *The End of Capitalism*.

79 Jon Sobrino, *The True Church and the Poor*, trans. Matthew J. O'Connell (Maryknoll, New York: Orbis, 1984), 166.

80 Gutiérrez, *Praxis de Liberación y Fe Cristiana*, 21; translation my own.
81 Karl Marx, *The Eighteenth Brumaire of Louis Bonaparte* (New York: International Publishers, 1966), 1.

CHAPTER 5

Liberation Theology, Institutional Imagination and Historical Projects

Chapter 4's analysis of liberation theology and capitalism reveals a third reason why liberation theology is unable to think in terms of historical projects. Remember that the first reason is external to liberation theology and lies in the inescapable fact that the worldwide context today is dramatically different from the time of the movement's birth and development. Currently, liberation theologians possess neither a supportive ecclesial context nor a context where revolution seems possible. Socialism is gone as an option and the Vatican no longer supports liberation theology. Liberation theology's three main positions at present – reasserting core ideas, reformulating basic categories and critiquing idolatry – acknowledge and make this fact their starting point. The second reason is internal to liberation theology and lies in the fact that its methodological statements do not make the construction of historical projects a priority. The upshot can be seen in liberation theology's inability to go beyond the analysis and condemnation of stagnant democracy as seen in Chapter 3. Chapter 4, however, uncovered another internal (and unacknowledged) reason why liberation theology is unable to develop historical projects: its own approach to capitalism as a social system. In liberation theology, capitalism is understood as an indivisible, monolithic entity encompassing all social relations. This understanding of capitalism and society turns an idol into God and works as a brake on any attempt to think in terms of new historical projects. A new approach to capitalism and society, or family of approaches, is needed.

This chapter attempts to provide a new approach. However, let me stress from the outset that my goal is not to provide a ready-made historical project. Here, as throughout this work, my goal is to contribute to the task of clearing spaces from which new historical projects may emerge. Established modes of thinking about liberation theology's methodology, as seen in Chapter 2, as well as established modes of thinking about capitalism and society, as seen in Chapter 4, have become roadblocks that obstruct the very goal of liberation. Thought too can hold us in chains. My task, therefore, is to provide liberation theology with a different set of intellectual tools. In order to do so, this chapter will bring together liberation theology and Roberto Unger's social theory. While the potential use of Roberto Unger's social theory by liberation theology has been acknowledged it has yet to be fully developed.[1] Since Unger's concern lies in the deepening of democracy and the expansion of economic opportunity, this is somewhat surprising, especially given that Unger himself is Brazilian and thus native to a country where liberation theology thrives. Unger has written extensively in the major Brazilian newspapers so ignorance of his work is unlikely.

The most likely explanation for the lack of interest on the part of liberation theologians lies in the fact that, as will become evident shortly, Unger's theoretical approach to capitalism and society is radically opposed to that of liberation theologians. Despite this opposition, this chapter will show that Unger's work is highly relevant to liberation theology. More specifically, I suggest that in order to devise new historical projects liberation theology must incorporate Unger's practice of institutional imagination: the step-by-step imaginative construction of alternative political and economic institutions. Rather than offer a specific historical project, what I do here is lead liberation theology through Unger to a point where the imagination of new historical projects once again seems possible. My argument develops in the following fashion: First, I briefly map liberation theology's understanding of society generally, and capitalism and democracy in particular, unto Unger's social theory. I suggest that liberation theology remains prey to a diluted version of what Unger call the naturalistic premise, the belief that there exist only a limited number of ways society may be organized. The naturalistic premise can be seen in liberation theology's espousal of deep structure social theory and the mistake of institutional fetishism. Second, I outline the assumptions and tools behind Unger's practice of institutional imagination. Finally, I give two examples, one in relation to the economy, the other in relation to the state, of how liberation theology can put institutional imagination into practice and construct new historical projects.

Liberation Theology and the Naturalistic Premise

It may come as a surprise to find liberation theology accused of retaining a diluted version of the belief that there is a natural order to society. After all, Gustavo Gutiérrez's foundational *A Theology of Liberation* includes a narrative of emancipation – from the 15th century to the Enlightenment, to Hegel, Marx and Freud – where the individual progressively 'perceives himself as creative subject' and as 'an agent of history responsible for his own destiny'.[2] Indeed, for Gutiérrez politics 'is the sphere for the exercise of a critical freedom which is won through history. It is the universal determinant and the collective arena for human fulfillment ... Nothing lies outside the political sphere understood in this way'.[3] Yet, despite this rhetoric, Gutiérrez and liberationists generally retain a version of the naturalistic premise in that they participate in modes of thinking that set strict limits to the available scope of social and political change.

Liberation Theology as an Instance of Deep Structure Social Theory

The first way that liberation theology retains a diluted view of the belief that there is a natural order to society lies in the espousal of what Unger calls 'deep structure' social theory. Deep structure social theories are based on three main assumptions.[4]

The first assumption Unger describes as the 'closed list idea'. According to the closed list idea there are a small number of possible institutional systems such as, in the traditional Marxist story, feudalism, capitalism and socialism, or a market economy and a command economy. The closed list idea acquires further force through deep structure's second assumption, the 'indivisibility idea'.[5] According to this idea the institutional systems within the closed list form indivisible wholes. They stand or fall in one piece. For this reason, within deep structure social theory all politics is either revolutionary, the exchange of one system for another, or reformist, the humanization of a system that remains unchallenged at its core. The third assumption is the 'determinist idea' according to which necessary and lawlike conditions (such as the imperative of profit or technological advancement) govern the emergence, actualization and spread of social systems. Liberation theology retains all three of these assumptions. The closed list idea, on the one hand, lies behind the liberationist belief that the death of socialism posits a crisis of alternatives. Yet this is the case only if institutional systems follow this closed list pattern, in which case the demise of socialism leaves liberation theology only with a monolithic capitalism that must be accepted as a whole. Otherwise, different options would be available. The indivisibility idea, on the other hand, lies at the root of liberation theology's claim that capitalism cannot be overcome piece by piece but must be rejected as a whole and replaced by some other system. Finally, the determinist idea leads liberation theology to postulate that capitalism possesses dynamics that make it necessarily exploitative. Thus, the determinist idea comes together with the indivisibility idea to make the complete overcoming of capitalism the only viable option.

Liberation Theology and Institutional Fetishism

Liberation theology's espousal of deep structure social theory is symptomatic of a deeper problem, the conceptual mistakes of 'false necessity' and 'institutional fetishism'. False necessity is the belief that there is a natural content for contingent categories. An example of false necessity would be to stipulate that a woman's natural place lies in the household. In this case, rather than realizing that this conception of women is the contingent historical product of a Victorian understanding of womanhood and its place within a wider family and social structure, a historical product is taken as necessary to women as such. Institutional fetishism is the specific political expression of false necessity. Institutional fetishism identifies 'institutional conceptions, such as a representative democracy, a market economy, and a free civil society, with a single set of institutional arrangements'.[6] Liberation theology's understanding of capitalism or market systems as necessarily evil, monolithic entities is an example of institutional fetishism because it implicitly assumes that there is only one form a market economy can take.

Every liberationist depiction of capitalism given in the previous chapter serves as an example of institutional fetishism. Take, as one more example, Leonardo and

Clodovis Boff's comment, 'Capitalism can be more or less *immoral*; it can never be more or less *moral*. You do not eliminate the ferocity of the wolf by filing down its teeth ... It is just as impossible to create a moral market system as it is to build a Christian brothel.'[7] Boff and Boff display liberation theology's wider perspective according to which capitalism and the market are synonymous categories with a predefined content, possessing laws or dynamics that make them by definition immoral. Take also Gutiérrez's claim that 'capitalist development is *of its very nature* detrimental to the masses'.[8] Because capitalism is theorized as having a necessarily evil nature, gradual reform is futile and so the only option becomes the replacement of capitalism by another system. Prey to institutional fetishism, liberation theology is unable from the outset to envision a version of capitalism or market that could distribute the benefits of ownership more democratically.

Another example of institutional fetishism is the belief, found in contemporary North American social science work on democracy in Latin America, as seen in Chapter 2, that a well functioning democracy must take the form of the limited American procedural or the European parliamentary models. The abstract concept of democracy is imbued with a particular content which then seems natural. Institutional fetishism is also found in liberation theology's analysis of stagnant democracy in the fact that liberation theologians criticize the emancipatory potential of current Latin American democracies without ever asking how their institutional form, inherited from the First World, limits that very potential. They thus tacitly acknowledge in practice that the shape of democracy is set, that variations in the institutional framework we have come to identify as 'democracy' are not possible. They do not question, and thus take for granted, the background governmental structure of society. In their criticism of capitalism and democracy, liberation theologians reduce them to a single, and thus natural, institutional form.

Liberation Theology and Institutional Imagination

At the center of Unger's practice of institutional imagination – the step-by-step construction of alternative political and economic institutions – lies the idea of alternative pluralisms. Contrary to institutional fetishism that supposes that there is one natural form that 'capitalism' or 'democracy' takes, alternative pluralisms argue that representative democracies, market economies and civil societies can in fact take many different institutional forms.[9] Alternative pluralisms thus suggest that abstract concepts such as capitalism, the market and democracy have no necessary content; such concepts hide more than they reveal about the way life chances and scarce resources may be institutionally realized.[10] To incorporate the idea of alternative pluralisms and engage in the practice of institutional imagination, however, liberation theology must follow Unger and make three moves. First, liberation theology will have to theorize society generally, and the economy in particular, as the product of historical accident and contained political conflict.

Second, liberation theology will have to replace its abstract and monolithic view of capitalism with the recognition and analysis of the wide variety of market systems in actual existence in the world today. Once in place, these two moves make room for the third move: incorporating Unger's methodology of mapping and criticism as the means to balance ideals and institutions in the formulation of historical projects.

Society as Frozen Politics

The first step liberation theology must take lies in the incorporation of Unger's belief that 'society is made and imagined, that it is a human artifact rather than the expression of an underlying natural order'.[11] According to Unger, the organization of society – its political and economic institutions – is *only* the outcome of political contest. He rejects any psychological, economic or organizational constraints on the variety of shapes society may take. Society 'works and assumes a definite form because the fighting over all these terms of order is partly interrupted and contained'.[12] Society, as Unger puts it, is merely 'frozen politics'.[13] Central to Unger's understanding of society is the notion of contingency in society, that is, the artificial, contextual and haphazard nature of economic and political institutions. If institutions are the contingent product of historical accident, in conjunction with the victories and defeats of groups in political struggle, then their shape and form are not set in stone. Support for this thesis can be found in multiple locations, such as Charles Sabel's understanding of the economy, the critical legal studies movement's view on law, and Ernesto Laclau's and Chantal Mouffe's post-Marxist political theory.

For example, within economic history Michael Piore and Charles Sabel have shown that the rise of industrial capitalism was the result of political struggle between social groups and the choices implied in that struggle.[14] As they put it: 'From the perspective of late twentieth century scholarship ... even the successes of mass production seem less the outcome of mechanization than an interplay of social and political forces.'[15] In his more recent work, Sabel in alliance with Jonathan Zeitlin, radicalizes this thesis by bringing to the forefront the political and contingent nature of the economy.[16] Their starting point is composed of three elements: first, 'the sense of fragility, and especially institutional fragility as a continuing, perhaps permanent feature of economic life';[17] second, the experience of 'recombinability and interpenetration of different forms of economic organization: the rigid and the flexible, the putatively archaic and the certifiably modern, the hierarchical and the market-conforming, the trusting and the mistrustful';[18] third, the claim that economic actors, as they decide and act on particular courses of action, make structure at the same time that they are constrained by structure. These elements come together in a view of the economy as always in transition, its form always in question: 'Our analysis of economic actors as knitting together and redefining the past and future in their moment-to-moment strategic choices suggests ... that even the most apparently tranquil epochs of economic history never have the matter-of-factness that the notion of grand periodization almost inevitably imposes on them.'[19] History is always more open than historical writing allows.[20] Sabel and Zeitlin's perspective rejects a periodization of economic history into grand epochs that requires the distinction between open and closed periods, periods where institutions are so settled they appear objective and natural, in which the multiple instabilities that make society are lost.[21] For them, therefore, modern capitalism is a hodgepodge of diverse and often contradictory institutions devoid of any systematic unity.

Furthermore, the critical legal studies movement has undermined the view of law generally and judicial decision making in particular as neutral and apolitical.[22] Take, for example, mainstream North American legal thought's obsession with the way judges decide cases. This obsession stems from the problem – in terms of democracy – of delegating power to a set of non-elected officials such as judges. The mainstream response to this problem has been to 'posit adjudication as an objective and rationally-bounded process, in stark contrast to the nonrational, often arbitrary, character of political decisionmaking'.[23] Judges, therefore, do not exercise discretion when deciding cases. The law or some non-political principle behind the law or guiding the law decides the case. For CLSers,[24] however, the idea of law as neutral and apolitical rests on an implicit belief that one can find neutral and apolitical rules by which to organize society. Law, in this case, is merely the incarnation and expression of an underlying natural order. If this were not the case, the law could not be apolitical. Its neutrality stems from the claim to map a prepolitical order. Instead, CLSers contend that the law does not possess a single and coherent view of human relations; rather, a number of different and competing views can be found on key issues with different consequences for the distribution of resources in society, nor is there any objective way to adjudicate between the competing views.[25]

Yet, as Allan Hutchinson and Patrick Monahan argue, mainstream contemporary legal thought has tried to retain an apolitical understanding of law through three major failed strategies.[26] First, some scholars appeal to conventional morality. The argument states that even though society is pluralistic values come together to form a coherent body of norms. Judges must apply this societal consensus. The upshot, however, is that the judge gives a legal gloss to the particularities of a time and place. Here the law is not so much separate from politics, but sanctifies politics with its legal blessing.[27] Second, other scholars claim that there exists a set of fundamental rights inherent to liberal society. The tactic here is to get to the purposes and principles behind legal doctrine. The problem with this position is that purposes and principles themselves contradict and are indeterminate.[28] Third, scholars within law and economics appeal to a criterion of allocative efficiency for evaluating the law. But any resort to allocative efficiency is meaningful within a given scheme of distribution and thus cannot be separated from the existing distribution of legal entitlements. Thus it loses its claim to apolitical and objective legitimacy.[29] Finally, the attempt to envision law as discursively justified – and thus justified through political deliberation – is closer to CLS than any of these previous options. However, such an emphasis still remains linked to the search for a justification for legal structure and thus a search for stability that is integral to mainstream legal thought.[30] CLS goes in exactly the opposite direction; the quest is for the inherent instabilities in legal doctrine. The upshot of critical legal thought's attack on the attempt to uphold the ideal of legal neutrality is to reveal the law, similarly to what Sabel does for the economy, as politically created at the level of legal process and at the level of legal structure itself.

Finally, Ernesto Laclau and Chantal Mouffe have demolished the idea of historical laws in Marxist political theory, showing that socialism was the result of localized political contests rather than the necessary unfolding of capitalism's contradictions.[31] Instead, they develop a theoretical framework where the definition of society through political struggle takes priority. Within their post-Marxist framework society is divided into two parts whose boundary remains fluid: 'the political' and 'the social'. 'The political' are areas of society that remain fought over and thus have yet to be fully settled and defined, while 'the social', are areas of society where a truce has contained the fighting. Politics creates society and so society remains a contingent and historical product. Once the repository of economic laws awaiting discovery on the part of the classical Marxist (or dependency theorist), 'the social' is now viewed as areas of society that temporarily fall outside the scope of political struggle. Society, rather than being constructed around the existence of necessary capitalist dynamics, is stabilized insofar as political struggle over its shape is contained. All of society is the product of political strife and therefore historical and contingent, the outcome of a myriad of contests; society is a 'social construction of human beings which is not grounded on any metaphysical "necessity" external to it – neither God, nor "essential forms", nor the 'necessary laws of history".'[32]

The outcome of the belief that society is fully defined through politics – some areas more settled, others less settled – is that there is no fundamental nodal point upon which a revolution can be constructed. Neither capitalism nor society forms a coherent and systemic whole waiting to be toppled and replaced by another whole. Society has no a priori foundation and remains constantly constructed, deconstructed and reconstructed through a variety of discursive and political struggles. Since there is no master key to history, neither is there a class in possession of such a key. The area of social struggle is extended into multiple forms of resistance and emancipation such as class, gender, culture and ethnicity in which none has any self-evident privileged position over the other. The only difference between parts of society, whether the economic, political or cultural realms, is that some areas are temporarily more removed from political strife and thus temporarily more immune to critique than others.[33]

Capitalism(s) Revised

The second step liberation theology must take lies in replacing its abstract and monolithic understanding of capitalism with a more subtle view that recognizes the existence of a variety of market systems in place in the world today. As Geoffrey Hodgson puts it, 'pronouncements of the "end of history" ignore the tremendous variety of forms of capitalism itself'.[34] While liberation theologians rightly reject the end of history thesis, they remain tied to it insofar as they fail to see the various market systems lying beneath their monolithic understanding of capitalism. For proponents of the end of history capitalism is a good thing; for liberation theologians capitalism is a bad thing. Yet for both it is one thing. However, if societies are constituted through political struggle and historical accident, and those accidents and struggles as well as their outcomes differ across nations, then one would expect to find important differences in the way societies organize their political and economic life.

For Unger, the abstract concept of capitalism is merely a blanket term that gets in the way of detailing and understanding the particularities of each social order. He argues that the very concept 'capitalism' is either too general or too specific, too inclusive or too exclusive, to possess descriptive or explanatory power. The definition of capitalism must, on the one hand, remain sufficiently general and inclusive to incorporate countries that organize production, labor and capital very differently. One common definition claims, for example, that capitalism is 'an economic system based on private ownership of the means of production, in which personal profit can be acquired through investment of capital and employment of labor'.[35] This definition, however, remains too broad for as Unger argues many non-European societies of antique history meet the threefold requirements of private property, free labor and capital investment.[36] According to this definition, China during the Sung dynasty, 19th-century England and present day United States are all equally capitalist. So the definition must be made more specific through the incorporation of other traits such as the replacement of small-scale family farms with large estates and mass migration from countryside to cities (in addition to the already cited traits of private property, free wage labor and investment of capital).

This definition, however, remains too inclusive, since there are periods in the history of the agrarian empires when these traits are met, and too exclusive in that it excludes 19th-century Holland and France (both kept family size holdings as the agricultural norm) from a model of 'capitalist' development that is essentially English. So another trait needs to be added, such as the rollback of government from the economy to allow private groups to act and invest on their own. In this case, however, neither Japan nor Germany would be capitalist since government agencies such as public banks played a central role in industrialization and government continues to shape their economies through cross holdings, industrial policy and ownership of industry. According to Unger, the problem in defining the concept cannot be avoided: 'Every addition to the list of defining traits produces a category that seems to include both too much and too little and to have an arbitrary relationship to the more abstract conceptions of capitalism. If you go far enough, you no longer have a concept at all but the summary description of particular developments that took place in particular countries, with particular outcomes that resulted from time to time.'[37]

Once the inescapably abstract nature of 'capitalism' as an analytical concept is accepted, liberation theology can use political economy to give specific and localized content to the term as well as find institutions and practices to inform institutional design; institutions that work in one place can perhaps be adapted to work elsewhere. For example, the most influential analysis of the 'variety of capitalisms' in contemporary political economy, developed by Peter Hall and David Soskice, divides economies into a spectrum within which they fall: coordinated market economies (CMEs such as Germany, Japan, Sweden, Norway, Switzerland, Austria) and liberal market economies (LMEs including England, the United States, Ireland, Canada, Australia).[38] These economies differ in the organization of their industrial relations, their training systems, their inter-company relations and their financial systems. They represent different institutional matrixes. Table 5.1 outlines these differences.

Table 5.1 Institutional matrixes

	Coordinated market economies	Liberal market economies
Industrial relations	1 Centralized/industry collective bargaining 2 Employee representation on boards in the form of work councils	1 Individual/company-level bargaining 2 Weak employee representation, no restrictions on hiring or firing
Training system	Strong vocational training system (because of a focus on long-term hiring)	Strong general education
Inter-company relations	1 Cooperative standard setting 2 Collaborative research and development programs 3 Interlocking directorships (and thus possible to sit on multiple boards)	1 Standards set through competition 2 Strong antitrust legislation
Financial system	1 Restrictive takeover legislation (makes hostile takeovers difficult) 2 Bank financing central (banks are also shareholders and thus have considerable power in determining company strategy) 3 Patient capital	1 Liberal takeover legislation 2 Stock equity 3 Risk-willing capital
Outcome	Diversified quality products	Radical innovation

The institutional frameworks of CMEs encourage long-term cooperative relations between the different actors in the system: between companies, companies and employees, and between companies and their owners.[39] LMEs, on the other hand, grant companies little capacity to coordinate their activities collectively. The LME state, like the CME state, is at arm's length from business but, unlike the CME state, cannot work out frameworks with business collectively. Such an institutional framework, based on market deregulation, works by favoring shorter terms and more competitive relations.

The differences between models are so significant that Hall and Soskice argue that production regimes favor some types of economic activity over others; some economies compete better in certain areas than others. Central to the varieties of capitalism approach, therefore, lies the notion of 'comparative institutional advantage' in that 'the institutional structure of the political economy provides firms with advantages for engaging in specific kinds of activities. Firms produce some kinds of goods more efficiently than others because of the institutional support they receive for their activities, and the relevant institutions are not distributed evenly across nations'.[40] So, on the one hand, firms in more LMEs are better at radical product innovation because they combine unilateral control by management, freedom to buy and sell subsidiaries, freedom to hire and fire workers through deregulated markets, all this marked by the general unavailability of access to long term capital. These elements come together to give a company great leeway to combine and recombine capital, labor and technology at whim in the pursuit of new products and markets. Firms in more CMEs, on the other hand, are better at the incremental innovation of established products because their institutional framework favors cooperation between clusters of companies, between management and labor, within a context in which long term capital is available. The framework thus supports a process of production as cooperative problem solving where firms within an industry or group can share information and capital in pursuit of improvements in the product line.[41]

Hall and Soskice, moreover, contend that the differences between capitalisms are not destined to disappear under the weight of economic globalization. Economic globalization is based on the belief that the massive change in the size of flows of investment, services and goods across nation states has become so great that governments are no longer able to regulate and manage economic policy.[42] The conventional presumption is that businesses will thus pressure governments into deregulating their economies, and thus, for example, CMEs would slowly merge into LMEs.[43] This view, however, ignores the fact that in CMEs businesses benefit from the dense regulatory framework that composes their comparative institutional advantage. So, while LMEs could very well choose to deregulate further, especially since firm activity is already coordinated by market mechanisms that can often be made more effective through further selective deregulation, business interests in CMEs would likely be concerned to preserve or adapt regulation at the basis of their comparative advantage.[44]

Indeed, there is no consensus on how to understand or define globalization. Some analysts point to evidence suggesting that the thesis has been greatly exaggerated, so that, for example, in reality the percentage of exports/GDP of industrialized nations is not much higher than in 1913. Financial flows, moreover, which have increased have done so only within the industrialized nations, so globalization may be excluding the Third World rather than sweeping through it.[45] Multinational companies, moreover, still keep most of their operations and investment in their home countries, undermining the assumption that firms pick up and move their productive processes abroad at whim.[46] This evidence should caution liberation theology against views such as Pablo Richard's: 'it is not possible to live *outside* the system, since globalization integrates everything, but it is possible to live *against* the spirit of the system'.[47] Here an extreme view of economic globalization is presented as a given: 'For the "people" [el pueblo] (the popular sectors, social movements at the base) political power has become impossible (the system does not allow for the orientation of political power in benefit of popular interest), political power become*s irrelevant* (since everything is determined by market logic and it is impossible to govern against that logic).'[48] This extreme understanding of globalization runs rampant within liberation theology,[49] yet Hall and Soskice as well as other political economists show that to accept the thesis in this form is to unjustifiably delimit too sharply the options available for historical projects.[50]

In order to use political economy as a set of tools for institutional design liberation theology must, however, be wary of the institutional fetishism present within the varieties approach itself. Unger, in fact, argues that contemporary political economy generally forgets that 'the distinctive institutional and social character of every such order is itself the singular and surprising product of practical and institutional conflict'.[51] Take Soskice's categorization of CMEs and LMEs presented above. For him 'there are strong *interlocking complementarities* between different parts of the institutional framework. Each system depends on the other systems to function effectively'.[52] Each part of the institutional framework reinforces the others and 'gives a partial reason for there being only a limited number of possible constellations of institutional frameworks'.[53] Yet it remains unclear why there should be a limited number of possibilities. Just because institutional development is path-dependent does not mean that other more efficient and more democratic institutions could not exist in principle. Nor does it mean that the institutions that emerge must form such a coherent whole. As Soskice and Hall recognize, there are many hybrid models, such as France and Italy, that do not clearly fall into the categories generated by current models. There are also important differences between countries within the same model, so that CMEs can be differentiated between those whose business coordination takes place within the industrial sector or branch and those whose coordination takes place within groups of companies.[54] The latter, East Asian variant CMEs, are also characterized by a much closer integration of the national state with private enterprise than that found within industry-based CME.[55]

Indeed one could criticize Hall and Soskice in the same way Julie Graham criticizes Marxist economic holism. Even though the varieties school posits a set of different models of capitalist organization, each model is presented as centered rather than decentered and thus contradictions are mediated or stalled: 'Once again a stable, coherent, and hegemonic formation has been placed in the path of the forces of change.'[56] Yet once one starts to analyze the differences between overarching models of the market or capitalism, and then goes on to look at the minutiae within the representatives of different models themselves, it becomes hard to hold on to the claim that the interconnection between different aspects of the system are as necessary as they appear at first glance.[57] Only then can one see that technologies and markets are never fully determinative of the economy, and societies thus have important alternatives in regard to the way they want to run their respective forms of economic organization and, in turn, what kind of society they want to be or become.[58]

Mapping and Criticism

The third step, the incorporation of Unger's methodology of mapping and criticism, can only take place when the first two steps have been taken. Unless society is first seen as frozen politics and capitalism is demoted from a monolithic whole to a set of particular and localized institutions, the possibility of mapping and criticism remains hidden. Without mapping and criticism, moreover, the full implications of the first two steps for understanding society and social change remain undeveloped. Mapping, Unger explains, is the attempt to construct a picture of a particular society's institutions.[59] Mapping seeks to 'understand the existing institutional situation as the complex and contradictory structure that it really is, as the strange and surprising settlement that you could never guess from abstractions like "the mixed economy", "representative democracy", or "industrial society"'.[60] Criticism sets the agenda for mapping in that 'to understand society deeply is always to see the settled from the angle of the unsettled'.[61]

The aim of mapping is thus not so much to give a detailed or comprehensive overview but rather to highlight the 'deviant' cases that reveal the contingent nature of institutions. Small deviations and contradictions in the political, economic and legal structure between and within societies provide clues to possible projects of social reconstruction.[62] Criticism, therefore, is the moment when we focus on the disharmonies of institutions and the way in which ideal conceptions such as 'democracy' are truncated in their development by their institutional realization. The task of mapping and criticism is thus to find these contradictions and develop them by thinking of the possible institutional realization of our ideals.

Given this, Unger argues that mapping and criticism reveal an intimate link between thinking about ideals and thinking about institutions. We give content to, and thus define, a social ideal such as 'democracy' by thinking of its possible institutional realization. Different institutions, moreover, will develop our ideals in different directions. When thinking about ideals and institutions two mistakes can emerge, both of which are made by liberation theology as it fails to construct historical projects. I already exemplified the first mistake at the beginning of this chapter, institutional fetishism, that is, identifying an abstract concept such as democracy with a particular set of institutions. Here the mistake stems from the inevitable fact that the meaning of a social ideal such as democracy is largely defined and thus constrained by the institutional practices and social arrangements that today embody that ideal.

The second mistake consists of voicing the ideal without attempting to define its institutional incarnation. John Dewey once put it thus: 'As for ideals, all agree that we want the good life ... But as long as we limit ourselves to generalities, the phrases that express ideals may be transferred from conservative to radical or vice versa, and nobody will be the wiser. For, without analysis, they do not descend into the actual scene nor concern themselves with the generative conditions of realization of ideals.'[63] Here the ideal remains empty of content and thus undefined, the intended meaning unclear. Chapter 1 examined the cooption of terms such as the preferential option for the poor and liberation at the hands of liberation theology's opponents which makes the dangers of this mistake urgently present. The solution is to realize that thinking about ideals and thinking about institutions do not represent two separate activities; each influences the other. Thinking in terms of institutions is the means to define our ideals, while thinking about ideals is the means to avoid becoming prey to the institutions we currently possess. Institutions embody our ideals, but our ideals are never fully exhausted by existing institutions.[64]

The absence of mapping and criticism in liberation theology can be seen in the fact that liberationists never even attempt to examine the way the legal minutiae of the variety of existing capitalisms affect the distribution of resources in society. Yet, when specifically examined, a market economy is a particular legal regime and so law, in the form of the regime choice, influences the distribution of income achieved.[65] Through the process of mapping and criticism liberation theology can focus on the way the legal rules that compose different market economies affect distributional struggles.[66] As Duncan Kennedy explains, social interactions (for example, the bargaining between labor and capital over wages) can be analogized to a game played under a set of rules.[67] Even if the rules are stated in a way that applies equally to all, they can be examined for their impact on each player's chances of success. The rules of basketball, for example, could be changed to affect the advantage tall players have over short players; lowering the height of the hoop would affect the relative ability of each player.

Similarly, the legal rules that set the terms by which capital and labor negotiate are generally deemed 'background' and thus part of the neutral rules of the game. In this perspective, law only plays a role in distributing power and privilege when it actively intervenes in society to resolve a conflict. Intervention is the exception rather than the rule; the rule being that the law merely sets the apolitical ground rules within which conflict and cooperation can take place. Yet, if one imagines alternative rules, the background rules are brought forward as far from neutral. Rules are only 'background' rules from the point of view of analyses that operate under the assumption of *ceteris paribus* – other things being equal – that is, the assumption that those rules remain constant. When the background conditions change, however, they undermine analyses that assume them constant.[68] Laws pertaining to collective bargaining, unionization, duration of strikes, the nature and scope of picketing and many other details necessarily tilt the scale of power in one direction or another. To change these rules is to change the bargaining power of the groups involved which, in turn, affects the distributional consequences of the capitalism in question. The legal ground rules themselves can take many different forms.

Liberation theology's handling of the concept of property provides a striking example of the way that an approach that fails to focus on mapping and criticizing legal detail hides the indeterminate and reformable nature of society's 'background rules', thereby blocking the imagination of alternatives. Liberation theology's understanding of capitalism, as well as its preferred socialist alternative, implicitly relies on an outdated Blackstonian conception of property as 'thing ownership', in which property, as the foundation of an economy, is understood as the absolute and exclusive dominion exercised by an owner over a unified item.[69] Take Juan Luis Segundo's classic essay, 'Capitalism–Socialism: a Theological Crux', where he writes: 'We give the name socialism to a political regime in which the ownership of the means of production is removed from individuals and handed over to higher institutions whose concern is the common good. By capitalism we understand the political regime in which the ownership of the goods of production is open to economic competition.'[70] While he contrasts capitalism and socialism as opposing systems, in both cases property is implicitly theorized as a unified right owned or administered by isolated individuals or overarching institutions. This vision of property impedes the development of more sophisticated and realistic alternatives than the replacement of capitalism by an abstract socialism.[71]

Liberation theology could instead appropriate critical legal thought's understanding of property as a 'bundle of rights'; instead of emphasizing the relationship between an individual or institution and a unitary thing, liberation theology would focus on the relationship between various rightholders who possess limited rights over disaggregated property.[72] One example of disaggregated property rights is the fast-growing Chinese shareholding cooperative system (SCS).[73] SCSs emerged in the 1980s from the problem of how to dismantle the property of the People's Communes fairly. The peasants realized that some forms of property, such as vehicles, were indivisible. Consequently they decided to issue equal shares to each peasant worker. They then further realized, however, that previous generations of peasant-workers, in addition to local governments that had invested in the communes, also had stakes in the property. They thus set aside a number of shares as 'collective shares' that were designed to be held by outside corporate bodies like local government agencies, other companies inside and outside the locality, banks, universities and research institutions. Given this organization, in the Zhoueun District of China 10 per cent of the profits of a SCS enterprise go into a workers' welfare fund; 30 per cent into a firm development fund, and 60 per cent go into a share fund composed of both collective and individual shares.[74] Here the liberationist distinction between private/capitalist property and collective/socialist property is blurred. Neither adjective accurately describes the property regime.

Historical Projects: Two Examples

The three steps outlined thus far enable a practice of institutional imagination centered on 'alternative pluralisms', the idea that representative democracies, market economies and civil societies can take different institutional forms. From the standpoint of alternative pluralisms, the fall of socialism gives liberation theology the opportunity to revise its understanding of capitalism and society themselves. Without positioning socialism as its opposing unified totality, a placement that made possible the imaginative leap from capitalism to socialism, capitalism too is deprived of its abstract unity. In this case, the focus falls on the piecemeal traits hiding behind abstract concepts such as capitalism, society and democracy and therefore avoids dualisms such as capitalism/socialism, capitalism/life and even market/state. The task, therefore, is not to counterpoise different systems but to find the gradual steps that will democratize access to political and economic opportunity.

Institutional imagination has the following traits. First, it theorizes society as mixed rather than unitary, heterogeneous rather than homogeneous.[75] Society, as a historical and social product, possesses no systematic unity. The mixed nature of society is a permanent condition of the assumption that the political and economic institutions which compose society are 'frozen politics', the result of contained political and ideological strife. These institutions do not fit into a neat system that must be overthrown all at once, but rather remain always partial, fragmented and incomplete.

Second, institutional imagination is contextually based, (or as Unger claims, 'the argument begins in the middle of the stuff'[76]) finding its starting point in already existing debates about economic and political reconstruction and their relationship to received ideals about democracy and economic opportunity. Since the starting point is concrete, change can be envisioned in a step-by-step process rather than the empty imaginative leap between a monolithic capitalism to an equally monolithic socialism or abstractly defined participatory democracy. Liberation theology would pay the same attention to the literature on comparative political economy and law – raiding them for ideas on political and economic diversity and possibility – as it does to the critique of the prophets of economic liberalism such as Friedrich Hayek and Milton Friedman.

Third, institutional imagination relaxes the distinction between periods of stability and periods of transition or change to better recognize the existence of conflicts at all periods. It prioritizes a type of change which is neither revolution (the wholesale change of one structure for another) nor reform (the humanization of the existing structure) but revolutionary reform: the step-by-step change of the formative context of society. This formative context includes, for example, the shape and distribution of property rights, the relations between branches of government, the relation between the state and private enterprise, the relation between private enterprises, rules of inheritance, voting rules and means of campaign: in short, the background legal rules of the game.[77]

Now let me give two examples of the way institutional imagination connects ideals to institutions, thereby avoiding both institutional fetishism and the problem of leaving ideals institutionally undefined and thus empty of content. The first example focuses on the organization of the economy, the second focuses on the organization of the state. What shape might the ideal of an economy with wider access to productive resources today take? As we saw earlier in this chapter, within liberation theology the debate around the impact of property rights on the nature of society juxtaposes private property as the 'natural' form of capitalism to collective or social property as the socialist mode of ownership. For example, in *A Theology of Liberation*, Gutiérrez argues for social over private property as the foundation of socialism over capitalism.[78] He writes that 'we refer to the progressive radicalization of the debate concerning private property ... the history of private ownership of the means of production makes evident the necessity of its reduction or suppression for the welfare of society. We must hence *opt for social ownership of the means of production*'.[79]

For this view, the change of regime (from, say, a capitalist to a socialist society or vice versa) would also necessitate the replacement of one type of property by another. This debate thus counterpoises two systems, capitalism and private property on the one hand, socialism or social property on the other. Note, moreover, that this dichotomy is also found in mainstream policy-making circles. In this case, with the demise of socialism in the Eastern bloc, and statism in Latin America, private ownership became the ruling paradigm for the organization of the economy. When framed in these terms, however, the debate around property suffers from institutional fetishism in that it assumes there are just two forms property can take. Moreover, in addition to framing property in institutional fetishist terms, liberation theology often makes the mistake of stating the ideal of wider property access without developing its institutional shape. Leonardo Boff, for example, agrees with Gutiérrez that capitalism's principal contradiction 'lies in the fact that all, by their labor, contribute to the production of goods, but only certain ones – those who hold capital – acquire ownership of these goods, to the exclusion of the others.' He claims that what is needed is 'a new form of organization for the whole of society – no longer from a point of departure of the capital held in the hands of a few, but an organization of society based on everyone's labor, with everyone sharing, in the means and the goods of production as well as in the means of power. And this is called liberation'.[80] Yet the actual institutional shape of this 'liberation' is never explored.[81]

However, as Unger shows, tools acquired from political economy and critical legal thought enable us to reject the false dichotomy between capitalism and socialism and give content to the abstract ideal of Boff's 'shared' and Gutiérrez's 'social' property by exploring and extending examples of disaggregated property found in economic vanguardism or flexible specialization regimes.[82] Currently this type of production takes place in regions of India, Brazil and Malaysia as well as parts of the developed world; the most successful economic districts today follow this pattern. Flexible specialization's success is built upon the disaggregation of property and ownership into its diverse parts – use rights, income rights, control rights and transfer rights – enabling the creation of associational networks within the economy that allow small firms to tap large resources. In the 'Third Italy', for example, local governments aided in the creation of industrial parks, consortia and other types of inter-firm productive associations.[83]

The end result is a region where firms engage in cooperative competition, that is, continue to compete in terms of the final product but cooperate through the pooling of financial, commercial and technological resources. These regimes disaggregate the property right, rejecting the dominant view of property as an exclusionary power of the owner over the things that he or she possesses, see property as a bundle of rights and vest those rights in governments, intermediate organizations, communities and firms.[84] Economies of scale and the intimacy of small enterprise are reconciled through the disaggregation of property for use by multiple stakeholders. Such a property system distributes the benefits of property ownership more democratically, by restricting the absolute claim any person or institution can make on its productive base.[85] The end result is neither capitalism nor socialism, but a democratized market economy.[86]

My second example focuses on the organization of the state. Recall liberation theology's discussion of democracy in Chapter 2, especially the dichotomy between Leonardo Boff's high hopes for participatory democracy and the current analysis of stagnant democracy. Liberation theologians are right to express skepticism about the emancipatory potential of current Latin American democratic regimes. As Enrique Dussel writes: '*Formal* democracy, of which we must applaud many positive aspects, covers up also a great injustice.'[87] They are wrong, however, insofar as their analysis tacitly equates the institutional shape of democracy with its North American and European forms. In the same way that the institutional fetishist straitjacket of a monolithic capitalism must be escaped, so too must an understanding of democracy constrained by the imitation of received forms. Once again the task is to envision a series of reforms that would lead, step by step, to a more radical democracy. Leonardo Boff once wrote: 'More than a social form, democracy supposes an attitude that must be lived in all spheres of life, in our intersubjectivity and society itself. Democratic ideals are profoundly revolutionary;

they subvert all forms of domination. Democracy is also one of the West's most ancient aspirations. It possesses a utopian dimension that illuminates every aspect of life and cannot be exhausted in any particular historical form.'[88] The key question Boff ignores, however, lies in what institutional framework might begin to approach this ideal. What institutional shape might a more radical democracy take?

For example, Unger argues that the dominant constitutional tradition today draws on two main sets of ideas. The first set prioritizes constitutional forms that fragment power, favors deadlock between branches of government and places legal and practical obstacles to the transformative aspirations of a political program. Both the North American system of checks and balances and the need for broad consensus among a parliamentary political class are examples of this tradition. The second set of ideas is the adoption of rules that keep society at a low level of political mobilization. However, once the assumptions that make up institutional imagination are in place there exists no reason to remain prey to this particular form of institutionalizing democracy. Instead, one could imagine a democratic regime with rules of mandatory voting, proportional representation, free access to the media for political parties at stipulated periods before elections and public financing of campaigns. This could be coupled with a system that resolves impasse between branches of government by appealing, through plebiscites or referenda, to the general populace.

The system would work in the following way. First, reform programs would be given priority over episodic legislation. Second, when the president and parliament disagreed over a certain issue, the situation would be resolved via plebiscites or referenda. Third, if the different branches disagreed on the terms of popular consultation, either branch could call for anticipated elections faced by both branches at the same time. Impasse is thus resolved by appealing to the people at large.[89] While such a democratic regime offers a much wider scope for popular participation, and thus gives institutional content to Boff's participatory democracy as well as liberation theology's focus on the poor as subjects rather than objects of political power, it may have another advantage as well: such a democracy would be less easily preyed upon by parasitic moneyed elites and thus would be better equipped to enact policy for the nation as a whole.[90]

Conclusion

In the introduction to a 1974 special edition of *Concilium* dedicated to Latin American liberation theology, Claude Geffre asserted that liberation theology's special topic was 'the relations between an historical practice of liberation and eschatological salvation'.[91] Over 20 years later, Enrique Dussel echoed 'that which is most specific to liberation theology is precisely the articulation of political projects of liberation and God's reign'.[92] Following still this line of thinking, José Míguez Bonino recently highlighted the differences between liberation theology and North Atlantic theology in the following fashion: 'Latin American authors try to specify Christian liberating praxis in terms of very concrete decisions related to specific issues – economic, political, social ... the need to move from general definitions of oppression and liberation to specific structural, anthropological, cultural and even religious analysis and the discussion of definite – however imperfect or conjectural – projects continues to be central to our theological work and, in our view, a dangerous shortcoming in the work of many of our European friends.'[93]

Yet if these men are right, and I believe they are, liberation theology has lost its distinctive mark. As we have seen, liberation theology has no historical projects to relate to God's reign. Fully half of the liberationist project is missing. Small wonder then that, as José Comblin states, 'even "liberation" as a theme is becoming more indefinite, and is being replaced by "life" as a theme'.[94] For him 'liberation theology is ceasing to be reflection on a praxis and is becoming a prophetic theology, that is, a theology without a historical subject, a theology of denouncement and announcement in a world of utopia, of pure hope, rather than in the real world of history'.[95] Despite Bonino, present day liberation theology is closer to German political theology than it is to the early liberation theology that criticized an exclusive reliance on negative critique.[96]

This chapter showed that liberation theology need not settle for negative critique by presenting a practice of institutional imagination as the means to make room for the development of new historical projects. Simply put, institutional imagination requires that liberation theology cease to think in terms of monolithic wholes and recognize the contingent nature of institutions. Instead of seeing a world made up of large building blocks offering two (or a few) options, the world should be seen as constructed from myriad tiny blocks that can be mixed, shifted and reconstituted for creating the world liberation theologians seek. In order to practice institutional imagination, liberation theology must take the three steps delineated in this chapter: theorizing society as frozen politics, recognizing the variety of capitalisms, and incorporating critical legal thought's process of mapping and criticism. Once taken, these steps allow for reading capitalist hegemony as a dominant discourse *within* liberation theology, a discourse that must be overcome, rather than the reflection of a monolithic and practically inescapable social reality.[97] This shift in the location of hegemony reveals the possibility of alternative pluralisms and makes room for a way of thinking that avoids generalized conceptions of capitalism and democracy to focus on their concrete expressions. Since the starting point is concrete rather than abstract – in the institutional here and now of society – the imaginative leap from an empty capitalism to an empty alternative is avoided. One can envision step by step historical projects that take liberation theology far beyond the mere denunciation of capitalism. The dual traps of resistance within a monolithic and ultimately unchangeable system (unless it were to collapse of its own accord) and millenarian revolutionary fervor are overcome. In the same fashion, to understand that the institutional form of democracy is not set in stone, but that more radical versions can be devised piecemeal with materials already at hand, is to expand the imaginative space available for the construction of historical projects.

According to Cornel West, 'the lack of a clear-cut social theory prevents the emergence of any substantive political program or social vision ... Without this clear-cut social theory about what is, it is difficult to say anything significant about what can be. The possibility of liberation is found only in the depths of the actuality of oppression. Without an adequate social theory, this possibility is precluded'.[98] What West wants for African American theology is what I have tried to provide here for Latin American theology. The next, and final, chapter reviews the argument of this work as a whole and relates it to contemporary theological trends.

Notes

1 For previous attempts to relate liberation theology and Unger see Ivan Petrella, 'Latin American Liberation Theology, Globalization, and Historical Projects: From Critique to Construction', in *Latin American Perspectives on Globalization: Ethics, Politics, and Alternative Visions*, ed. Mario Saenz (Lanham, MD: Rowman and Littlefield Publishers, 2002) and Ivan Petrella, 'Liberation Theology and Democracy: Toward a New Historical Project', *Journal of Hispanic/Latino Theology*, 7(4) (May 2000), 50–67. See also Robert Araujo SJ, 'Political Theory and Liberation Theology: The Intersection of Unger and Gutiérrez', *The Journal of Law and Religion*, XI(1) (1994), 63–83. Araujo's article, however, takes as paradigmatic Unger's 1974 *Knowledge and Politics*, a work that Unger himself, in a postscript to the second edition, in 1984, abandons, and completely ignores Unger's three-volume *Politics*, which sets out in a very different direction from his earlier work. On Unger generally, see Robin Lovin and Michael Perry (eds), *Critique and Construction: A Symposium on Roberto Unger's Politics* (Cambridge: Cambridge University Press, 1990); Andrew Altman, *Critical Legal Studies: A Liberal Critique* (Princeton, NJ: Princeton University Press, 1990); Richard Rorty, 'Unger, Castoriadis, and the Romance of a National Future', in *Richard Rorty, Essays on Heidegger and Others* (Cambridge: Cambridge University Press, 1991); Stephen Holmes, *An Anatomy of Anti-Liberalism* (Cambridge: Harvard University Press, 1993); Anthony Kronman, *The Lost Lawyer: Failing Ideals of the Legal Profession* (Cambridge, MA: Harvard University Press, 1993) and Bojan Bugaric, 'Courts as Policy-Makers: Lessons from Transition', *Harvard Journal of International Law*, 42(1) (Winter 2001), 247–88.

2 Gustavo Gutiérrez, *A Theology of Liberation: History, Politics and Salvation*, ed. Caridad Inda and John Eagleson (New York: Maryknoll, 1985), 67.

3 Gustavo Gutiérrez, *A Theology of Liberation*, 47.

4 For an extended discussion, see Roberto Mangabeira Unger, *Social Theory: Its Situation and Its Task*, in *Politics: A Work in Constructive Social Theory*, introduction (Cambridge: Cambridge University Press, 1987), 87–120; for a brief discussion, see Roberto Mangabeira Unger, *Democracy Realized: The Progressive Alternative* (New York: Verso, 1998), 22. The discussion of Unger and deep structure social theory in Altman, *Critical Legal Studies*, is also helpful.

5 These elements have their root in classical social theory. Marx's notion of different 'modes of production' posits a closed list of possible types of society (feudalism, capitalism, socialism) that are mutually incompatible, overcome by revolutionary change, a change that in the final analysis is the byproduct of historical laws. See, for example, Marx's 'Manifesto for the Communist Party'. The idea that societies form whole systems can also be seen in Durkheim's distinction between organic and mechanical solidarity, as well as in Weber's typology of legal forms (although the latter is not as clear-cut in the case of Weber owing to his insistence that his regimes are ideal types devised for analytical

use). See Emile Durkheim, *The Division of Labor in Society*, trans. George Simpson, reprint, 1933 (New York: Free Press, 1964) and Max Weber, *Economy and Society: An Outline of Interpretive Sociology*, ed. Guenther Roth and Claus Wittich (Berkeley: University of California Press, 1978). For an example of a Marx open to a messier, non unilinear, view of history with no clear-cut classes, see Karl Marx, *The Class Struggles in France* (New York: International Publishers, 1955) and Karl Marx, *The Eighteenth Brumaire of Louis Bonaparte* (New York: International Publishers, 1966).

6 Unger, *Democracy Realized*, 25. On false necessity, see Roberto Mangabeira Unger, *False Necessity: Anti-Necessitarian Social Theory in the Service of Radical Democracy*, in *Politics: A Work in Constructive Social Theory*, part 1 (Cambridge: Cambridge University Press, 1987). False necessity is often tied to essentialism, the belief that any apparent complexity can be uncovered to reveal a simplicity at its core. Essentialism was first rejected in projects that questioned and destabilized gender and sexual categories. On essentialism in gender and queer theory see Judith Butler, *Gender Trouble: Feminism and the Subversion of Identity* (New York: Routledge, 1990); Judith Butler, 'Against Proper Objects', *Differences: A Journal of Feminist Cultural Studies*, 6 (Summer–Fall 1994), 1–24; Diana Fuss, *Essentially Speaking: Feminism, Nature, and Difference* (New York: Routledge, 1989); Eve Kosofsky Sedgwick, *Epistemology of the Closet* (Berkeley and Los Angeles: University of California Press, 1990) and Eve Kosofsky Sedgwick, *Tendencies* (Durham: Duke University Press, 1993). For a provocative combination of Latin American liberation theology and queer theory, see Marcella Althaus-Reid, *Indecent Theology*.

7 Leonardo and Clodovis Boff criticizing the US Bishops' pastoral letter, *Economic Justice for All*; quoted in Arthur McGovern, *Liberation Theology and Its Critics: Toward an Assessment* (Maryknoll, NY: Orbis Books, 1989), 139.

8 Gustavo Gutiérrez, *The Power of the Poor in History* (Maryknoll, NY: Orbis Books, 1983), 85; emphasis added.

9 Unger, *Democracy Realized*, 27.

10 Herbert Kitschelt, Peter Lange, Gary Marks and John Stephens, 'Convergence and Divergence in Advanced Capitalist Democracies', in *Continuity and Change in Contemporary Capitalism*, ed. Herbert Kitschelt, Peter Lange, Gary Marks and John Stephens (Cambridge: Cambridge University Press, 1999), 427.

11 Unger, *Social Theory: Its Situation and Its Task*, 1. See also Unger, *False Necessity: Anti-Necessitarian Social Theory in the Service of Radical Democracy* and Roberto Mangabeira Unger, *Plasticity Into Power: Comparative–Historical Studies on the Institutional Conditions of Economic and Military Success: Variations on Themes* (Cambridge: Cambridge University Press, 1987). For Unger's more recent work, see Roberto Mangabeira Unger, *What Should Legal Analysis Become?* (New York: Verso, 1996); Unger, *Democracy Realized* and Roberto Mangabeira Unger and Cornel West, *The Future of American Progressivism* (Boston: Beacon Press, 1998). For work on Unger, see Lovin and Perry, *Critique and Construction*, and relevant sections in Altman, *Critical Legal Studies*. For a particularly vicious misreading of Unger's social theory, see Holmes, *An Anatomy of Anti-Liberalism*.

12 Unger, *Social Theory: Its Situation and Its Task*, 19.

13 Ibid., 11.

14 See Michael Piore and Charles Sabel, *The Second Industrial Divide: Possibilities for Prosperity* (New York: Basic Books, 1984). Their groundbreaking work can be related to Alexander Gerschenkron's classic study of 19th century English, French, German and Russian industrialization highlighting the conscious political nature of industrialization. In each case, they invented economic institutions – public development banks serve as one notable example – that had not existed before. See Alexander Gerschenkron, *Economic Backwardness in Historical Perspective* (Cambridge: Harvard University Press, 1962). For another recent work in this line see Liah Greenfeld, *The Spirit of Capitalism: Nationalism and Economic Growth* (Cambridge, MA: Harvard University Press, 2001).

15 Piore and Sabel, *The Second Industrial Divide*, 20.

16 For what could be called this approach's 'manifesto', see Charles Sabel and Jonathan Zeitlin, 'Stories, Strategies, Structures: Rethinking Historical Alternatives to Mass Production', in *World of Possibilities: Flexibility and Mass Production in Western Industrialization*, ed. Charles Sabel and

114   *The Future of Liberation Theology*

Jonathan Zeitlin (Cambridge: Cambridge University Press, 1997). For a short review, see Peter Hall, 'The Political Economy of Europe in an Era of Interdependence', in *Continuity and Change in Contemporary Capitalism*, ed. Herbert Kitschelt, Peter Lange, Gary Marks and John Stephens (Cambridge: Cambridge University Press, 1999), 135–63. For Sabel's earlier yet related views in addition to Piore and Sabel, *The Second Industrial Divide*, see also Charles Sabel, *Work and Politics: The Division of Labor in Industry* (Cambridge: Cambridge University Press, 1982). Paul Hirst and Jonathan Zeitlin, 'Flexible Specialization Versus Post-Fordism: Theory, Evidence, and Policy Implications', in *Pathways to Industrialization and Regional Development*, ed. Michael Storper and Allen Scott (New York: Routledge, 1992), 70–115 is also helpful.

    17 Sabel and Zeitlin, 'Stories, Strategies, Structures', 2.

    18 Ibid.

    19 Ibid., 29.

    20 See Geoffrey Hawthorn, *Plausible Worlds: Possibility and Understanding in History and the Social Sciences* (Cambridge: Cambridge University Press, 1991). For an account of the way surveys of the field of economics create the very field being surveyed see E. Roy Weintraub, *Stabilizing Dynamics* (New York: Cambridge University Press, 1991). See also the exchange between Weintraub and Roger Backhouse in *Journal of the History of Economic Thought*, 14, Fall 1992.

    21 Sabel and Zeitlin, 'Stories, Strategies, Structures', 29. They point out that these opposing viewpoints on the form of society and the nature of the social transformation are reproduced in the philosophy of science. The position Sabel embraces sides with Feyerabend, Lakatos and Popper against Kuhn. In Kuhn's classic *The Structure of Scientific Revolutions*, the history of science is seen as the movement from periods of tranquility (normal science) to periods of upheaval (revolutionary science) in which the transition from one paradigm to another takes place. He thus reproduces the strict distinction between periods of continuity and periods of change. Instead, according to Feyerabend, Lakatos and Popper, normal science and revolutionary science – orthodoxy and heresy – are much more closely intertwined than allowed for in Kuhn's sharper distinction.

    22 The view of law as neutral and apolitical found its defining expression in Christopher Langdell, who sought to ground law on a geometric model of the scientific method. For Langdell, to understand any branch of the law scientifically, one had first to identify the basic principles upon which it was based by surveying the case law in the area. Once identified, scholars then needed to derive the subordinate principles entailed by the first principles. The law in a particular area is known once all the principles are derived, stated in proper propositional form, and the relations between them described and clarified. In the same way that geometry merely unfolds the meaning of its first principles, so too the doctrinal details of any legal branch can be drawn from its first principles. See Christopher Langdell, *A Selection of Cases on the Law of Contracts: With a Summary of the Topics Covered by the Cases* (Boston: Little, Brown, 1879) and Christopher Langdell, *Summary of the Law of Contracts* (Boston: Little, Brown, 1880). On Langdell, see Kronman, *The Lost Lawyer*. This overview draws on pages 170–85. For a general overview of the structure of 19th-century legal thought see Morton Horwitz, *The Transformation of American Law, 1870–1960: The Crisis of Legal Orthodoxy* (Oxford: Oxford University Press, 1992), 9–31.

    23 The following discussion of different legal approaches is taken from Allan Hutchinson and Patrick Monahan, 'Law, Politics, and the Critical Legal Scholars: The Unfolding Drama of American Legal Thought', *Stanford Law Review*, 36 (1984), 207.

    24 'CLSers' is a common umbrella term used to refer to critical legal studies scholars.

    25 Many CLS arguments were spearheaded by the North American legal realists of the early 20th century. On legal realism see Duncan Kennedy, *A Critique of Adjudication* (Cambridge, MA: Harvard University Press, 1997); Duncan Kennedy, *Sexy Dressing Etc.: Essays on the Power and Politics of Cultural Identity* (Cambridge, MA: Harvard University Press, 1993), 83–125; Kronman, *The Lost Lawyer*, 185–225; Horwitz, *The Transformation of American Law, 1870–1960*; Joseph William Singer, 'Legal Realism Now', *California Law Review*, 76 (1988), 465–544; and Andrew Altman, 'Legal Realism, Critical Legal Studies, and Dworkin', *Philosophy & Public Affairs*, 15(3) (Summer 1986), 205–35.

26 See Hutchinson and Monahan, 'Law, Politics, and the Critical Legal Scholars'.

27 Hutchinson and Monahan cite Guido Calabresi, *A Common Law for the Age of Statutes* (Cambridge: Harvard University Press, 1982) as representative of this approach.

28 Hutchinson and Monahan cite Ronald Dworkin, *Taking Rights Seriously* (Cambridge, MA: Harvard University Press, 1978) as representative of this approach.

29 Hutchinson and Monahan cite Richard Posner, *The Economic Analysis of Law* (Boston: Little, Brown, 1986) as representative of the law and economics school.

30 For this stance on law, see Jurgen Habermas, *Between Facts and Norms* (Cambridge: Massachussetts Institute of Technology Press, 1996).

31 See Ernesto Laclau and Chantal Mouffe, *Hegemony and Socialist Strategy: Towards a Radical Democratic Politics* (New York: Verso, 1985).

32 Ernesto Laclau, *New Reflections on the Revolution of Our Time* (New York: Verso, 1990), 129.

33 Laclau, *New Reflections on the Revolution of Our Time*, 36. Laclau and Mouffe trace the roots of this theoretical perspective to Antonio Gramsci. Gramsci broke from a 'conception according to which there were aprioristic laws of capitalism imposing and dictating a necessary course to historical events. Against it he asserted the primacy of politics: the pragmatic formulation of collective wills through contingent articulations whose success was entirely context-dependent'. See Chantal Mouffe (ed.), *Deconstruction and Pragmatism* (New York: Routledge, 1996), 62. On Gramsci, see also Giuseppe Fiori's beautiful biography: Giuseppe Fiori, *Antonio Gramsci: Life of a Revolutionary* (London: NLB, 1969). For another attempt to rid Marxism of its determinist bias, see Stephen Resnick and Richard Wolff, *Knowledge and Class: A Marxian Critique of Political Economy* (Chicago: The University of Chicago Press, 1987).

34 Geoffrey Hodgson, 'Varieties of Capitalism and Varieties of Economic Theory', in *Institutions and Economic Change: New Perspectives on Markets, Firms, and Technology*, Bjorn Johnson and Klaus Nielsen (eds) (Cheltenham, UK: Edward Elgar Publishing, 1998), 215.

35 Barbara Chernow and George Vallasi (eds), *The Columbia Encyclopedia* (New York: Columbia University Press, 1993), 449.

36 Unger, *Social Theory: Its Situation and Its Task*, 104; this discussion draws on his critique of the concept of capitalism on pp.99–113.

37 Unger, *Social Theory: Its Situation and Its Task*, 109.

38 On the varieties of capitalism approach see, most recently, Peter Hall and David Soskice (eds), *Capitalism: The Institutional Foundations of Comparative Advantage* (Oxford: Oxford University Press, 2001). Also see Peter Hall, 'The Evolution of Economic Policy in the European Union', in *From the Nation-State to the European Union*, ed. Anand Menon and Vincent Wright (Oxford: Oxford University Press, 2001); Hall, 'The Political Economy of Europe in an Era of Interdependence'; David Soskice, 'Divergent Production Regimes: Coordinated and Uncoordinated Market Economies in the 1980s and 1990s', in *Continuity and Change in Contemporary Capitalism*, ed. Herbert Kitschelt, Peter Lange, Gary Marks and John Stephens (Cambridge: Cambridge University Press, 1999), 101–34; Peter Hall, 'The Political Economy of Adjustment in Germany', in *Okonomische Leistungsfahigkeit und Institutionelle Innovation: Das Deutsche Produktions und Politikregime Im Globalen Wettbewerb*, ed. Frieder Naschold, David Soskice and Bob Hancke (WZB-Jahrbuch, 1997), 293–317; David Soskice, 'German Technology Policy, Innovation and National Institutional Frameworks', *Industry and Innovation*, 4 (1997), 75–96; Michael Storper and Robert Salais, *Worlds of Production: The Action Frameworks of the Economy* (Cambridge, MA: Harvard University Press, 1997); John Groenwegen, 'Institutions of Capitalisms: American, European, and Japanese Systems Compared', *Journal of Economic Issues*, XXXI(2) (June 1997), 333–47; David Soskice, 'The Institutional Infrastructure for International Competitiveness: A Comparative Analysis of the UK and Germany', in *The Economics of the New Europe*, ed. Anthony Atkinson and Renato Brunetta (London: Macmillan, 1991); Michel Albert, *Capitalisme Contre Capitalisme* (Paris: Seuil, 1991) and David Soskice, 'Reinterpreting Corporatism and Explaining Unemployment: Coordinated and Uncoordinated Market Economies', in *Labour Relations and Economic Performance*, ed. Renato Brunetta and Carlo Dell'Aringa (London: Macmillan, 1990).

39 Soskice, 'Divergent Production Regimes', 106.

40 Hall and Soskice, *Capitalism*, 22.

41 The institutional setting of an economy, moreover, came to the forefront in explaining national rates of growth as soon as economists working within endogenous growth theory began to observe that such rates could not be fully explained by incremental additions to capital and labor stocks and fixed rates of technical change (Hall and Soskice, *Capitalism*, 22).

42 The most comprehensive book available on globalization is David Goldblatt, David Held, Anthony McGrew and Jonathan Perraton, *Global Transformations: Politics, Economics and Culture* (Stanford: Stanford University Press, 1999).

43 See the introduction to Hall and Soskice, *Capitalism*, and Hall, 'The Political Economy of Adjustment in Germany', 302–13.

44 Hall, 'The Political Economy of Adjustment in Germany', 302–3.

45 See Paul Bairoch, 'Globalization Myths and Realities: One Century of External Trade and Foreign Investment', in *States Against Markets: The Limits of Globalization*, ed. Robert Boyer and Daniel Drache (New York: Routledge, 1996), 173–92.

46 See Paul Doremus, William Keller, Louis Pauly and Simon Reich, *The Myth of the Global Organization* (Princeton, NJ: Princeton University Press, 1998).

47 Pablo Richard, 'Teología de la Solidaridad en el Contexto Actual de Economía Neoliberal de Mercado', in *El Huracan de la Globalización*, ed. Franz Hinkelammert (San José, Costa Rica: DEI, 1999), 228, original emphasis.

48 Richard, 'Teología de la Solidaridad en el Contexto Actual de Economía Neoliberal de Mercado', 233, original emphasis.

49 The title of the collection within which Richard's essay is included refers to globalization as a 'hurricane'. See Franz Hinkelammert (ed.), *El Huracan de la Globalización* (San José: DEI, 1999).

50 Another critique of an extreme economic globalization thesis states that globalization is not an economic or technology-driven phenomenon, but rather stems from a politically charged US agenda that seeks to support Wall Street's interest in entering emerging markets. The important claim is that globalization is then not a natural extension of the search for efficiency but carries a covert political agenda and can only take place through political pressure. Here see Robert Wade, 'A Clash of Capitalisms', *APSA-CP*, 10(1) (1999 Winter 1999), 23–6. For more on globalization, see Robert Wade, 'Globalization and Its Limits: Reports of the Death of the National Economy Are Greatly Exaggerated', in *National Diversity and Global Capitalism*, ed. Suzanne Berger and Ronald Dore (Ithaca: Cornell University Press, 1996), 60–89; the essays in Robert Boyer and Daniel Drache (eds), *States Against Markets: The Limits of Globalization* (New York: Routledge, 1996) and Suzanne Berger and Ronald Dore (eds), *National Diversity and Global Capitalism* (Ithaca: Cornell University Press, 1996) and Ramesh Mishra, *Globalization and the Welfare State* (Cheltenham: Edward Elgar Publishing Limited, 1999).

51 Unger, *What Should Legal Analysis Become?*, 25. For Unger's critique of political economy and economics generally, see 22–5 and Unger, *Social Theory: Its Situation and Its Task*, 120–35.

52 Soskice, 'Divergent Production Regimes', 109.

53 Ibid., 110.

54 Industry coordinated economies (northern Europe) allow for industry-defined unions, technical norm setting within the industry, technology transfer and diffusion within the industry, industry based development of vocational training standards and training of engineers and other specialists within an industry framework. Group coordinated economies (such as Japanese *Keiretsu* and Korean *Chaebols*) allow for company based unions, technology diffusion and development within the group of companies, company based vocational training, and technical standard setting within the group (Soskice, 'Divergent Production Regimes', 106).

55 On the East Asian model of 'capitalism' see, most recently, Alice Amsden, *The Rise of the 'Rest': Challenges to the West from Late-Industrializing Economies* (Oxford: Oxford University Press, 2001). Also helpful are Robert Wade, *Governing the Market: Economic Theory and the Role of Government in*

East Asian Industrialization (Princeton, NJ: Princeton University Press, 1990); Stephen Haggard, *Pathways from the Periphery: The Politics of Growth in the Newly Industrializing Economies* (Ithaca: Cornell University Press, 1990) and Alice Amsden, *Asia's Next Giant: South Korea and Late Industrialization* (New York: Oxford University Press, 1989).

56 Julie Graham, 'Post-Fordism as Politics: The Political Consequences of Narratives on the Left', *Environment and Planning D: Society and Space*, 10 (1991), 393.

57 On the debate over 'tightness of fit in national systems of production', see Berger and Dore, *National Diversity and Global Capitalism*, 21–3. Geoffrey Hodgson makes a similar argument via what he calls 'the impurity principle': 'However, whilst the impurity principle contends that different kinds of subsystem are necessary for the system as a whole to function, it does not specify the particular kind of subsystem nor the precise boundaries between each subsystem and the system as a whole. Indeed, a variety of types of system and subsystem can feasibly be combined. Furthermore, the boundaries between subsystem and dominant system are likely to be highly variable. Significantly, the nature of the combination and the precise boundaries of the demarcation profoundly affect the nature of the specific variety of the capitalist system. A corollary of the impurity principle is the contention that an immense variety of forms of any given socio-economic system can exist' (Hodgson, 'Varieties of Capitalism and Varieties of Economic Theory', 226). See also Geoffrey Hodgson, *Economics and Utopia: Why the Learning Economy is not the End of History* (London: Routledge, 1999).

58 Here I am paraphrasing from Colin Crouch and Wolfgang Streeck, 'Introduction: The Future of Capitalist Diversity', in *Political Economy of Modern Capitalism: Mapping Convergence and Diversity*, Colin Crouch and Wolfgang Streeck (eds) (London: Sage Publications, 1997), 1.

59 Unger, *What Should Legal Analysis Become?* 133.

60 Ibid., 132.

61 Unger, *Social Theory: Its Situation and Its Task*, 65.

62 Unger, *What Should Legal Analysis Become?*, 1–2.

63 John Dewey, *Individualism Old and New* (New York: Milton, Balch & Company, 1930), 147. For more on the connection between thinking about ideals and thinking about institutions, see Unger, *Democracy Realized*, 16; Unger, *What Should Legal Analysis Become?* 4; Unger, *False Necessity: Anti-Necessitarian Social Theory in the Service of Radical Democracy*, 10.

64 Unger, *Democracy Realized*, 16–19. Unger is highly critical of what he calls 'the dominant styles of normative philosophy today' (read Rawls, Dworkin and liberalism generally) that treat the definition of ideals and the design of institutions as two separate activities. In this dominant conception you first derive your principles and then you come up with institutions. In this way, you assure the independence of the principles from the institutional background of society. For Unger, however, this theory's failure to acknowledge that ideals are shaped by institutional preconceptions has exactly the opposite effect of delivering them into the hand of their historical setting: 'No wonder so much of their speculation remains a philosophical gloss upon the distinctive practices of redistributive tax-and-transfer and individual-rights protection in the postwar industrial democracies' (Unger, *Democracy Realized*, 18–19).

A similar debate, dealt with in the concluding chapter, is found between liberation theology, German political theology and the Vatican. Both the Vatican and political theology criticize liberation theology for moving too quickly from religious ideals to historical projects. Instead, they argue that you first need to develop principles and criteria for making judgments about society. Here let me make two points. First, liberation theologians are right when they assert (in a way that parallels Unger) that those principles are empty until defined institutionally through historical projects. Second, liberation theologians are wrong when they suggest that scripture itself provides a warrant for siding with the oppressed and from that scriptural warrant comes the need for historical projects. Instead, the construction of historical projects always already takes place within the context of reconstructive interpretations of a religious tradition, background theories, retroductive warrants and communities of discourse. See Francis Schüssler Fiorenza, 'Systematic Theology: Tasks and Methods', in *Systematic Theology: Roman Catholic Perspectives*, ed. Francis Schüssler Fiorenza and John Galvin (Minneapolis: Fortress Press, 1991), 70–85 for these elements. For the two Vatican instructions on liberation theology see chs 45 and

53 in Alfred Hennelly SJ, *Liberation Theology: A Documentary History* (Maryknoll, NY: Orbis Books, 1990). Chapter 6 deals with this issue.

65 Kennedy, *Sexy Dressing Etc.*, 97.

66 See the classic legal realist text, Robert Hale, 'Coercion and Distribution in a Supposedly Non-Coercive State', *Political Science Quarterly*, 38(470) (1923). For an excellent discussion of Hale, see Kennedy, *Sexy Dressing Etc.*, 83–125.

67 The basketball example is taken from Kennedy, *Sexy Dressing Etc.*, 84–5.

68 Fred Block, *Postindustrial Possibilities: A Critique of Economic Discourse* (Berkeley: University of California Press, 1990), 30.

69 For a discussion of this classical view of property see Horwitz, *The Transformation of American Law, 1870–1960*.

70 Juan Luis Segundo, 'Capitalism–Socialism: A Theological Crux', in *The Mystical and Political Dimension of the Christian Faith*, ed. Claude Geffre and Gustavo Gutiérrez (New York: Herder and Herder, 1974), 115.

71 For an excellent discussion of property and democratic reconstruction that takes Eastern Europe as its starting point see Karl Klare, 'Legal Theory and Democratic Reconstruction: Reflections on 1989', in *A Fourth Way? Privatization, Property, and the Emergence of New Market Economies*, ed. Gregory Alexander and Grazyna Skapska (New York: Routledge, 1994), 310–33.

72 The North American legal realists pioneered the critique of the classical conception of property and were the first to systematize property as a bundle of rights (including, for example, use rights, income rights, control rights and transfer rights). For the foundational realist critique of the classical understanding of property, see Wesley Hohfeld, 'Some Fundamental Legal Conceptions as Applied in Judicial Reasoning', *Yale Law Journal*, 23 (1913), 28–59. For an overview of the realist approach to property, see Horwitz, *The Transformation of American Law, 1870–1960*. See also Thomas Grey, 'The Disintegration of Property', *Nomos*, XXII (1980), 69–86; Joseph Singer, 'The Reliance Interest in Property', *Stanford Law Review*, 40 (1988), 614–726, and Joseph William Singer, 'Legal Realism Now'.

73 See Zhiyuan Cui, 'Privatization and the Consolidation of Democratic Regimes: An Analysis and an Alternative', *Journal of International Affairs*, 50(2) (Winter 1997), 675–92; Zhiyuan Cui, 'The Discourse on Property Rights in the Chinese Reform Context', *Social Text 55*, 16(2) (Winter 1998), 1–17.

74 Here see Cui, 'The Discourse on Property Rights in the Chinese Reform Context'.

75 See Suzanne Berger and Michael Piore, *Dualism and Discontinuity in Industrial Societies* (Cambridge: Cambridge University Press, 1980), 142.

76 Unger, *What Should Legal Analysis Become?*, 128.

77 The notions of 'revolutionary reform', and 'formative context' are taken from Roberto Unger, as well as the examples of revolutionary reform provided in the pages that follow. Andre Gorz provides another way to understand revolutionary reform: 'A reformist reform is one that subordinates its objective to the criteria of rationality and practicability of a given system and policy. Reformism rejects those objectives and demands – however deep the need for them – which are incompatible with the preservation of the system ... On the other hand, a not necessarily reformist reform is one which is conceived not in terms of what is possible within the framework of a given system and administration, but in view of what should be made possible in terms of human needs and demands' (Andre Gorz, *Strategy for Labor*, Boston: Beacon Press, 1964, 7).

78 Gutiérrez, *A Theology of Liberation*, 66–7. See also Gustavo Gutiérrez, *La Fuerza Histórica de los Pobres* (Lima: Centro de Estudios y Publicaciones, 1979), 66.

79 Gutiérrez, *A Theology of Liberation*, 111–12; original emphasis.

80 Clodovis Boff and Leonardo Boff, *Salvation and Liberation: In Search of a Balance Between Faith and Politics* (Maryknoll, NY: Orbis Books, 1984), 8.

81 It remains an open question, moreover, whether by 'social' or 'shared' property Gutiérrez and Boff have in mind property placed in the hands of Segundo's 'higher institutions'. A further question is whether by 'higher institutions' Segundo means the state.

82 For the best short introduction to this model of political economy, see Hirst and Zeitlin, 'Flexible Specialization and Post-Fordism'. For more on flexible specialization, see Sabel and Zeitlin, 'Stories, Strategies, Structures' and Piore and Sabel, *The Second Industrial Divide*.

83 For the political and cultural background required for flexible specialization as well as its role in the affluence of northern Italy, see Robert Putnam, *Making Democracy Work: Civic Traditions in Modern Italy* (Princeton: Princeton University Press, 1993). On the 'Third Italy', see Michael Best, *The New Competition: Institutions of Industrial Restructuring* (Cambridge: Harvard University Press, 1990) and Tamara Lothian, 'The Democratized Market Economy in Latin America (and Elsewhere): An Exercise in Institutional Thinking Within Law and Economy', *Cornell International Law Journal*, 28(1) (Winter 1995), 169–217.

84 See Thomas Grey for one formulation of the disaggregated property right: 'The growth of power of non-shareholding management is only one aspect of the general phenomenon of the dispersion of lawful power over the resources involved in the modern corporation. Not only managers and common shareholders, but also other classes of shareholders, directors, bondholders, other creditors, large suppliers and customers (through contractual arrangements), insurers, government regulators, tax authorities, and labor unions – all may have some of the legal powers that would be concentrated in the single ideal thing-owner of classical property theory.' (Grey, 'The Disintegration of Property', 80).

85 The notion of property as a bundle of rights and the examples of disaggregated property rights (the Chinese SCS and flexible specialization regimes such as the 'Third Italy') can be understood as developing and giving concrete content to John Paul's reflections on property in *Centesimus annus*. In that encyclical, John Paul moves away from a property paradigm of 'thing ownership' grounded in the ownership of land and natural resources to one based on know-how, technology and skill. In the same way that no one has an absolute right over natural resources, no one has an absolute right over these goods; their moral purpose is to serve the human community. For this reason they must be organized into 'ever more extensive working communities' bound 'by a progressively expanding chain of solidarity'. The question, of course, is how this ideal is realized institutionally. The examples here provided give two possibilities. For a succinct review of the discussion of property in *Centesimus annus* see David Hollenbach, 'Christian Social Ethics After the Cold War', *Theological Studies*, 53(1) (March 1992), 75–95. (I have quoted from page 85).

86 See Unger, *Democracy Realized*, 95–105; Unger, *What Should Legal Analysis Become?*, 12–13; Unger, *False Necessity: Anti-Necessitarian Social Theory in the Service of Radical Democracy*, 480–506; see also Block, *Postindustrial Possibilities*, 191–4. For another attempt to rework and escape the socialism/capitalism dichotomy, see Hodgson, *Economics and Utopia*.

87 Enrique Dussel, *The Underside of Modernity: Apel, Ricoeur, Rorty, Taylor, and the Philosophy of Liberation*, Eduardo Mendieta (New York: Humanity Books, 1998), 230.

88 Leonardo Boff, 'Libertad y Liberación. Puntos de Contacto y de Fricción en el Primer y Tercer Mundo', *Revista Latinoamericana de Teología*, 14 (May–August 1988), 201–2.

89 Unger calls this model of democracy 'mobilizational democracy'. See Unger, *Democracy Realized*, for a summary, pages 264–6; also Unger, *What Should Legal Analysis Become?*, 15–17, 163–9, Unger, *False Necessity: Anti-Necessitarian Social Theory in the Service of Radical Democracy*, 444–76.

90 A large body of political economy literature stresses the importance of a 'hard state' for economic progress. See, most recently, Amsden, *The Rise of the 'Rest'*. See also Amsden, *Asia's Next Giant*; Haggard, *Pathways from the Periphery*; Wade, *Governing the Market*. Hard states, however, have often been achieved through authoritarianism. What is most interesting about the reforms briefly outlined here is that they may soften the tension between the radical changes often needed for development and the incrementalism that is part of democracy. This is the challenge that a 'democratic developmental state' must meet. See Adrian Leftwich, 'Forms of the Democratic Developmental State: Democratic Practices and Developmental Capacity', in *The Democratic Developmental State: Politics and Institutional Design*, ed. Mark Robinson and Gordon White (Oxford: Oxford University Press, 1998), 52–83. For more on developmental states, see the volume as a whole.

91 Claude Geffre and Gustavo Gutiérrez (eds), *The Mystical and Political Dimension of the Christian Faith* (New York: Herder and Herder, 1974), 8.

92 Ibid.; see also Enrique Dussel, *Teología de la Liberación: Un Panorama de Su Desarrollo* (Ciudad de Mexico: Potrerillos Editores, 1995), 183.

93 José Míguez Bonino, 'Reading Jürgen Moltmann from Latin America', *The Asbury Theological Journal*, 55(1) (Spring 2000), 111.

94 José Comblin, 'La Iglesia Latinoamericana Desde Puebla a Santo Domingo', in *Cambio Social y Pensamiento Cristiano en América Latina*, ed. José Comblin, José I. González Faus and Jon Sobrino (Madrid: Editorial Trotta, 1993), 40.

95 Comblin, 'La Iglesia Latinoamericana Desde Puebla a Santo Domingo', 41.

96 For an explicit attempt to move liberation theology in the direction of negative critique see José Ignacio González Faus, 'Una Tarea Histórica: De la Liberación a la Apocalíptica', *Revista Latinoamericana de Teología*, XII (September–December 1995), 281–90.

97 For an attempt to shift capitalist hegemony from society to discourse in the realm of feminist political economy see J.K. Gibson-Graham, 'Re-Placing Class in Economic Geographies: Possibilities for a New Class Politics', in *Geographies of Economies*, Roger Lee and Jane Wills (eds) (London: Arnold, 1997), 88. Judith Butler engages in the same type of argument in the realm of feminist and queer theory. She writes, for example, 'even if we accept Foucault's proposal to consider "sex" as a fictional unity, a speculative ideal, which compounds the semantic senses of sex as identity, sensation, and practice, to name a few, are we to accept Foucault's presumption that "sex" is a monolithic and unified category as it seems? Does "sex" not gain that appearance of a monolithic unity, a speculative ideal, to the extent that it covers over "sexual difference" or, rather assimilates sexual difference to the category of "sex"? In so far as lesbian and gay studies rely on *this* notion of sex, it then appears to take as one of its grounds, its founding methodological claims, a refusal of sexual difference in the theoretical constitution of "sex" as a proper object of study ... Sexual difference, irreducible to "gender" or to the putative biological disjunction of "female or male", is rhetorically refused through the substitution by which a unitary sex is installed as the proper object of inquiry' (Butler, 'Against Proper Objects', 3–4).

98 Cornel West, *Prophesy Deliverance: An Afro-American Revolutionary Christianity* (Philadelphia: Westminster Press, 1982), 111–12.

Liberation Theology as the Construction of Historical Projects Revisited

Theodor Adorno once wrote that 'perspectives must be fashioned that displace and estrange the world, reveal it to be, with its rifts and crevices, as indigent and distorted as it will appear one day in the messianic light'.[1] I flatter myself by hoping that the argument of this work may contribute, in the smallest way, to fashioning such perspectives. My reconstruction of liberation theology around the notion of a historical project enables it to uncover and exploit the rifts and crevices of a world that too often denies the majority their full humanity, a world where full redemption is outside our merely human grasp. However, while the messianic light is not ours to shine, we can still pursue the limited redemptions that historical projects provide. This book outlines one way to do so.[2]

This chapter brings my argument back full circle. First, I look back at liberation theology's main trends and methodological statements presented in Chapters 1 and 2 to show how the argument of the book as a whole remedies their deficiencies. Second, I bring my argument in contact with four contemporary theological trends. In the first place, I present and assess political theology's objection that my vision of liberation theology as the construction of historical projects turns theology into ideology. For political theology, theology should either restrain itself to negative critique or should only indirectly make claims on the political realm through a political ethic. In the second place, I evaluate the most recent reconstruction of liberation theology to emerge from the North Atlantic academy – radical orthodoxy. While I disagree with the shape of this reconstruction, it currently stands as the most important alternative understanding of liberation theology to emerge. Finally, I examine Latina and Black liberation theology from the perspective of my own argument. I suggest that, much like present day Latin American liberation theology, they are incapable of truly pursuing their stated goal of liberation.

Liberation Theology: its Present

Today liberation theology is characterized by a minor theological victory and an almost complete political defeat.[3] If imitation is the sincerest form of flattery, then the cooption of liberation theology's terminology is a tribute to its impact within theology and beyond; even the IMF and the Vatican espouse the preferential option for the poor, liberation and the reign of God. Victory in a battle, however, means little if tied to defeat in a war. Take José Comblin's reaction to the Vatican's incorporation of liberation theology's terminology. He notes that in 1984 the Vatican's 'Instructions on Certain Aspects of the Theology of Liberation' denounced liberation theology in no uncertain terms. More recently, though, documents such as *Libertatis Nuntius* and *Libertatis Conscientia* take up the notions of liberation and the preferential option for the poor. This move can be seen as a tribute to liberation theology's impact, its themes being incorporated into official teaching. Comblin, however, is skeptical: 'The words are there, but always in a context that avoids all possibility of conflict: this is a poor and a liberation with which all social classes can identify themselves. Noone feels denounced. In this way liberation theology's themes acquire a level of generality, abstraction and also of insignificance so that they become valid for all continents, for all peoples.'[4] The less liberation theology is a threat to established powers the easier it can be coopted by those powers. Indeed the cooption of its terminology highlights liberation theology's non-threatening present.

This cooption stems from liberation theology's inability to construct historical projects that would give terms such as 'liberation', 'the preferential option' and 'Reign of God' concrete sociopolitical content beyond the celebration of civil society. The vacuity of the terminology reflects the lack of historical projects that would enable liberation theology to place its stated goal – liberation – at the forefront of its task. The emptiness of liberation theology's key concepts is not an academic issue. In the final analysis, at stake is not liberation theology's continued relevance – lives are at stake. None of liberation theology's current trends are able to truly engage liberation by developing historical projects. Position one, reasserting core ideas, disentangles key liberationist concepts such as the preferential option for the poor or liberation from Marxism as a social scientific mediation and from socialism as a historical project. To reassert core ideas, the theologian argues that liberation theology was never instrinsically tied to any particular social–scientific mediation or historical project, and thus the discrediting of any mediation or project cannot affect liberation theology's core ideas.

Position one has no answer to liberation theology's cooption; position one, in fact, aids that cooption by drawing a strict distinction between the paradigm and the mediation that gives that paradigm content. Position one separates what early liberation theology – via the historical project – refused to separate. It ends, therefore, by facilitating the emptying and subsequent takeover of liberation theology's basic terminology. Position one is an active pawn in liberation theology's domesticated present.

Position two, revising basic categories, goes beyond reasserting core ideas by reformulating aspects of early liberation theology to open up a space for the implementation of new sociocultural mediations. It eliminates the dichotomy between reform and revolution, rejects the belief in a unified revolutionary subject and embraces popular culture and civil society as the privileged arenas for liberation. These moves have far-reaching implications: undoing the sharp division between reform and revolution prioritizes piecemeal change, often belittled by liberation theologians; rejecting the belief in the poor as a unified revolutionary subject forces liberation theology to search for alliances across classes both within the nation and around the globe, and the focus on civil society concentrates attention on the struggles for rights of once ignored actors such as indigenous peoples, ecological activists and women occupying other disenfranchised groups.

The problem with position two stems, however, from a lack of rigorous political and economic analysis and the subsequent inability to devise a positive program beyond the call for conversion and concertation at the community level. Position two thus revises liberation theology but has yet to build upon the new foundation. Construction would require the initial elaboration of a new historical project, going beyond the promotion of civil society that is position two's constructive proposal. In this way, position two also fails to address fully the increasing vacuity of the language of liberation. Liberation remains little threat to the powers that be.

Position three, critiquing idolatry, develops a critique of capitalism and modernity that uses the sustainability of human life as a criterion for evaluating institutions and social systems. Critiquing idolatry claims that idolatry presents itself wherever upholding abstract laws, such as the the law of profit in capitalism, is valued over life. Hinkelammert, for example, uses this argument to differentiate liberation theology's use of the preferential option for the poor from that of the IMF. While the IMF claims to embrace the preferential option, it continues to support structural adjustment policies geared toward debt servicing that privilege the interests of wealthy foreign bankers over poor local populations. The continued enrichment of one sector is placed above the mere survival of another. The critique of idolatry concludes that while liberation theology and the IMF may use the same terminology they do not serve the same God: one worships the God of life while the other prostrates itself before an idol. The problem with the critique of idolatry, however, stems from its inability to devise an alternative to the policies espoused by the IMF and other dominant economic groups. These groups argue that their policies do, in fact, support life and that increasing poverty in the short term is the necessary price to pay for development in the long term.

The real question for liberation theology, therefore, comes after the critique of idolatry and yet this position does not provide an alternative to the IMF's understanding of the means by which liberation might be achieved. For this reason, position three cannot give any more content to liberation theology's central terms than positions one or two. Now the key question is not whether liberation theology is valid as theology but how its insights are to be translated into the sociopolitical realm. The key issue is what historical projects will define what 'liberation' actually means.

Liberation Theology as the Construction of Historical Projects

Liberation theology need not resign itself to a life of quiet domestication. It need not do so because the inability to construct historical projects is due primarily to problems internal to liberation theology itself – the restricted understanding of 'theology' in its methodological statements, its understanding of capitalism and society – rather than to the shift in context captured in the fall of socialism. Indeed, this work shows that, through the practice of institutional imagination, liberation theology can engage in a wholesale transformation of society piecemeal, by focusing on changing society's background legal rules, rather than settling for mere defiant resistance or grass-roots activism as the primary default opposition to capitalism after the failure of revolution.

A distinct advantage of my argument lies in that while critical of details, it is supportive of the liberationist project as a whole. Details, however, can make or break the project. With position one, I believe that liberation theology's core ideas remain relevant and worth defending. With position two, I believe that the dichotomy between reform and revolution must be superseded, that capturing state power need not be the obsessive focus of politics and that the poor can no longer be elevated to the exclusive bearers of liberation. Yet the pursuit of liberation requires refusing to accept their limitations. In both, the failure of revolution leads to a call for solidarity and community that ends up leaving society's political and economic framework untouched. That change is not possible at these levels is a bias that must be overcome. The focus on civil society (and its emphasis on culture, gender and ecology) needs to be complemented by a focus on the reconstruction of the market and the state. The critique of idolatry can also be strengthened through the construction of historical projects. In this case, the best way to combat the idolatrous nature of capitalism is to develop alternatives that reveal the idol as idol. Liberation theology thus must approach both democracy and capitalism as partial, fragmented, haphazard entities opening up space for political and economic possibility. Only then can the development of new historical projects take place. Without such projects, liberation theology freezes political struggle to the existing forms and institutions of society, despite the initial rejection of society as it stands. The idols, then, are granted the final say.

Centering liberation theology around the construction of historical projects also shows that Boff and Sung can be read as highlighting different parts of a theological task which should be understood as a single process that includes the construction of historical projects. Boff's canonical statement sees liberation theology as composed of a social scientific mediation, a hermeneutic mediation and a practical mediation. The first uses the social sciences to understand the causes of oppression, the second judges oppression through the lens of the Bible and tradition, and the third develops programs for action to remedy that oppression. Within this statement the social sciences only play a role in the analysis of the causes of oppression; they do not return in the development of programs for action, programs that thus remain little more than vague calls for reform. For the canonical statement, moreover, it is only the rereading of the Bible and tradition in the light of society that is formally theological. The social sciences themselves have no theological worth. The construction of historical projects is pushed out of a scheme that relegates the social sciences to the social scientific mediation and denies any strictly theological relevance to the construction of historical projects.

Sung's marginal statement argues that liberation theology's theological background – the ideas of a God of life, a unitary anthropology and a unitary history – requires a closer link between theology and the social sciences. Here the social sciences do not just read reality, the social sciences are the realm where God's promise of life fails or succeeds. They occupy a theological space in themselves and thus the critique of idolatry within the social sciences becomes a central part of doing liberation theology as theology. In addition, the marginal position recognizes the importance of constructing concrete institutional alternatives to the status quo. However, like the canonical position, it too fails to develop the theological import of this construction. A discipline like economics is a theological space in that it helps to decide who will eat and who will go hungry, but the use of economics to develop institutions that could help more people afford a meal are not seen as an intrinsic part of doing liberation theology. Once again the construction of historical projects is relegated to a minor role, if not forgotten altogether.

The key difference with each position lies in where the emphasis is placed. One focuses on reconstructing Christian concepts, the other on tackling idolatry within society. However, it is only by constructing historical projects that liberation theology can fully take as its starting point the challenge posed by the non-person and fully take liberation as its goal. Tackling that challenge and striving for that goal does require, insofar as Christianity remains a force in Latin America and the rest of the Third or '2/3' World, a rereading of the Christian tradition around notions such as a God of life, a unitary anthropology and history, the preferential option for the poor, the reign of God and liberation.[5] It also requires what could be called a critical use for the social sciences; that is, if your starting point is the non-person, and your goal is liberation, then you need the social sciences to uncover the causes of oppression. By themselves, however, the rereading of Christianity and the critical use of the social sciences are not enough. If your starting point is the non-person, and your goal really is liberation, you also need a constructive use for the social sciences in the imagination of historical projects that can lift people out of their need. At its best, liberation theology was able to combine all these elements. I have shown that it can still do so.

Alistair Kee recently argued that liberation theology has forgotten the second part of Marx's famous eleventh thesis on Feuerbach: 'the philosophers have only interpreted the world in various ways; *the point is to change it*'.[6] For him, liberation theology has merely interpreted the world of the poor: 'Liberation theology has provided the poor with an interpretation of their own poverty. It has given it meaning and value. It has even given the poor status. God has chosen the poor. They are the Chosen people with whom He is well pleased. Their suffering now has a place in the grand scheme of liberation.'[7] Liberation theology, by only interpreting the world of the poor, by giving their poverty theological significance, 'makes the intolerable tolerable'.[8] In focusing on the first part of Marx's thesis while forgetting the second, therefore, Kee suggests liberation theology may have unwittingly become a painkiller, 'the opium of the people'.⁹ Perhaps Kee is right; perhaps liberation theology has only interpreted poverty theologically. If so, the revision of liberation theology around historical projects is all the more urgent a task.

Liberation Theology and Contemporary Theology

Latin American Liberation Theology and Johann Baptist Metz's Political Theology

Johann Baptist Metz's work provides the classic objection to my view of liberation theology as the construction of historical projects. For him, my collapsing of the theology and sociopolitical analysis dichotomy runs the risk of making theology ideology. He thus make that dichotomy a basis for his understanding of theology.

For Metz the secular sphere has emancipated itself from the religious sphere and operates according to its own criteria and laws.¹⁰ This separation, moreover, is necessary to ensure the individual's freedom from a state subject to the permanent temptation to require an all-encompassing allegiance from its citizens. The separation between theology and sociopolitical analysis thus serves to protect against totalitarian idolatries in which limited historical projects make absolute claims and take the place of God. However, the separation is not an absolute divorce, theology can make claims on the political sphere; the gospel's eschatological message is public and universal and to leave the secular sphere completely independent would be to limit the promise of God's Reign found in the New Testament – freedom, peace, justice, reconciliation – to a merely private affair.¹¹ The gospel's message, however, must be expressed only in negative terms via a negative critique of society: 'Christianity can only formulate the decisiveness ("absoluteness") and universality of its message without falling into an ideology when it formulates it as critical negation (of and in given situations).'¹² Only by restraining theology to the realm of negative critique can a proper balance between the universality of the Christian message and the autonomous rights of the secular sphere be mantained and the totalitarian temptation kept at bay. To this negative critique Metz then adds the 'dangerous memory' of past suffering as a source for aiding judgments about the political realm.¹³

I disagree with his position for three reasons. First, and most basically, I disagree with the eschatology and religious/secular divide that underlie his position. For liberation theologians, God's reign does not relate to human history from a position of complete otherness. They stress that the supernatural should be understood as perfecting the natural order, rather than as standing in complete opposition to it. Metz's negative critique, however, is the twin of his 'eschatological proviso' by which every institution falls under the judgment of God's reign.¹⁴ The absolute transcendence of God's reign leads to an understanding of eschatology where it is difficult, if not impossible, to find a connection between earthly history and the history of salvation. In addition, liberation theologians see modern society as idolatrous rather than secular. To posit a 'secular' space which, because secular, is safe from theological encroachment ends by safeguarding idolatry. Both moves deprive of theological backing our limited ability, yet ability nonetheless, to build a more just world.

Second, Metz follows a long line of German thought in taking a particular German problem and universalizing it into an absolute rule for theology the world over.[15] In fact, to focus only on eschatology as the source of the separation between theology and historical projects is to overlook the Eurocentrism at the heart of his understanding of theology. As is well known, Metz's focus on negative critique stems from his reflections on the relation between church and state in Nazi Germany. In the Nazi era important German theologians not only supported Hitler's state but lent that state theological backing; they gave those policies divine foundation. Metz's focus on negative critique is the product of such a context. Because theology was once used in Germany to disguise bloodthirsty idolatry in divine garb, he is universally opposed to drawing any link between theology and historical projects. For Metz the obsession with separating theology from sociopolitical analysis and historical projects, through either negative critique or a political ethic, is tied to his taking a reaction to a particular German experience and setting it up as a general rule for all theology.

Indeed, implicit in the construction of historical projects is liberation theology's demotion of Western philosophy and theology to undeniably influential, yet often colonialist and provincial schools of thought which mistakenly understand themselves as the history of philosophy and theology per se.[16] Part of the process of constructing historical projects is the undermining of claims to exclusivity found in Western philosophy and theology, as well as their characteristic political and economic institutions. Such an undermining is necessary because within these schools of thought Europe positioned itself as the carrier of reason and civilization for the rest of the world. Similarily, Latin American elites' desire to emulate political and economic forms received from the 'First World' rests on the assumption that Europe and the United States possess something of universal significance that the rest of the world lacks. But if this North Atlantic tradition is one flawed tradition among many, its primary exports today, capitalism and liberal democracy, need not be taken as the end points of social development.[17] If this assumption is dropped, the critique of Western philosophy and theology, the critique of modernity, can open itself up to a critique of inherited versions of the market economy and of democracy. In this way, liberation theology can strike a balance between the theological critique of modernity and the institutional reconstruction of society: the former must inform the latter, but the latter should be the ultimate goal.[18]

Third, his view of eschatology and his Eurocentrism render theology powerless in the face of massive material human suffering. It functions to retain a pure space for theology, a space where theology need not deal with the ugly realities of global inequality. As Hugo Assmann suggests, 'in the name of a "political theology",

theology is made apolitical, because what really counts politically is the supposedly secular and autonomous ethical sphere'.[19] In reality, however, this pure space is nowhere to be found and can only be simulated by emptying theological terminology of concrete content. For Metz, 'wherever a party, group, race, nation, or class – even the class of technocrats – tries to define itself as this subject [subject of divine will], the Christian *memoria* must oppose that, and unmask this attempt as political idolatry, as political ideology with a totalitarian or – in apocalyptic terms – a "bestial" tendency'.[20]

Here is the eschatological proviso and negative critique that liberate political life from totalitarianism, a valid yet limited move. To his credit, Metz wants more: 'this liberation is now utopian in orientation and not undefined. The Christian memory of suffering is in its theological implications an anticipatory memory: it intends the anticipation of a particular future of man as a future for the suffering, the hopeless, the oppressed, the injured and the useless of the earth'.[21] Note how vague Metz's 'not undefined' idea of liberation remains.[22] This vagueness is the characteristic byproduct of every attempt to posit a divide between theology and the constructive use of the social sciences in the elaboration of historical projects. Surprisingly, Metz also states that, in his view, 'nothing is more urgently needed today than a moral and political imagination springing from a messianic Christianity and capable of being more than merely a copy of accepted political and economic strategies'.[23] I agree, but Metz's limitation of theology to negative critique and *memoria* ensures his inability to contribute to this task.[24]

Once one grasps that the emptiness of theological ideals, whether in liberation theology, political theology or Catholic social teaching, is tied to strategies which carve out a purified theological realm where theology is excused from responsibility for suffering, there emerges an option to take the opposite road and corrupt theology by forcing it into the feared unholy matrimony with the social sciences. That, of course, was the road taken in this book.[25]

Latin American Liberation Theology and Radical Orthodoxy

Currently, in addition to this book, another new approach to liberation theology has emerged from an unlikely source, the 'radical orthodoxy' movement within the contemporary North American and English academy which, spearheaded by John Milbank and Stanley Hauerwas and further developed by their students, can be read as having staked out a position through a critique of liberation theology and its turn to the social sciences.[26] Recently, though, radical orthodoxy has moved from criticism toward revising liberation theology around its own theological framework. This move is evident in the most recent work to emerge from this school, and the study most specifically directed toward liberation theology, Daniel Bell Jr's *Liberation Theology After the End of History: the Refusal to Cease Suffering*. In reality, however, radical orthodoxy's move from criticism to revision is merely the very same move from opposition to cooption previously made by the IMF and the

Vatican. While my argument presupposes and strengthens liberation theology's framework – the understanding of a God of life, a unitary history and a unitary anthropology – radical orthodoxy takes concepts such as the preferential option and liberation and inserts them in a theological framework that is in overt conflict with the liberationist understanding of these ideas. Here I focus on Bell in the context of radical orthodoxy as a whole.[27]

Bell and I hold three points in common. Like myself, Bell wants to revitalize liberation theology in the face of an apparant capitalist triumph. In addition, he sees liberation theology's political paralysis as mostly self-inflicted, the product of the wrong way of thinking about capitalism and its relationship with the social sciences. Finally, he too wants to collapse the distinction between theology and politics in order to stress the material reality of faith.

The way he develops these points in common, however, is diametrically opposed to my own position. The kernel of his argument lies in four steps. First, he criticizes liberation theology's understanding of capitalism. Bell argues that liberation theology actually *underestimates* the utter pervasiveness of capitalist relations. For him, capitalism's victory 'is not simply economic; it is, more insidiously, ontological'.[28] Capitalism functions not just through economic exploitation 'but by capturing and distorting the constitutive human power, desire'.[29] Everything at every level has been taken over, 'the capitalist axiomatic is like a megapolis of which all the nations constitute neighborhoods'.[30] For this reason, attempts to reform the state along more democratic lines, from the top down through socialist takeover or from the botton up through civil society, are destined to failure.

Second, Bell declares that the only way to oppose capitalism is through another system of desire. Drawing on Augustine, Bell suggests that human beings are constituted by desire for God. However, humans are fallen and desire needs to be set straight. Christianity 'is a therapy, a way of life that releases desire from its bondage, that cures the madness so that desire may once again flow as it was created to do'.[31] The conflict between Christianity and capitalism is thus a conflict around two opposing disciplines of desire.

Third, Bell argues that liberation theology needs a more substantive ecclesiology to enact this program. According to Bell, even as liberationists insist that the theological and the political must be correlated, they keep a division between the two. The division stems from the belief that theology must be applied to politics rather than 'reclaiming the theological as material, that is, as a fully social, political, economic reality'.[32] The ensuing consequence is that the Church is rendered only indirectly political; politics takes place at the level of statecraft. Instead, Bell's ecclesiology collapses religion and politics by recognizing the church as an 'uncivil society'. For him 'the Church's politics is not defined by the secular order. Thus, it finds no home in civil society. The Church's politics culminates not in the centralized rule of the state and its civil society but in the Kingdom of God'.[33]

Fourth, Bell suggests that liberation theology need go no further than its base communities to find the agents for his approach: 'As poor Christians come together in non-hierarchical, participatory gatherings to celebrate informal liturgies, as they reflect on scripture, as they share food, visit the sick, establish cooperatives or undertake a joint work project, and occasionally engage in some form of protest or petition the ruling powers, they are clearly about politics.'[34] Such a model of the church 'explodes the secular order's categories of "public" and "private", "religious" and "political", as it worships with the victims of AIDS, offers sanctuary to illegal immigrants, and operates soup kitchens in places not "zoned" for such activities. Likewise, its practice of baptism escapes the private realm of values as it challenges the boundaries of political loyalties, and celebrating the Eucharist directly threatens the economic order by offering and providing sustenance'.[35]

I disagree with Bell's approach on a number of points. His understanding of capitalism is an example of the institutional fetishism I criticize in Chapter 4 and overcome in Chapter 5. For Bell, capitalism is once again an abstract, monolithic and all encompassing entity from which, in this case, there is no escape other than the church.[36] Yet, even if one grants him this view of capitalism, why assume that the church can escape capitalism at all? Why does Bell think the church can succeed where every other social body has failed? Why is his view not the mere abandonment of wider society to oppressive capitalism? His answer comes in a footnote: 'the anti-statist position I put forward only leaves one naked before the forces of the market if the Spirit is not forming alternative communities capable of resisting'.[37] This answer highlights the different understandings of history present in Bell and radical orthodoxy over and against my argument and liberation theology. Underlying the whole radical orthodoxy movement lies Milbank's and Hauerwas's retrieval of an Augustinian view of history in which the *Civitas terrena* and the *Civitas Dei* stand diametrically opposed to each other. In this view, the *Civitas terrena* is inescapably corrupt while the *Civitas Dei* embodies God's politics. Grace, therefore, is found only within the latter.[38]

This dichotomy underlies Bell's understanding of capitalism and the church. Capitalism represents the *Civitas terrena*; the church represents the *Civitas Dei*. Thus, on the one hand, capitalism, civil society and the state (conquered as they are by capitalism) are absolutely corrupt; their regeneration is impossible. The church, on the other hand, is safeguarded from corruption by 'the Spirit'. This dichotomy also forces Bell to turn inward into Christian tradition as the means to make theology material. Theology can only use its own resources, scripture and tradition, since to turn outward into the social sciences means turning outwards into the *Civitas terrena*. Only corruption can ensue. Milbank, for example, argues that theology does not need the social sciences; theology itself is already an alternative social science.[39] Yet without political science, economics and law, theology is a social science that deprives itself of the means to give institutional content to its terminology.[40] The upshot is that in Bell liberation theology's politics is not radicalized but reduced to acts of social charity and the fostering of community.

In addition to subscribing to a dualistic view of history, Bell and radical orthodoxy also embrace an understanding of God as a God of peace that is different from liberation theology's understanding of God as a God of life. For example, for Milbank the notion of a God of peace helps 'unthink' the necessity of a social order based on violence. Viewing God as a God of peace thus stops a spiral of violence since the belief in the necessity of violence inevitably leads to further violence. More importantly, however, Milbank argues that this notion grounds a specific Christian form of resistance to violence: 'it indicates that there is a way to act in a violent world which assumes the ontological priority of non-violence, and this way is called "forgiveness of sins"'.[41] In practice, this means that the church and the Christian should 'echo God, not in punishing, but in suffering, for the duration of the *saeculum*, the consequences of sin, beyond considerations of desert and non-desert'.[42]

Bell's application of these ideas to liberation theology highlights their problematic character. Bell, like Milbank, asserts the priority of forgiveness over justice. For Bell, liberation theologians are mistaken to assign priority to justice for the pursuit of justice merely reproduces the violence that is inherent to capitalism: 'Justice in the distributive sense that liberationists invoke may actually exacerbate conflict and violence precisely in the name of restoring violated rights'.[43] The pursuit of justice, moreover, fails to overcome the essentially possessive and acquisitive nature of capitalism because one is seeking to acquire and possess just desert. In Bell's scheme the pursuit of justice and capitalism operate according to a similar logic: 'The liberationists face capitalism and demand that it render what is due; capitalism responds that that is exactly what it does. Liberationists face the poor and encourage them to become acquisitive; so, too, does capitalism ... a troubling family resemblance remains'.[44] Following Milbank, Bell proposes forgiveness as the means to overturn the spiral of violence to which both capitalism and justice are prone. He argues that only by abandoning calculi of reciprocity and desert can the spiral of violence be broken. Only through forgiveness can the victim be free from enmity and the victimizer free from the burden of having committed injustice. Forgiveness gives them the chance to start a relationship anew. Justice, in this sense, is not abandoned but reconceived as 'fundamentally a matter of recreation and reconciliation, of living in communion and love'.[45] As such, it is forgiveness that makes justice revamped possible. In practice, however, this means that the poor must no longer seek justice in terms of the distribution of rights. As I have shown, Bell believes that such a strategy remains prey to capitalist logic. Instead, he argues that the Christian resistance strategy lies in 'the refusal to cease suffering', that is, in 'entering into suffering, bearing it, in the hope of bearing it away'.[46] For Bell, this refusal to cease suffering is ultimately an act of hope in God.[47]

From a liberationist perspective, radical orthodoxy forgets that life is prior to peace; that is, concrete bodily human life is a prerequisite for peace to exist. Life is the precondition for all other conditions, thus liberation theologians argue that God most basically is a God of life. Moreover, the refusal to cease suffering as a strategy implicitly buys into a dualistic view of history. Once again, within this view, earthly struggles for a better world can only lead to greater violence. Release from suffering can only come from beyond history. For this reason all Bell can appeal to is hope in God, hence his description of the refusal to cease suffering as a wager on God.[48] Finally, the very notion of the refusal to cease suffering downplays the material plight of the Latin American (and world's) poor. At stake is not just suffering or non-suffering but, as liberation theologians repeatedly stress, life and death. In this case, the refusal to cease suffering emerges as a death sentence. In life one may refuse to cease suffering, until death.

Latin American Liberation Theology and Liberation Theologies

What of theologies that share the underlying theological foundation of Latin American liberation theology? What of theologies that share the idea of a God of life, the same eschatology, a unified anthropology and history? While today a proliferation of liberation theologies with different emphases exist – Black, Womanist, Feminist, Mujerista, Latina, Queer, Hispanic, to name a few – none places the development of historical projects at the forefront of their task.[49] Liberation theology outlined as I outline it remains unique, its approach is not followed by any contemporary theological movement. Here I cannot comment on each type of theology, nor is their just one 'Hispanic' or 'Womanist' or 'Latina' theology. Many trends and foci coexist under each label. However, it is precisely those theologians who seek to intervene most directly in societal reform who find themselves most disabled by the lack of a social vision and political program which defines liberation. Let me exemplify this point by examining the discrepancy between the stated goal and the central features and tasks of, on the one hand, Maria Pilar Aquino's Latina theology, and, on the other hand, Dwight Hopkins' Black liberation theology.

In her programmatic statement, 'Latina Feminist Theology: Central Features', Aquino writes that 'Latina/Chicana feminism is a critical framework to analyze systematic injustice, both locally and globally, to determine effective strategies for its elimination and the actualization of authentic justice.'[50] She seeks to 'use the power of theology with its liberating traditions as a religious force which contributes to personal and social transformation and the elimination of suffering born of violence and social injustice'.[51] Given this liberationist thrust, Aquino provides an analysis of the current 'material geopolitical' context which determines the method, the principles for theologizing and the tasks for Latina theology.[52] This context has several levels. The first level is characterized by global poverty, inequality, social exclusion and social insecurity brought about by 'the current capitalist, neoliberal global economic paradigm'.[53] The second level is characterized by poverty in the United States and the fact that the poverty rates for children, minorities and families headed by women are well above average of the United States as a whole.[54] The third level is characterized by the exclusion of Latina women from theological activity.[55]

Following her analysis of Latina theology's context, Aquino moves to highlight its central features. These features include preconditions such as 'entering *Nepantla*; fostering *la facultad*; *honesty* with the real; *empapamiento* of hope; and an *evolving* truth'.[56] Entering *Nepantla* means that the theologian must be willing to explore God and ourselves from the borders; *la facultad* stresses that the theologian must have the capacity to transform and relocate him or herself to best make signs to the dispossessed and keep theology vital and dynamic; *honesty* with the real requires recognizing that the world is marred by injustice; *empapamiento* refers to the need to saturate oneself with hope to better engage the transformative imagination; finally, *evolving* truth means that truth is not given once and for all, but is the evolving product of culturally plural truths. Latina theology's central features also include, among the major methodological characteristics and principles, a focus on the varied daily life (*la vida cotidiana*) experiences of excluded women as the starting point for critical reflection, a focus on popular religion as both oppressive and liberative, the feminist option for the poor and the oppressed and claim that salvation should be understood as 'liberation from every oppression'.[57]

Aquino ends her programmatic essay by relating Latina theology's four major tasks.[58] The first task lies in developing further Latina theology's theological foundations by bringing a feminist critical approach to its sources: mestizaje, popular religion, Scripture, the Magisterium, interdisciplinary studies, intercultural theories and philosophical hermeneutics. The second task lies in Latina women continuing to claim their right to intellectual construction and the development of means and resources for the theological education of Latinas. The third task is drawing a closer connection between theology and spirituality in feminist terms. Finally, the fourth task lies in continuing the theological analysis of capitalist neoliberal globalization and its effects on the life of grassroots Latinas.

Notice that as Aquino develops Latina theology the background of global economic marginalization as well as the marginalization of the United States' poor recedes from view, while the theological exclusion of Latinas comes to the forefront. This happens in several ways. First, Aquino explicitly relegates the critique of economic conditions to the fourth task Latina theology must tackle. Access to theological education and intellectual construction comes first. So does developing further the foundation of Latina theology. Helping people become theologians is given priority over helping them raise themselves from social misery. It seems, therefore, that the focus of Latina theology is middle class Latinas, rather than the poor.[59] Second, among the sources she names for Latina theology disciplines that might help tackle global and local economic marginalization are conspicuously absent. Not only are political economy and legal theory excluded from her sources, but Aquino stresses elements that threaten neither religious orthodoxy nor the academy: mestizaje, popular religion, Scripture, the Magisterium, interdisciplinary studies and philosophical hermeneutics. These are elements that both the Vatican and the mainstream North Atlantic academy easily accept as part of theology. Here there is no danger of turning theology into ideology or of being accused of doing 'pop sociology', but neither is there the possibility of concretely addressing economic marginalization. Third, the end result of the two prior moves is a theological focus that deals almost exclusively with seeking to address cultural marginalization through integration at the level of the academy, exemplified in one instance by Aquino's penchant for incorporating words from Nahautl and Spanish into a North Atlantic theological discourse dominated by English, French and German.

Let me stress that I wholeheartedly support feminist theological projects and agree with Aquino that the cultural exclusion of Latinas in the United States as well as their underrepresentation in the academy are problems that must be addressed. I also agree that English, French and German have dominated theology for too long. Aquino is right to try to give Latinas a voice. But this focus is too narrow and makes scarcely visible either global poverty or the poverty of the vast majority of Latinas in the United States. For this reason the focus on culture needs to be part of a wider project of social reconstruction if the benefits of cultural inclusion are not going to be restricted to members of the middle class. Issues of cultural politics must be tied to an egalitarian program of economic and political reconstruction. To do this, however, Latina theology will have to incorporate different elements. It will have to include, for example, political economy and legal theory, not just for the critique of social structure, but also for the development of new social structures. Without the incorporation of these tools the elaboration of programs for liberation will be unable to move beyond wishful thinking.[60] It will also have to refuse to remain confined within the narrow limits of what the Magisterium defines as theology. Instead, it must explode those limits and view the construction of historical projects as integral to the theological task itself.

Aquino writes that 'salvation is understood by Latina Feminist theology as liberation from every oppression' and that 'the historical process of liberation from poverty, social injustice, and exclusion becomes the most effective and credible manifestation of God's salvation'.[61] Yet the tasks she outlines for Latina theology as well as the elements that make it up relegate liberation from poverty and social injustice to an afterthought. What really has priority is the inclusion of Latinas in the United States' mainstream; yet if that is her social vision Cornel West's early critique of Black theology applies here as well: 'It roughly equates liberation with American middle class status, leaving the unequal distribution of wealth relatively untouched ... Liberation would consist of including Black people [and Latinas] within the mainstream of liberal capitalist America. If this is the social vision of Black [and Latina] theologians, they should drop the meretricious and flamboyant term "liberation" and adopt the more accurate and sober word "inclusion".'[62]

Contemporary Black theology itself, however, fails to address Cornel West's early critique. West criticized first-generation Black theology for 'its absence of a systemic social analysis' and its 'lack of a social vision, political program, and concrete praxis which defines and facilitates socioeconomic and political liberation'.[63] Black theology today, as defined by Dwight Hopkins, arguably its preeminent representative, is incapable of addressing this challenge. For Hopkins, 'the key is liberation and the practice of freedom for all human beings'.[64] Once again, 'the key to all talk about God from the perspective of the black poor is the spirit of liberation'.[65] But who are the poor? For Hopkins, 'the *poor* indicates first the material poor; those who own or control no wealth'.[66] Indeed, he stresses that class is the normative thread that runs throughout Black theology.[67] Hopkins thus embraces the preferential option for the poor as a central element of Black theology, an option which involves a 'faith engaged in a radical redistribution of power and wealth on behalf of those whose voices aren't taken seriously in the United States'.[68] For this reason, 'one of the key challenges for black theology is to understand adequately the negative effects of US monopoly capitalism on African American poor and working communities. Faith and practice based on liberation theology must include the need for freedom from the oppressive control of global capital'. Hopkins is aware that facing this challenge requires a new economic and political vision that mediates between the present and an ultimate future when God-given ideal human relations – a new self and new commonwealth – are established:

> In addition, between the cutthroat reality of the now, on the one hand, and the period of the ultimate goal, on the other hand, we envision an intermediate period. Here the preferential option for the poor becomes even more clear. During the in-between time, we envision the poor, the least sectors of society, and the marginalized people among us owning and controlling the wealth of this land. A true majority of society will govern. With this condition in place, issues of universal healthcare, housing, employment, vacations, recreations, education, day care, and all of the issues that ensure a positive quality of daily life for those who were suffering from poverty will become easily attainable. The sole criterion during this interim period will be how we participate in the process of eliminating the system of poverty and the host of related forms of brokenness in the human family.[69]

Hopkins' political and economic vision, however, suffers from a vagueness that is endemic in contemporary Black theologies.[70] The reason for this vagueness is to be found in the five sources that he makes central to Black theology: the Bible, the African American Church, a faith tradition of struggle for liberation, culture (art, literature, music, folktales, black English and rhythm) and radical politics.[71] As with Aquino, the focus of Hopkins' sources is the fostering of identity and the safeguarding of orthodoxy. Thus Black identity is fostered through the Black church and Black culture; religious orthodoxy is safeguarded by the primary status of the Bible and the Black church. Radical politics is included as a source but it is a radical politics without a compass. Hopkins states that 'here politics is the ability to determine the direction that the African American community can pursue'.[72] Yet how is that direction to be determined without the incorporation of a more concrete social analysis and the development of a more concrete social vision? Hopkins' earlier work recognized this need and explicity incorporated political economy into Black theology's sources: 'While interacting with other disciplines, theology seeks to discover how best to get at divine vocation for concrete liberation. For instance, political economy surfaces the issue of power control of politics, culture, and economics ... Furthermore, political economy paints the constructive contours of the new democratic society.'[73] Even when he made political economy constitutive of Black theology, however, Hopkins still refused to turn to current social, political, legal and economic theory, preferring instead to draw on the work of Martin Luther King, Jr and Malcom X. While these two men are obvious potential sources for Black theology, they are not the most current resource if one is interested in developing a political and economic vision of content applicable to the 21st century.[74]

In Hopkins' recent work, disciplines like political economy have been abandoned and his Black theology of liberation suffers without them. They have been adandoned, I believe, because of the perceived need to emphasize theology's blackness in much the same way that Aquino feels the need to emphasize her theology's Latina nature. He tells us that 'we must avoid an amorphous type of black theology that omits the crucial phrase of *liberation of the poor*. In ambiguity lies the danger'.[75] Yes, in ambiguity lies the danger. But one cannot avoid ambiguity by relying on the cachet of the term 'liberation'. Rather, one must do the hard work of developing the relation between liberation and historical projects. Insofar as Hopkins fails to do so the upshot, yet again, is a theology that states as its goal liberation of the poor – by which Hopkins means primarily the *material* poor – yet is incapable of doing anything about their real physical poverty.

Conclusion

Liberation theology invites the theologian to place at his or her heart the problems of the majority of humankind. Recall the data used to illustrate Guitérrez's use of the terms 'non-person' and 'non-human' at the end of Chapter 1. Better yet, let me refresh your memory with just one statistic: It would take 13 billion dollars of additional yearly investment to guarantee basic health and nutrition for every single person in the developing world; 17 billion are spent on pet food in Europe and the United States combined. Indeed, the tragic nature of our world order lies reflected in that a theology that takes as its starting point the non-person starts from the commonplace, starts from the mainstream. The dichotomy revealed by these numbers is not extreme or unusual; it captures the way most of the world lives, or, to be more accurate, barely lives. From a global perspective, it is the European and North American standard of living that is extreme and unusual in that it represents an extreme and unusual case of affluence in the midst of routine poverty. From a global perspective, affluence is the exception and lack is the rule. No understanding of liberation theology that fails to make the construction of historical projects a central element fully takes the plight of humanity's majority to heart.

Allow me to conclude, perhaps unwisely, by mentioning two aspects of the general relation between liberation theology and historical projects that I do not deal with but nonetheless need to be acknowledged and developed as future areas of research. In the first place, any attempt to open a space in which to develop localized alternatives to the reigning economic order must also be tied to a transformation of the world-system as a whole.[76] This requires paying attention to the cultural, economic, political and ecological linkages between the rich and the poor nations, and how those linkages hinder, block and deny attempts by the latter to become masters of their own fate.[77] Second, throughout this book I stress the indissoluble link between the theological and the political in liberation theology. While I focus on the implications of this link for recovering the notion of a historical project in an attempt to reconstruct liberation theology for the 21st century, I also believe that liberation theology is a spiritual exercise, a call to both social and personal conversion, as well as a hope for ultimate redemption.

Let us not forget that, to paraphrase Georges Friedmann, in order to prepare for the revolution, we must seek, in addition, to become worthy of it.[78]

Notes

1 Theodor W. Adorno, *Minima Moralia: Reflections from Damaged Life*, trans. E.F.N. Jephcott (London: Verso Editons-NLB, 1978), 247.

2 I realize, however, that Adorno would likely not be sympathetic to my attempt to place the development of historical projects at the center of liberation theology.

3 For discussions on liberation theology after the fall of socialism, see Daniel M. Bell Jr, *Liberation Theology After the End of History: The Refusal to Cease Suffering* (London: Routledge, 2001); Marcella Althaus-Reid, *Indecent Theology: Theological Perversions in Sex, Gender and Politics* (New York: Routledge, 2000); Marcella Althaus-Reid, 'Bien Sonados? The Future of Mystical Connections in Liberation Theology', *Political Theology: The Journal of Christian Socialism*, 3 (Nov 2000), 44–63; Ian Linden, 'Liberation Theology: Coming of Age?', *Political Theology: The Journal of Christian Socialism*, 3 (Nov 2000), 11–29; Alistair Kee, 'The Conservatism of Liberation Theology: Four Questions for Jon Sobrino', *Political Theology: The Journal of Christian Socialism*, 3 (Nov 2000), 30–43; Rolando Alvarado, 'Teologia de la Liberación en el Post-Socialismo', *Revista Latinoamericana de Teología*, 47 (May–August 1999), 173–87; Kee, 'The Conservatism of Liberation Theology'; José Comblin, *Called for Freedom: The Changing Context of Liberation Theology*, ed. Phillip Berryman (Maryknoll, New York: Orbis Books, 1998); Rui Manuel Gracio das Neves, 'Neoliberalismo, Teología de la Liberación y Nuevos Paradigmas', *Alternativas*, 9 (1998), 57–96; G. De Schrijver (ed.), *Liberation Theologies on Shifting Grounds: A Clash of Socio-Economic and Cultural Paradigms* (Louvain, Belgium: Leuven University Press, 1998); Daniel Bell JR, 'Men of Stone and Children of Struggle: Latin American Liberationists at the End of History', *Modern Theology*, 14(1) (Jan 1998), 113–41; J. Amando Robles Robles, 'Postmodernidad y Teología de la Liberación', *Cristianismo y Sociedad*, 137 (1998), 49–66; Adolfo Galeano, 'Desafios de la Postmodernidad a la Teología en América Latina', *Cristianismo y Sociedad*, 137 (1998), 67–85; David Batstone, Eduardo Mendieta, Lois Ann Lorentzen and Dwight Hopkins (eds), *Liberation Theologies, Postmodernity, and the Americas* (New York: Routledge, 1997); Enrique Dussel, 'Transformaciones de los Supuestos Epistemologicos de la Teología de la Liberación', *Cuadernos de Teología*, XVI(1–2) (1997), 129–37; José Maria Vigil, 'Cambio de Paradigma en la Teología de la Liberación?', *Alternativas*, 8 (1997), 27–46; José Ignacio González Faus, 'Veinticinco años de la Teología de la Liberación: Teología y Opción por los Pobres', *Revista Latinoamericana de Teología*, 42 (September–December 1997), 223–42; see also *Exodo*, 38 (March–April 1997) an issue dedicated to the future of liberation theology; Gustavo Gutiérrez, 'Una Teología de la Liberación en el Contexto del Tercer

Milenio', *El Futuro de la Reflexion Teologica en América Latina* (Bogota, Colombia: CELAM, 1996), 97–166; Diego Irarrazaval, 'Nuevas Rutas de la Teología Latinoamericana', *Revista Latinoamericana de Teología*, 38 (May–August 1996), 183–97; Jon Sobrino, 'La Teología y el "Principio Liberación"', *Revista Latinoamericana de Teología*, 35 (May–August 1995), 115–40; Jung Mo Sung, *Economia: Tema Ausente en la Teología de la Liberación* (San José, Costa Rica: DEI, 1994); Hugo Assmann, 'Teologia de la Liberación: Mirando Hacia el Frente', *Pasos*, 55 (September–October 1994), 1–9; Edward A. Lynch, 'Beyond Liberation Theology?', *Journal of Interdisciplinary Studies*, 6(1–2) (1994), 147–64; Duncan B. Forrester, 'Can Liberation Theology Survive 1989?', *Scottish Journal of Theology*, 47(2) (1994), 245–53; José Comblin, José I. González Faus and Jon Sobrino (eds), *Cambio Social y Pensamiento Cristiano en América Latina* (Madrid: Editorial Trotta, 1993); Max Stackhouse, 'Now That the Revolution is Over', *The Reformed Journal*, 40(7) (September 1990), 16–20; Alistair Kee, *Marx and the Failure of Liberation Theology* (Philadelphia, PA: Trinity Press International, 1990). This list is not exhaustive; it merely hints at the dual sense of impasse and ferment in current liberation theology.

4 José Comblin, 'La Iglesia Latinoamericana Desde Puebla a Santo Domingo', *Cambio Social y Pensamiento Cristiano en América Latina*, ed. José Comblin, José I. González Faus, and Jon Sobrino (Madrid: Editorial Trotta, 1993), 51.

5 I find neither the notion of 'Third World' nor '2/3' world entirely adequate. The first rightly highlights a disparity in power, the second rightly highlights the majority status of the 'Third World.'

6 Cited in Kee, 'The Conservatism of Liberation Theology', 34.

7 Kee, ibid.

8 Ibid.

9 Karl Marx, *On Religion*, ed. and trans. Saul Padover (New York: McGraw-Hill, 1974), vol. 5 of *The Karl Marx Library*, 36.

10 For Metz's initial development of this idea, see Johann Baptist Metz, *Theology of the World* (New York: Herder and Herder, 1969).

11 Johann Baptist Metz, 'Political Theology', *Encylopedia of Theology*, ed. Karl Rahner (New York: Seabury Press, 1975), 1241.

12 Ibid.

13 See the essays in Johann Baptist Metz, *A Passion for God: The Mystical–Political Dimension of Christianity* (New York: Paulist Press, 1998).

14 See Metz, *Theology of the World*, 114.

15 Of course, the granting of a particular Western European problematic or event universal significance is common to his theological and philosophical tradition. See, for example, the view of the European Enlightenment in Immanuel Kant, 'What is Enlightenment?', *The Philosophy of Kant: Moral and Political Writings*, ed. Carl Friedrich (New York: The Modern Library, 1949), 132–9; the view of European history in Georg Wilhelm Friedrich Hegel, *The Philosophy of History*, preface by Charles Hegel, trans. and preface by J. Sibree, introduction by E.J. Friedrich (New York: Dover, 1956); and the view of the German Reformation, the European Enlightenment and the French revolution in Jürgen Habermas, *The Philosophical Discourse of Modernity: Twelve Lectures*, trans. Frederick Lawrence, Studies in Contemporary German Social Thought (Cambridge, Massachusetts: MIT, 1987). The best critique of this hubris lies in Enrique Dussel, *Etica de la Liberación en la Edad de la Globalización y de la Exclusión* (Madrid: Editorial Trotta, 1998).

16 For this argument see Dussel, *Etica de la Liberación* and Enrique Dussel, *The Underside of Modernity: Apel, Ricoeur, Rorty, Taylor, and the Philosophy of Liberation*, Eduard Mendieta (New York: Humanity Books, 1998). For a book that seeks to give different world philosophies equal standing see David Cooper, *World Philosophies: An Historical Introduction* (Cambridge, MA: Blackwell Publishers Ltd., 1996).

17 See Francis Fukuyama, 'The End of History', *The National Interest* Summer (1989), 3–18 and Francis Fukuyama, *The End of History and the Last Man* (New York: Free Press, 1992).

18 One way to understand the construction of historical projects is to see it as part of a continuing wide reflective equilibrium among interpretations of tradition, background theories, retroductive

warrants and communities of discourse. It would also require, however, recognizing the place of institutional imagination and thus the constructive role of the social sciences as an additional element in the theological enterprise. One way to understand institutional imagination's placement in this process is to grasp that within the reflective equilibrium of the above four elements, there must be another reflective equilibrium, demonstrated in the previous chapter, where the understanding of ideals and institutions progress in unison and reinforce each other. Within this critical interaction between ideals and institutions one comes to recognize that the separation between theology and political construction posited by Metz is a mistake because theological ideals are empty without the development of historical projects. From the perspective of a reflective equilibrium, there is no strict divide between ideals and the projects, the former guides the latter, while the latter gives shape to the former. There is no need to find a special linkage because the link is already present when one starts to think through theological ideals. Unless one postulates the reflective equilibrium between ideals and institutions as part of theology proper, the construction of historical projects cannot get off the ground. Without it, the attempt to move beyond critique and concretely define theological ideals will fail. On this reflective equilibrium, see Francis Schussler Fiorenza, 'Systematic Theology: Tasks and Methods', *Systematic Theology: Roman Catholic Perspectives*, ed. Francis Schüssler Fiorenza and John Galvin (Minneapolis: Fortress Press, 1991), 70–85, and Francis Schüssler Fiorenza, *Foundational Theology: Jesus and the Church* (New York: Crossroad, 1984), ch. 11.

19 Hugo Assmann, *Teología Desde la Praxis de la Liberación* (Salamanca: Ediciones Sigueme, 1973), 91.

20 Johann Baptist Metz and Jürgen Moltmann, *Faith and the Future: Essays on Theology, Solidarity, and Modernity* (Maryknoll, NY: Orbis Books, 1995), 15.

21 Ibid., 115.

22 Note also that Metz's critique of idolatry is usually vaguely directed; that is, it rarely tackles a specific issue. In this way it is far less powerful than either Hinkelammert's or Sung's brand of such critique.

23 Metz and Moltmann, *Faith and the Future*, 24. In that statement Metz contradicts his own espousal of pure negative critique. In fact, his more recent work repeatedly contradicts his central concepts of negative critique and eschatological proviso. He has even come to write that 'for Christianity there is only one history, since to talk about two histories dualistically avoids the seriousness and risk of historical life' (Metz, *A Passion for God*, 37). Within such an understanding of history Metz should no longer be opposed to the construction of historical projects.

24 Cardinal Joseph Ratzinger relies on Catholic social teaching to link theology to the political sphere, yet the result is the same. The Vatican's 'Instruction on Christian Freedom and Liberation' stresses two main principles: the principle of solidarity by which human beings must contribute to the common good of society at its many levels and the principle of subsidiarity by which the state should never substitute for itself the initiative and responsibility that a smaller organization or individuals themselves can accomplish. But what do these principles concretely mean for the way society is organized? Ratzinger fails to realize that they are indeterminate; they can be developed institutionally in different directions with different consequences for society and lack definition until that development takes place. Ratzinger would claim that theology provides the background upon which the principles of a political ethic rest, the actual concretization of the principles is then taken up by politics. The actual vagueness of the theological vocabulary is first excused and then enshrined as good theology. Theology thus delimited remains, insofar as the goal is social liberation for the non-person, irrelevant. See also Joseph Ratzinger, *Church, Ecumenism and Politics: New Essays in Ecclesiology* (New York: Crossroads, 1988).

25 My argument also goes beyond Marsha Hewitt's Metz-like focus on negative critique. Drawing on the Adorno–Horkheimer–Benjamin critical theory tradition, she sees as a virtue the refusal to move beyond 'negative confrontation with the world as it is'. Such negative confrontation 'does not indulge in romantic programmatic speculations about what an alternative society will look like' (Marsha Hewitt, *Critical Theory of Religion: A Feminist Analysis*, Minneapolis: Fortress Press, 1995, x). Like Metz she

thinks that such a constructive move would deprive critical theory of its power for critique. Of course, I think she is mistaken and hope to have shown that the construction of historical projects need not be merely 'romantic'.

26 See Peter Scott, '"Global Capitalism" vs "End of Socialism": Crux Theologica? Engaging Liberation Theology and Theological Postliberalism', *Political Theology*, 4 (May 2001), 36–54, for the only comparison of radical orthodoxy and liberation theology to date.

27 For Milbank, see the foundational John Milbank, *Theology and Social Theory: Beyond Secular Reason* (Oxford: Blackwell, 1990). For a popular introduction to Hauerwas see Stanley Hauerwas and William Willimon, *Resident Aliens: Life in the Christian Colony* (Nashville: Abingdon Press, 1989); for his thoughts on liberation theology see Stanley Hauerwas, 'Some Theological Reflections on Gutiérrez's Use of 'Liberation' as a Theological Concept', *Modern Theology*, 3(1) (1986), 67–76; most recently, see Stanley Hauerwas, *A Better Hope: Resources for a Church Confronting Capitalism, Democracy, and Postmodernity* (Michigan: Brazos Press, 2000). For more work by their students that deals with liberation theology, see Daniel M. Bell Jr, *Liberation Theology After the End of History*; Stephen D. Long, *Divine Economy: Theology and the Market* (New York: Routledge, 2000) and William Cavanaugh, *Torture and Eucharist* (Oxford: Blackwell Publishers Ltd, 1998).

28 Daniel M. Bell Jr, *Liberation Theology After the End of History*, 9.

29 Ibid.

30 Ibid., 17.

31 Daniel M. Bell Jr, *Liberation Theology After the End of History*, 3. Bell here draws on Milbank's reading of Augustine. See Milbank on Augustine and desire, in Milbank, *Theology and Social Theory*, 400.

32 Daniel M. Bell Jr, *Liberation Theology After the End of History*, 72.

33 Ibid., 73.

34 Ibid.

35 Ibid., 72–3.

36 Bell remains unaware of liberation theology's move toward world system theory and its tendency to undertheorize capitalism. In both cases liberation theology often does depict capitalism's scope as ontological rather than merely economic. Witness Leonardo Boff: 'the dominant system today, which is the capitalist system ... has developed its own ways of collectively designing and constructing human subjectivity ... The capitalist and mercantile systems have succeeded in penetrating into every part of the personal and collective human mind. They have managed to decide the individual's way of life, the development of the emotions, the way in which an individual relates to his or her neighbors or strangers, a particular mode of love or friendship, and, indeed, the whole gamut of life and death' (Leonardo Boff, *Ecology and Liberation: A New Paradigm*, New York: Orbis Books, 1995, 33–4).

37 Daniel M. Bell Jr, *Liberation Theology After the End of History*, 83.

38 For a critique of political augustinianism from a liberationist perspective, see José-Míguez Bonino, 'Historical Praxis and Christian Identity', *Frontiers of Theology in Latin America*, ed. Rosino Gibellini (Maryknoll, NY: Orbis Books, 1983), 269–80.

39 For Milbank, 'a re-reading of the *Civitas Dei* will allow us to realize that political theology can take its critique, both of secular society and of the Church, directly out of the developing Biblical tradition, without recourse to any external supplementation' (Milbank, *Theology and Social Theory*, 389). See also pp.245–9, as well as the entirety of Chapter 12 ('The Other City: Theology as Social Science').

40 I agree with Milbank when he writes that 'the attempt to envision, as a sort of "general *topos*", a universally normative human society, may represent not so much a deduction from metaphysical or theological first principles, as rather an attempt to more exactly articulate or concretely envision *in what those principles consist*, such that one is not here talking about any merely secondary "entailment"'. Milbank, however, seems to think that this process can be done from within theology alone. Against liberation theology, he advocates a 'complex space' which he sees best explained in papal social teaching through concepts such as 'personalism, distributism, solidarism, subsidarity, household independence, free association and balance between the rural and urban environments'. At no point, however, does he

begin to explain 'in what those principles consist', which would require working out the possible shapes of their institutional realization. See John Milbank, *The Word Made Strange: Theology, Language, Culture* (Cambridge, MA: Blackwell Publishers, 1997), 270–71.

41 Milbank, *Theology and Social Theory*, 411.

42 Ibid., 422.

43 Daniel M. Bell Jr, *Liberation Theology After the End of History*, 128.

44 Ibid., 129.

45 Ibid., 187.

46 'The refusal to cease suffering' is the subtitle of Bell's book and the focus of its final chapter. See Daniel M. Bell Jr, *Liberation Theology After the End of History*, 193.

47 Daniel M. Bell Jr, *Liberation Theology After the End of History*, 195.

48 Ibid., 193.

49 For Black liberation theology, see the work of James Cone, Cornel West, Gayraud Wilmore, Victor Anderson and Dwight Hopkins; for Womanist theology, see the work of Delores Williams, Jacquelyn Grant, Cherly Townsend Gilkes and Emilie Townes; for Feminist liberation theology see the work of Elisabeth Schüssler Fiorenza, Marsha Hewitt, Mary Daly, Rosemary Radford Ruether and Susan Brooks Thistlethwaite; for Mujerista theology see the work of Ada Maria Isasi-Diaz; for Latina theology, see the work of Maria Pilar Aquino, for queer liberation theology, see the work of Marcella Althaus-Reid; and for Hispanic theology see the work of Virgilio Elizondo, Justo González, Fernando Segovia and Roberto Goizueta. This list is a small sample of representatives of each strand.

50 Maria Pilar Aquino, 'Latina Feminist Theology: Central Features', *A Reader in Latina Feminist Theology: Religion and Justice*, ed. Maria Pilar Aquino, Daisy Machado and Jeanette Rodriguez (Austin: University of Texas Press, 2002), 136.

51 Ibid., 139.

52 Ibid., 140.

53 Ibid.

54 Ibid., 144.

55 Ibid., 145.

56 Aquino, 149; original emphasis.

57 Aquino, 151.

58 See Aquino, 153–4.

59 Indeed, the middle class often seems to be the focus of Latina theology: 'Since the option for the poor arose within a Latin American context marked by a great disparity between the very rich and the very poor, the lacuna in U.S. discourse is located in the underdevelopment of an understanding and articulation of the role of those who find themselves in the middle. While there is no disputing the existence of a disparity in wealth, access, and resources between the very rich and the very poor, in the United States these represent extremes, with the majority of people falling economically somewhere between these two poles' (Carmen Marie Nanko, 'Justice Across the Border: The Preferential Option for the Poor in the United States', *A Reader in Latina Feminist Theology: Religion and Justice*, ed. Maria Pilar Aquino, Daisy Machado and Jeanette Rodriguez, Austin: University of Texas Press, 2002, 189).

60 According to Susan Brooks Thistlethwaite, 'a major roadblock to the emergence of liberation theology in the North American context is the failure of economic analysis to take hold [and] unless you do your economic homework, you can't pretend to be doing liberation theology': in Joerg Rieger (ed.), *Liberating the Future: God, Mammon and Theology* (Minneapolis, MN: Augsburg Press, 1998), 21 and 23. The problem, however, may run deeper. Economic analysis has taken hold among a small number of theologians – as the volume in which her essay is included attests – yet the analysis suffers from the problems I have sought to remedy in this book: vagueness, institutional fetishism, and the inability to make the move from critique to construction.

61 Aquino, 'Latina Feminist Theology', 151.

62 Cornel West, 'Black Theology and Marxist Thought,' *Black Theology: A Documentary History, Vol. I 1966–1979*, ed. James Cone and Gayraud Wilmore (Maryknoll, NY: Orbis Books, 1993) 413.

Similar critiques are emerging from within Latino theology itself. Benjamin Valentin has pointed out that Latino/a/Hispanic theologies have tended to restrict their discourse to the internal concerns and language of the churches. He also notes that the same theology has limited itself to issues of culture and identity to the exclusion of class and social politics. See Benjamin Valentin, 'Strangers No More: An Introduction to, and an Interpretation of, U.S. Hispanic/Latino/a Theology', *The Ties That Bind: African American and Hispanic American/Latino/a Theologies in Dialogue*, Anthony Pinn and Benjamin Valentin (eds) (New York: Continuum, 2001), 51–3. For an excellent critique of Roberto Goizueta of similar thrust see Manuel Mejido, 'A Critique of the "Aesthetic Turn" in U.S. Hispanic Theology: A Dialogue with Roberto Goizueta and the Positing of a New Paradigm', *Journal of Hispanic/Latino Theology*, 8(3) (2001), 18–48.

63 Cornel West, 'Black Theology of Liberation as Critique of Capitalist Civilization', *Black Theology, A Documentary History: Volume II 1980–1992*, ed. James Cone and Gayraud Wilmore (Maryknoll, NY: Orbis Books, 1993), 416.

64 Dwight Hopkins, *Heart and Head: Black Theology – Past, Present and Future* (New York: Palgrave, 2002), 62.

65 Dwight Hopkins, *Introducing Black Theology of Liberation* (Maryknoll, NY: Orbis Books, 1999), 46.

66 Hopkins, *Heart and Head*, 24.

67 Dwight Hopkins and Linda Thomas, 'Womanist Theology and Black Theology: Conversational Envisioning of an Unfinished Dream', *A Dream Unfinished: Theological Reflections on America from the Margins*, Eleazar Fernandez and Fernando Segovia (Maryknoll, NY: Orbis Books, 2001), 86.

68 Hopkins, *Heart and Head*, 61.

69 Ibid., 73.

70 Another example: 'Those living in poverty, therefore, should participate in the stewardship and ownership of the major economic corporations and commercial businesses and wealth – the land, everything built on it, and scientific innovation. To carry out such a new democracy requires reallocation of current political economic structures toward sharing ... To facilitate this process and spirit of liberation, major corporations and financial institutions would be used to help poor and working people to set up small and mediumsize businesses in their communities as another form of collective participation and healthy renewal for the common good. Economic democracy, the ethics of this stewardship, provides various ways of unleashing the creative potential of previously untapped people and ideas.' I sympathize with Hopkins' vision, but what institutional mechanisms will realize this intermediate goal? What will the the ownership structure of these enterprises look like?

One more: 'Because the majority of the U.S. population is made up of poor and working people, the elected officials (on national, regional, and local levels) should be chosen from among that group ... The reason that this does not happen today is because now the first criterion to be elected in the United States is to own, control, and monopolize wealth or have access to resources and money.' Obviously, however, the reasons why Hopkins' vision does not happen are more complex. There are all sorts of institutional mechanisms that impede the presentation of third party or independent candidates that would have to be addressed. (Hopkins, *Heart and Head*, 180 and 181.)

71 Hopkins, *Introducing Black Theology of Liberation*, 42–6.

72 Ibid., 45.

73 Dwight Hopkins, 'Black Theology and a Second Generation: New Scholarship and New Challenges', *Black Theology, A Documentary History: Volume II 1980–1992*, ed. James Cone and Gayraud Wilmore (Maryknoll, NY: Orbis Books, 1993), 64. See also Dwight Hopkins, *Shoes That Fit Our Feet* (Maryknoll, NY: Orbis Books, 1993), 215 as well as chs 4–5.

74 See Hopkins, *Shoes That Fit Our Feet*, 170–206. A more recent essay reviews Foucault and Cone as sources for a political vision, Foucault for his micro analysis of power relations and Cone for his macro analysis. But Cone is still too vague, and why this insistence on staying within Black theology? Why not turn to contemporary social theory? See Dwight Hopkins, 'Postmodernity, Black Theology of Liberation and the USA: Michel Foucault and James H. Cone', *Liberation Theologies, Postmodernity, and the*

Americas, ed. David Batstone, Eduardo Mendieta, Lois Ann Lorentzen and Dwight Hopkins (New York: Routledge, 1997), 205–21.

75 Hopkins, *Heart and Head*, 162.

76 Note my use of 'world-system' over 'world system'. I agree with Dussel's analysis of the origin and dating of the current world-system, which sees 1492 as its inaugural event, over Andre Gunder Frank's. Dussel's position is closest to James Blaut's. For Blaut, see James Blaut, *1492: The Debate on Colonialism, Eurocentrism and History* (Trenton, NJ: Africa World Press, 1992). For the argument over 'world system' versus 'world-system' between Frank, Immanuel Wallerstein and others, see Andre Gunder Frank and Barry Gills (ed.), *The World System: Five Hundred Years or Five Thousand?* (New York: Routledge, 1993).

77 This must be done, however, without theorizing capitalism as a monolithic entity encompassing the whole globe. This is a flaw in current versions of world-system and world system theory.

78 Georges Friedmann, *La Puissance de la Sagesse* (Paris: Gallimard, 1970), 359. Cited in Pierre Hadot, *Philosophy as a Way of Life* (Cambridge, MA: Blackwell, 1995), 81 as well as in other essays in the collection.

CHAPTER 7

Conclusion

Following Soren Kierkegaard's dictum that life can only be understood backwards but must be lived forwards, this work looks back at liberation theology's past the better to look forward toward its future. It makes two sets of contributions, one interpretative, one constructive. This book presents, for the first time, liberation theology's responses to the fall of socialism. It provides a new evaluation of liberation theology's methodology and its methodological impasse. It updates the study of liberation theology's understanding of democracy and highlights from a new angle the pitfalls with liberation theology's approach to capitalism. Finally, the argument of the work as a whole provides a new perspective on liberation theology's present. The presentation and interpretation of liberation theology's past and present, however, seeks to influence liberation theology's future. The interpretative moves undergird a constructive project that can and should be pursued in different directions: the reconstruction of liberation theology for the 21st century. I chose the path of reconstructing liberation theology around its original notion of a historical project, others may choose another.

Born with the promise of making theology itself liberative, liberation theology today remains unable to move beyond a mere discourse on liberation. The reconstruction of liberation theology developed in this work breaks through this impasse by placing the development of historical projects at the heart of liberation theology as theology. Such a placement, however, requires accepting four main elements of the constructive argument developed in this work. First, the recognition that liberation theology's incapacity to develop historical projects stems primarily from internal deficiencies rather than the shift in historical context. Second, the claim that the first internal deficiency lies in the way liberation theology has come to understand its status as theology. Liberation theology's methodological statements bless the incapacity to construct historical projects with the status of good theology. This inability must instead be seen as a failure to be overcome, while the construction of historical projects must be seen as an integral part of the theological task. Third, the claim that the second internal deficiency lies in liberation theology's approaches to capitalism. These approaches block rather than facilitate the development of historical projects. Instead, an approach to capitalism and society that opens rather than closes political and economic possibility is required. The fourth element lies in the presentation of such an approach. While I base my understanding of political and economic systems on Roberto Unger's social theory, the concrete shape of this element may vary. The element itself, however, is urgently needed.

Jorge Luis Borges once wrote: 'Nothing is built on stone, everything is built on sand, yet our duty is to build on the sand as if it were stone.'[1] Today, perhaps more than ever, Borges seems to be in the right. Liberation theology is caught in a world where misery is rampant and the 'end of history' as the end of institutional experiments to address that misery is jubilantly proclaimed. In such a context, liberation theology seems more sand than stone, as its distinctive mark – relating theological concepts and ideals to institutions in historical projects – slips through the cracks at the same time that its relevance as a theological and political movement seems on the wane.[2] For there to be sand, however, there must first be stone. And since liberation theologians are not lacking in duty or heroism, in the face of persecution and martyrdom, they will find stone underneath the sand. I hope this work may aid that task.

Notes

1 Jorge Luis Borges, *Obras Completas 1923–1972* (Buenos Aires: Emece Editores, 1974), 1012.

2 Christopher Rowland recently wrote of a meeting with an important liberation theologian who 'treated me to a very gloomy set of predictions about the future of the theology of liberation: "All that will be left of it in a few years time will be our books", he said. In some respects, even that now looks optimistic. If book sales offered an accurate guide to its continuing influence, the situation would seem to be rather hopeless. Whereas books on the subject might have been expected to sell a decade ago, there is little market for them now' (Christopher Rowland (ed.), *The Cambridge Companion to Liberation Theology*, Cambridge: Cambridge University Press, 1999, 249). In fairness to Rowland, he relates a different conversation with another theologian who stresses the continued vitality of the base communities for a more nuanced picture.

The Present and Future of Latin American Liberation Theology: a Manifesto in Eight Parts

1 Latin American Liberation Theology's Past

At its best, in its pursuit of a *material* and *social* liberation for the non-person, liberation theology had two interrelated parts, one directed toward the Christian tradition, the other directed toward society. The former included a rereading of Christianity from history's underside. This had three elements: first, the notion of God as a God of concrete bodily life; second, a unified anthropology that made the body the locus of salvation and thus food, drink and shelter part of God's plan for all people; and third, a unified understanding of history in which the history of salvation is the very heart of human history. These elements formed the theological background for concepts such as the 'preferential option for the poor' and 'liberation'. The latter part included the use of the social sciences; liberation theologians incorporated economics, political science and sociology as intrinsic elements in the theological enterprise. They did so for two reasons, one critical and one constructive. First, liberation theologians sought to better understand the causes of oppression. If the goal is liberation, then there is a need to discover the underlying causes of oppression. Second, to develop 'historical projects' to achieve liberation. If the goal is liberation, then there is a need to develop models of political and economic organization that could contribute effectively to that cause. These elements, the rereading of Christianity, the critical and constructive use of the social sciences, worked together in the pursuit of liberation.

2 Latin American Liberation Theology's Present

Today, liberation theology has abandoned the construction of historical projects. This central element of early liberation theology – indeed, the element which, according to liberation theologians themselves, made their theology distinctive and different from North Atlantic theology – lies forgotten, a mere historical curiosity. Yet the development of historical projects remains central to liberation theology for two reasons. First and foremost, it is at this level that liberation is most truly pursued. Liberation is not abstract, it is social and material. Second, without historical projects liberation theology's terminology remains vacuous. It is through the development of such projects that liberation theology gives specific content to its theological terminology; it is not clear what 'liberation' and the 'preferential option for the poor' mean in the absence of historical projects: witness that even the IMF uses this terminology. The upshot is a theology powerless to define and pursue its own ideals, a domesticated theology that talks about liberation rather than concretely pursuing liberation where it matters most to most people – in the economic and political structure of society.

3   The Causes of Latin American Liberation Theology's Present

There are three main causes at the root of liberation theology's domestication. One cause is the shift in context emblematized by the fall of the Berlin Wall. This cause is inescapable; the other two, however, are not. The second lies in the way liberation theology has come to understand its status as theology. Once attacked for being a pseudo-politics, liberation theology now stresses its proper theological nature by focusing on Scripture and tradition as its privileged sources. The construction of historical projects is thus pushed out of theology proper; it becomes an afterthought to the orthodox theological enterprise. Indeed, what is not part of theology cannot be asked of the theologian. The third cause is the way liberation theology has chosen to theorize capitalism. Capitalism is seen as an abstract, monolithic and all-encompassing entity that must be overcome wholesale. It is a monster that cannot be defeated, only heroically resisted. The upshot is that alternative forms of economic organization seem perpetually out of reach.

4   Latin American Liberation Theology and North American Liberation Theologies

The various North American liberation theologies share an inability to place real material liberation at the forefront of their task. They say they do, but they do not. In fact, they cannot. North American liberation theologies have made a middle class-focused identity politics their rallying cry. This is done in four ways: First, by emphasizing sources that safeguard theological orthodoxy and particular identities (Scripture, Black or Latina culture, the Black or Latino church, and so on); second, by excluding disciplines like political economy and legal theory from their theological sources; third, by failing to see that the benefits of a program of 'naming' or voice giving will benefit only the already well-to-do middle class unless tied to a wider program of social reconstruction.; finally, by failing to see that to develop such a program one must give at least the same emphasis to the construction of historical projects that one does to the preservation of theological and identity purity. The right question is not, what makes theology Black? Or what makes theology Latino? The right question remains, what will make theology liberative to the materially poor?

5   Latin American Liberation Theology and Modern Philosophy/Theology

Liberation theology provincializes North Atlantic philosophy and theology not merely to make room for a new theology, but to help make room for alternative models of political and economic organization. The demotion of North Atlantic philosophy and theology to one school among many is not about books or currents of thought, it is to do with helping the majority of humankind have a better life. Seeing North Atlantic philosophy and theology as pinnacles of global culture feeds into the belief that the societies that produce this culture have reached the highest modes of political and economic organization. If the Enlightenment is the release from immaturity, then Europe is the first mature region of the world. Today the United States would carry that mantle with Europe – the rest of us must watch, learn and emulate, until caught up. Thus presidential democracy as in the United States and parliamentary democracy as in Europe become models for the rest of the world; and capitalism as practiced in the United States and Europe become the end goal for societies not yet fully developed. Within this worldview other regions of the globe are condemned to walk a beaten path that has the North Atlantic models as their final destination. We are unable to pave a path or reach a destination of our own – our alternatives are blocked.

6   The Liberation Theologian, the Community and Historical Projects

It is a mistake to think that historical projects can emerge only from the grassroots and that the theologian must wait until they so emerge. This assumes that there is a divide between the theologian and the community with which he or she identifies; the theologian reads theologically a historical project that emerges first from the community. Instead, this divide must be rejected and overcome. The theologian must be seen as an integral part of the community and thus through his or her work may contribute to the possible emergence of historical projects within a neighborhood, a region, a nation, and even the globe. In the same way that the theologian learns from the encounter with a community, so too the community can learn from the visions the theologian develops through multiple sources. In the final analysis, it is not the theologian as theologian that carries out a potential historical project, it is the community and thus also the theologian as part of the community that makes change happen.

7   Liberation Theologies, Theological Education and the Theological Profession

Theologians today are unprepared to tackle the challenge posed by the non-person. They are unprepared because theological education is geared toward the preservation of Christian identity and thus discourages the interdisciplinary work needed to train a budding liberation theology. Of course, future liberation theologians need to be aware of their rich theological heritage, but they must also receive training in disciplines such as comparative political economy, social theory and legal theory. They must learn to use these tools if there is to be any hope of placing liberation at the forefront of the theological task. However, there is a further problem. The professional practice of the theologian also discourages interdisciplinary work. This is so because theology suffers from lack of self-confidence. Within the academy, theology is often seen as not truly 'academic', as not truly rigorous. This attack has forced the theologian to retrench and focus more minutely on traditional theological concerns. As long as the concerns are traditionally theological, the theologian feels safe from outside criticism, master of his or her territory. The theologian who ventures outward, however, is ostracized on both fronts. Non-theologians see him as a dilettante, while theologians are afraid that his foolishness will reveal the foolishness of the profession as a whole. Any theologian who leans too heavily on disciplines deemed non-theological becomes a threat to the survival of the profession. His work is then judged as non-theological and he becomes an outcast.

8   The Way Forward

The time for liberation theology to reinvent itself is now. This reinvention requires three elements. First, liberation theology must be wrested from the stranglehold of church and academy. Both church and academy domesticate it by constraining liberation theology within a limited and 'proper' definition of theology. Only by releasing itself from this stranglehold can liberation theology's necessarily interdisciplinary nature come forth. Second, liberation theology must recover politics on a grand scale and see identity politics as part of a larger project of social, political and economic reconstruction. At best, identity politics without such a project serves the inclusion of minority middle-class groups into mainstream society; at worst, it degenerates into a quarrel among academics. Third, liberation theology must cease thinking of capitalism as a monolithic whole. As long as it continues to do so, avenues for change are blocked and liberation theology remains nailed to a capitalist cross. Instead, liberation theology must theorize political and economic systems as partial, incomplete and open to piece-by-piece change. These are the building blocks for a 21st century liberation theology. Let us start now. There is no better time to work for the future than the present.

References

Adorno, T.W. 1978, *Minima Moralia: Reflections from damaged life*, trans. E.F.N. Jephcott, London: NLB, Verso Editions.

Adriance, M. 1994, 'Base Communities and Rural Mobilization in Northern Brazil', *Sociology of Religion*, 55: 163–78.

Agnew, J. 1982, 'Sociologizing the Geographical Imagination: Spatial Concepts in the World-System Perspective', *Political Geography Quarterly*, 1(2), April: 159–66.

Aguero, F. and J. Stark (eds) 1998, *Fault Lines of Democracy in Post-Transition Latin America*, Miami: North–South Center Press, University of Miami.

Albert, M. 1991, *Capitalisme contre capitalisme*, Paris: Seuil.

Althaus-Reid, M. 2000, 'Bien Sonados? The Future of Mystical Connections in Liberation Theology', *Political Theology: The Journal of Christian Socialism*, 3 (November): 44–63.

—— 2000, *Indecent Theology: Theological Perversions in Sex, Gender and Politics*, New York: Routledge.

Altman, A. 1986, 'Legal Realism, Critical Legal Studies, and Dworkin', *Philosophy & Public Affairs*, 15(3), Summer: 205–35.

—— 1990, *Critical Legal Studies: A Liberal Critique*, Princeton, NJ: Princeton University Press.

Alvarado, R. 1999, 'Teología de la Liberación en el Post-Socialismo', *Revista Latinoamericana de Teología*, 47 (May–August): 173–87.

Amin, A. 1996, 'Beyond Associative Democracy', *New Political Economy*, 1(3): 309–33.

Amsden, A. 1989, *Asia's Next Giant: South Korea and Late Industrialization*, New York: Oxford University Press.

—— 2001, *The Rise of the 'Rest': Challenges to the West from Late-Industrializing Economies*, Oxford: Oxford University Press.

Andelson, R. and J. Dawsey 1992, *From Wasteland to Promised Land: Liberation Theology for a Post-Marxist World*, Maryknoll, NY: Orbis Books.

Anderson, G.E. 1990, *The Three Worlds of Welfare Capitalism*, Princeton, NJ: Princeton University Press.

Aquino, M.P. 2002, 'Latina Feminist Theology: Central Features', in *A Reader in Latina Feminist Theology: Religion and Justice*, ed. M.P. Aquino, D. Machado and J. Rodriguez, Austin: University of Texas Press, 133–60.

Araujo, R.S. 1994, 'Political Theory and Liberation Theology: The Intersection of Unger and Gutiérrez', *The Journal of Law and Religion*, XI(1): 63–83.

Arroyo, G. 1968, 'Pensamiento latinoamericano sobre subdesarrollo y dependencia', *Mensaje* 17: 516–20.

—— 1972, 'Consideraciones sobre el subdesarrollo de América Latina', in *Fe cristiana y cambio social en América Latina*, Salamanca: Ediciones Sigueme, 323–4.

—— 1973, 'Pensamiento latinoamericano sobre subdesarollo y dependencia externa', in *Fe cristiana y cambio social en América Latina*, Salamanca: Ediciones Sigueme, 305–22.

Assmann, H. 1972, 'Prologue', in *Habla Fidel Castro sobre los Cristianos Revolucionarios*, ed. H. Assmann, Montevideo: Nueva Tierra.

—— 1973, *Teología desde la Praxis de la Liberación*, Salamanca: Ediciones Sigueme.

—— 1975, *Theology for a Nomad Church*, ed. P. Burns, Maryknoll, NY: Orbis Books.

—— 1994, 'Teología de la Liberación: Mirando hacia el Frente', *Pasos*, 55 (September–October): 1–9.

—— 1997, 'Apuntes sobre el tema del sujeto', in *Perfiles teológicos para un nuevo milenio*, ed. J. Duque, San José: DEI, 115–46.

—— 1997, *La Idolatría del mercado*, San José, Costa Rica: DEI.

Aurelius, M. 1945, *Meditations*, New York: Walter J. Black.

Bairoch, P. 1996, 'Globalization Myths and Realities: One Century of External Trade and Foreign Investment', in *States Against Markets: The Limits of Globalization*, ed. R. Boyer and D. Drache, New York: Routledge, 173–92.

Barnes, T. 1997, 'Theories of Accumulation and Regulation: Bringing Life Back into Economic Geography', in *Geographies of Economies*, ed. R. Lee and J. Wills, London: Arnold, 231–47.

Batstone, D., E. Mendieta, L.A. Lorentzen and D. Hopkins (eds) 1997, *Liberation Theologies, Postmodernity, and the Americas*, New York: Routledge.

Bell Jr, D.M. 1998, 'Men of Stone and Children of Struggle: Latin American Liberationists at the End of History', *Modern Theology*, 14(1), January: 113–41.

—— 2001, *Liberation Theology After the End of History: The Refusal to Cease Suffering*, London: Routledge.

Belli, H. and R. Nash 1992, *Beyond Liberation Theology*, Grand Rapids, Michigan: Baker Book House.

Berger, S. and R. Dore (eds) 1996, *National Diversity and Global Capitalism*, Ithaca: Cornell University Press.

Berger, S. and M. Piore 1980, *Dualism and Discontinuity in Industrial Societies*, Cambridge: Cambridge University Press.

Best, M. 1990, *The New Competition: Institutions of Industrial Restructuring*, Cambridge: Harvard University Press.

Betto, F. 1986, 'As CEBs e o Projeto Político Popular', *Revista Eclesiastica Brasileira*, 41(162), December.

—— 1990, 'A Teología da Libertação: Ruiu com o Muro de Berlim?', *Revista Eclesiastica Brasileira*, 50(200), December: 922–29.

—— 1990, 'El fracaso del socialismo Alemán y los desafios de la izquierda latinoamericana', *Pasos*, 29 (May–June): 1–7.

—— 1990, 'O socialismo morreu. Viva o socialismo!', *Revista Eclesiastica Brasileira*, 50(197), March: 173–76.

Blaut, J. 1992, *1492: The Debate on Colonialism, Eurocentrism and History*, Trenton, NJ: Africa World Press.

Block, F. 1990, *PostIndustrial Possibilities: A Critique of Economic Discourse*, Berkeley: University of California Press.

Blomstrom, M. and B. Hettne 1984, *Development Theory in Transition: The Dependency Debate and Beyond – Third World Responses*, London: Zed.

Boff, C. 1978, 'Comunidades Cristãs e Política Partidária', *Revista Eclesiastica Brasileira*, 38 (September).

—— 1987, *Theology and Praxis*, Maryknoll, NY: Orbis Books.

—— 1990, 'Epistemología y Método de la Teología de la Liberación', in *Mysterium Liberationis: Conceptos Fundamentales de la Teología de la Liberación*, ed. I. Ellacuría and J. Sobrino, Madrid: Editorial Trotta, 79–114.

—— 1993, 'Epistemology and Method of the Theology of Liberation', in *Mysterium Liberationis: Fundamental Concepts of Liberation Theology*, ed. I. Ellacuría and J. Sobrino, Maryknoll, NY: Orbis Books, 57–84.

—— 2000, 'Como veo yo la teología latinoamericana treinta años después', in *El mar se abrio: Treinta años de teología en América Latina*, ed. L.C. Susin, Santander: Sal Terrae, 74–90.

Boff, C., and L. Boff 1984, *Salvation and Liberation: In Search of a Balance between Faith and Politics*, Maryknoll, NY: Orbis Books.

—— 1987, *Introducing Liberation Theology*, Maryknoll, NY: Orbis Books.

Boff, L. 1979, *Liberating Grace*, Maryknoll, NY: Orbis Books.

—— 1981, *Jesus Christ Liberator: A Critical Christology for our Time*, Maryknoll: Orbis Books.

—— 1988, 'Liberation Theology: A Political Expression of Biblical Faith', *Christian Jewish Relations*, 21(1), Spring: 12–21.

—— 1988, 'Libertad y Liberación. Puntos de contacto y de fricción en el primer y tercer mundo', *Revista Latinoamericana de Teología*, 14 (May–August): 187–206.

—— 1990, 'A Implosão da Socialismo Autoritario e a Teología da Libertacao', *Revista Eclesiastica Brasileira*, 50(197), March: 76–92.

—— 1995, *Ecology and Liberation: A New Paradigm*, New York: Orbis Books.

—— 1997, *Cry of the Earth, Cry of the Poor*, ed. Phillip Berryman, Maryknoll, New York: Orbis Books.

Bonino, J.M. 1975, *Doing Theology in a Revolutionary Situation*, ed. W.H. Lazareth, Confrontation Books. Philadelphia: Fortress Press.

—— 1976, *Christians and Marxists: The mutual challenge to revolution*, Grand Rapids: William B. Eerdmans.

—— 1981, 'For Life and Against Death: A Theology that takes Sides', in *Theologians in Transition*, ed. J. Wall, New York: Crossroad, 169–76.

—— 1983, 'Historical Praxis and Christian Identity', in *Frontiers of Theology in Latin America*, ed. R. Gibellini, Maryknoll, NY: Orbis Books, 260–83.

—— 1983, *Toward a Christian Political Ethics*, Philadelphia: Fortress Press.

—— 2000, 'Reading Jürgen Moltmann from Latin America', *The Asbury Theological Journal*, 55(1), Spring: 105–14.

Borges, Jorge Luis 1974, *Obras Completas 1923–1972*, Buenos Aires: Emece Editores.

Boron, A. 1995, *State, Capitalism, and Democracy in Latin America*, London: Lynne Rienner Publishers.

Boyer, R. and D. Drache (eds) 1996, *States Against Markets: The Limits of Globalization*, New York: Routledge.

Bugaric, B. 1996, 'From Plan to Market: One Way or Alternative Paths – a Critique of Institutional Reforms in Central and Eastern Europe', University of Wisconsin, Madison.

—— 2001, 'Courts as Policy-Makers: Lessons from Transition', *Harvard Journal of International Law*, 42(1), Winter: 247–88.

Burns, P. 1992, 'The Problem of Socialism in Liberation Theology', *Theological Studies*, 53(3), September: 493–516.

Butler, J. 1990, *Gender Trouble: Feminism and the Subversion of Identity*, New York: Routledge.

—— 1994, 'Against Proper Objects', *Differences: A Journal of Feminist Cultural Studies*, 6 (Summer–Fall): 1–24.

Caffarena, J.G. 1993, 'Diálogos y Debates', in *Cambio social y pensamiento cristiano en América Latina*, ed. J. Comblin, J.I. González Faus and J. Sobrino, Madrid: Editorial Trotta, 327–41.

Cammack, P. 1997, *Capitalism and Democracy in the Third World: The Doctrine for Political Development*, London: Leicester University Press.

Cardoso, F. H. 1972, 'Dependent Capitalist Development in Latin America', *New Left Review*, 74 (July–August): 83–95.

—— 1973, 'Associated-Dependent Development: Theoretical and Practical Implications', in *Authoritarian Brazil: Origins, Policies, and Future*, ed. A. Stepan, New Haven: Yale University Press, 142–78.

Cardoso, F.H. and E. Faletto 1979, *Dependency and Development in Latin America*, Berkeley and Los Angeles: University of California Press.

Castro-Gomez, S. 1996, *Crítica de la Razón latinoamericana*, Barcelona: Puvill Libros, S.A.

Cavanaugh, W. 1998, *Torture and Eucharist*, Oxford: Blackwell Publishers.

Cerutti Guldberg, H. 1983, *Filosofia de la Liberación latinoamericana*, Mexico: Tierra Firme.

Chalmers, D. 1997, *The New Politics of Inequality in Latin America: Rethinking Participation and Representation*, Oxford: Oxford University Press.

Chase-Dunn, C. and P. Grimes 1995, 'World Systems Analysis', *Annual Review of Sociology*, 21: 387–417.

Chernow, B. and G. Vallasi (eds) 1993, *The Columbia Encyclopedia*, New York: Columbia University Press.

Chilcote, R. (ed.) 1982, *Dependency and Marxism: Toward a Resolution of the Debate*, Boulder, Colorado: Westview Press.

—— 1984, *Theories of Development and Underdevelopment*, Boulder, Colorado: Westview Press.

Chilcote, R. and J. Edelstein (eds) 1974, *Latin America: The Struggle with Dependency and Beyond*, New York: Halsted Press.

CNBB 1981, *Reflexão Cristã sobre a Conjuntura Política*, San Pablo: Edições Paulinas.

Cobian, R.A. 1973, 'Factores Económicos y fuerzas politicas en el proceso de Liberación', in *Fe cristiana y cambio social en América Latina*, Salamanca: Ediciones Sigueme, 33–55.

Codina, V. 1994, *Creo en el Espíritu Santo. Pneumetología narrativa*, Santander: Sal Terrae.

Comblin, J. 1979, *The Church and the National Security State*, Maryknoll NY: Orbis Books.

—— 1993, 'La Iglesia Latinoamericana desde Puebla a Santo Domingo', in *Cambio Social y Pensamiento Cristiano en América Latina*, ed. J. Comblin, J.I. González Faus and J. Sobrino, Madrid: Editorial Trotta, 29–56.

—— 1998, *Called for Freedom: The Changing Context of Liberation Theology*, ed. Phillip Berryman. Maryknoll, NY: Orbis Books.

Comblin, J., J.I. González Faus and J. Sobrino (eds) 1993, *Cambio Social y Pensamiento Cristiano en América Latina*, Madrid: Editorial Trotta.

Cooper, D. 1996, *World Philosophies: An Historical Introduction*, Cambridge, MA: Blackwell Publishers.

Crouch, C. and W. Streeck 1997, 'Introduction: The Future of Capitalist Diversity', in *Political Economy of Modern Capitalism: Mapping Convergence and Diversity*, ed. C. Crouch and W. Streeck, London: Sage Publications, 1–18.

Cui, Z. 1997, 'Privatization and the Consolidation of Democratic Regimes: An Analysis and an Alternative', *Journal of International Affairs*, 50(2), Winter: 675–92.

—— 1998, 'The Discourse on Property Rights in the Chinese Reform Context', *Social Text 55*, 16(2), Winter: 1–17.

De Schrijver, G. (ed.) 1998, *Liberation Theologies on Shifting Grounds: A Clash of Socio-Economic and Cultural Paradigms*, Louvain, Belgium: Leuven University Press.

de Tocqueville, A. 1954, *Democracy in America*, rev. edn, vol. 1, ed. F. Bowen and P. Bradley, New York: Vintage.

—— 1956, *Democracy in America*, rev. edn, vol. 2, ed. F. Bowen and P. Bradley, New York: Vintage.

Dewey, J. 1910, *The Influence of Darwin on Philosophy*, New York: Henry Holt and Company.

—— 1930, *Individualism Old and New*, New York: Milton, Balch & Company.

—— 1957, *Reconstruction in Philosophy*, enlarged edn, Boston: Beacon Press.

—— 1960, *The Quest for Certainty: A Study of the Relation of Knowledge and Action*, New York: Putnam's, Capricorn.

Diamond, L., J. Linz and S. Lipset (eds) 1988, *Democracy in Developing Countries, Volume 2*, London: Adamantine Press.

Diamond, L., M. Plattner, Y.-h. Chu and Tien-Hung-mao (eds) 1997, *Consolidating the Third Wave Democracies: Themes and Perspectives*, Baltimore: Johns Hopkins University Press.

Documento de los Teólogos Latinoamericanos: Segunda Asamblea General de la Asociación Ecuménica de Teólogos del Tercer Mundo. 1986, *Revista Latinoamericana de Teología*, 3 (September–December): 303–25.

Doremus, P., W. Keller, L. Pauly and S. Reich 1998, *The Myth of the Global Organization*, Princeton, NJ: Princeton University Press.

Dos Santos, T. 1998, 'The Theoretical Foundations of the Cardoso Government', *Latin American Perspectives*, 25(1), January: 53–70.

Ducatenzeiler, G. and P. Oxhorn (eds) 1998, *What Kind of Democracy? What Kind of Market? Latin America in the Age of Neoliberalism*, Philadelphia, Pennsylvania: Pennsylvania State University Press.

Duque, J. and G. Gutiérrez 2001, *Itinerarios de la Razón Crítica: Homenaje a Franz Hinkelammert en sus 70 Años*, San José: DEI.

Durkheim, E. 1964, *The division of labor in society*, trans. G. Simpson, New York: Free Press.

Dussel, E. 1969, *El Humanismo Semita*, Buenos Aires: Eudeba.

—— 1978, 'A Specious Alternative: The Third Way', in *The Church at the Crossroads*, Rome: IDOC.

—— 1978, *Ethics and the Theology of Liberation*, Maryknoll, NY: Orbis Books.

—— 1993, 'Theology of Liberation and Marxism', in *Mysterium Liberationis: Fundamental Concepts of Liberation Theology*, ed. I. Ellacuría and J. Sobrino, Maryknoll, NY: Orbis, 85–102.

—— 1995, *Teología de la Liberación: Un Panorama de su Desarrollo*, Ciudad de Mexico: Potrerillos Editores.

—— 1997, 'Transformaciones de los Supuestos Epistemológicos de la Teología de la Liberación', *Cuaderno de Teología*, XVI(1–2): 129–37.

—— 1998, *Ética de la Liberación en la edad de la Globalización y de la Exclusión*, Madrid: Editorial Trotta.

—— 1998, *The Underside of Modernity: Apel, Ricouer, Rorty, Taylor, and the Philosophy of Liberation*, E. Mendieta. New York: Humanity Books.

Dworkin, R. 1978, *Taking Rights Seriously*, Cambridge, MA: Harvard University Press.

Eagleson, J. (ed.) 1975, *Christians and Socialism: The Christians for Socialism Movement in Latin America*, Maryknoll, NY: Orbis Books.

Eagleton, T. 1996, *The Illusions of Postmodernity*, Oxford: Blackwell Publishers.

Ellacuría, I. 1993, 'Utopia and Prophecy in Latin America', in *Mysterium Liberationis: Fundamental Concepts of Liberation Theology*, ed. I. Ellacuría and J. Sobrino, Maryknoll, NY: Orbis Books, 289–327.

Ellacuría, I. and J. Sobrino (eds) 1993, *Mysterium Liberationis: Fundamental Concepts of Liberation Theology*, Maryknoll, NY: Orbis Books.

Escobar, A. 1995, *Encountering Development: The Making and Unmaking of the Third World*, Princeton, NJ: Princeton University Press.

Ethier, D. (ed.) 1990, *Democratic Transition and Consolidation in Southern Europe, Latin America and Southeast Asia*, London: Macmillan Press.

Evans, P. 1987, 'Class, State, and Dependence in East Asia: Lessons for Latin Americanists', in *The Political Economy of the New Asian Industrialism*, ed. F. Deyo, Ithaca: Cornell University Press, 203–26.

Faus, J.I.G. 1995, 'Una Tarea Histórica: De la Liberación a la Apocalíptica', *Revista Latinoamericana de Teología*, XII (September–December): 281–90.

—— 1997, 'Veinticinco Años de la Teología de la Liberación: Teología y Opción por los Pobres', *Revista Latinoamericana de Teología*, 42 (September–December): 223–42.

Fe Cristiana y Cambio Social en América Latina, 1973, Salamanca: Ediciones Sigueme.

Fiori, G. 1969, *Antonio Gramsci: Life of a Revolutionary*, London: NLB.

Flint, C. 1996, 'Structure, Agency, and Context: The Contributions of Geography to World Systems Analysis', *Sociological Inquiry*, 66(4), November: 496–508.

Forrester, D.B. 1994, 'Can Liberation Theology Survive 1989?', *Scottish Journal of Theology*, 47(2): 245–53.

Foucault, M. 1979, *Discipline and Punishment: The Birth of the Prison*, trans. A. Sheridan, New York: Random House, Vintage.

—— 1980, *Power/Knowledge: Selected Writings and other Interviews 1972–1977*, ed. C. Gordon, trans. C. Gordon, L. Marshal, J. Mepham and K. Soper, New York: Pantheon.

—— 1980, *The History of Sexuality*, vol. 1, *An introduction*, trans. R. Hurley, New York: Random House, Vintage.

Frank, A.G. 1966, 'The Development of Underdevelopment', *Monthly Review*, 18 (September): 17–31.

—— 1967, *Capitalism and Underdevelopment in Latin America: Historical Studies of Chile and Brazil*, New York: Monthly Review Press.

—— 1991, *The Underdevelopment of Development*, ed. F. Vivekananda, Series in International Political Economy, vol. 2, Stockholm: Bethany Books.

—— 1992, 'Latin American Development Theories Revisited: A Participant Review', *Latin American Perspectives*, 19(73), Spring: 125–39.

Frank, A.G. and B. Gills (eds) 1993, *The World System: Five Hundred Years or Five Thousand?*, New York: Routledge.

Freire, P. 1970, *Pedagogy of the oppressed*, trans. M.B. Ramos, New York: Seabury Press, Continuum.

Friedmann, G. 1970, *La Puissance de la sagesse*, Paris: Gallimard.

Fukuyama, F. 1989, 'The End of History', *The National Interest*, Summer: 3–18.

—— 1992, *The End of History and the Last Man*, New York: Free Press.

Fuss, D. 1989, *Essentially Speaking: Feminism, nature, and difference*, New York: Routledge.

Galeano, A. 1998, 'Desafios de la Postmodernidad a la Teología en América Latina', *Cristianismo y Sociedad*, 137: 67–85.

Gallardo, H. 1994, 'La Teología de la Liberación como pensamiento latinoamericano', *Pasos*, 56 (November–December): 12–22.

Garrett, W. 1988, 'Liberation Theology and Dependency Theory', in *The Politics of Latin American Liberation Theology: The Challenge to U.S. Public Policy*, ed. R. Rubenstein and J. Roth, Washington, DC: Washington Institute Press, 174–98.

Geffre, C. and G. Gutiérrez (eds) 1974, *The Mystical and Political Dimension of the Christian Faith*, New York: Herder and Herder.

Gerschenkron, A. 1962, *Economic Backwardness in Historical Perspective*, Cambridge: Harvard University Press.

Gibson-Graham, J. 1996, *The End of Capitalism (as we knew it): A Feminist Critique of Political Economy*, Cambridge: Blackwell Publishers.

—— 1997, 'Re-Placing Class in Economic Geographies: Possibilities for a New Class Politics', in *Geographies of Economies*, ed. R. Lee and J. Wills, London: Arnold, 87–97.

Goizueta, R. 1988, *Liberation, Method and Dialogue – Enrique Dussel and North American Philosophical Discourse*, Atlanta: American Academy of Religion, Scholars Press.

Goldblatt, D., D. Held, A. McGrew and J. Perraton 1999, *Global Transformations: Politics, Economics and Culture*, Stanford: Stanford University Press.

Gorostiaga, X. 1993, 'La Mediación de las Ciencias Sociales', in *Cambio Social y Pensamiento Cristiano en América Latina*, ed. J. Comblin, J.I. González Faus and J. Sobrino, Madrid: Editorial Trotta, 123–44.

Gorz, A. 1964, *Strategy for Labor*, Boston: Beacon Press.

Gracio das Neves, R.M. 1998, 'Neoliberalismo, Teología de la Liberación y Nuevos Paradigmas', *Alternativas*, 9: 57–96.

Graham, J. 1991, 'Post-Fordism as Politics: The Political Consequences of Narratives on the Left', *Environment and Planning D: Society and Space*, 10: 393–410.

Greenfeld, L. 2001, *The Spirit of Capitalism: Nationalism and Economic Growth*, Cambridge, MA: Harvard University Press.

Gremillion, J. (ed.) 1976, *The Gospel of Peace and Justice: Catholic Social Teaching Since Pope John*, Maryknoll, NY: Orbis Books.

Grey, T. 1980, 'The Disintegration of Property', *Nomos*, XXII: 69–86.

Groenwegen, J. 1997, 'Institutions of Capitalisms: American, European and Japanese Systems Compared', *Journal of Economic Issues*, XXXI(2), June: 333–47.

Gutiérrez, G. 1973, *A theology of liberation: History, politics and salvation*, trans. and ed. S.C. Inda and J. Eagleson, Maryknoll, NY: Orbis.

—— 1974, 'Liberation, Theology and Proclamation', in *The Mystical and Political Dimension of the Christian Faith*, ed. C. Geffre and G. Gutiérrez, New York: Herder and Herder, 57–77.

—— 1974, *Praxis de Liberación y Fe Cristiana*, Madrid: Zero.

—— 1977, *Teología desde el reverso de la historia*, Lima, Peru: Ed. CEP.

—— 1979, *La Fuerza Histórica de los Pobres*, Lima: Centro de Estudios y Publicaciones.

—— 1983, *The Power of the Poor in History*, Maryknoll, NY: Orbis Books.

—— 1985, *A Theology of Liberation: History, Politics and Salvation*, ed. C. Inda and J. Eagleson, Maryknoll, NY: Orbis Books.

—— 1986, 'Teología y Ciencias Sociales', in *La verdad los hara libres*, Lima: CEP, 75–112.

—— 1988, 'Expanding the View', in *Expanding the View: Gustavo Gutiérrez and the Future of Liberation Theology*, ed. M. Ellis and O. Maduro, Maryknoll, NY: Orbis Books, 3–38.

—— 1990, *The Truth Shall Make You Free*, Maryknoll, NY: Orbis Books.

—— 1991, *The God of Life*, Maryknoll, NY: Orbis Books.

—— 1994, 'La Teología: Una Función Eclesial', *Páginas*, XIX(130), December: 10–17.

—— 1995, 'Renovar "la opción por los pobres"', *Revista Latinoamericana de Teología*, 36 (September–December): 269–90.

—— 1996, 'Una Teología de la Liberación en el Contexto del Tercer Milenio', in *El Futuro de la Reflexion Teologica en América Latina*, Bogota, Colombia: CELAM, 97–166.

Gwynne, R. and C. Kay 1999, *Latin America Transformed: Globalization and Modernity*, London: Arnold.

Habermas, J. 1987, *The Philosophical Discourse of Modernity: Twelve Lectures*, trans. F. Lawrence, Studies in Contemporary German Social Thought, Cambridge, Massachusetts: MIT Press.

—— 1996, *Between Facts and Norms*, Cambridge, MA: MIT Press.

Hadot, P. 1995, *Philosophy as a Way of Life*, Cambridge, MA: Blackwell.

Haggard, S. 1990, *Pathways from the Periphery: The Politics of Growth in the Newly Industrializing Economies*, Ithaca: Cornell University Press.

Hale, R. 1923, 'Coercion and Distribution in a Supposedly Non-Coercive State', *Political Science Quarterly*, 38(470).

Hall, P. 1997, 'The Political Economy of Adjustment in Germany', in *Okonomische Leistungsfahigkeit und Institutionelle Innovation: Das deutsche Produktions und Politikregime im globalen Wettbewerb*, ed. F. Naschold, D. Soskice and B. Hancke, WZB-Jahrbuch, 293–317.

—— 1999, 'The Political Economy of Europe in an Era of Interdependence', in *Continuity and Change in Contemporary Capitalism*, ed. H. Kitschelt, P. Lange, G. Marks and J. Stephens, Cambridge: Cambridge University Press, 135–63.

—— 2001, 'The Evolution of Economic Policy in the European Union', in *From the Nation-State to the European Union*, ed. A. Menon and V. Wright, Oxford: Oxford University Press.

Hall, P. and D. Soskice (eds) 2001, *Capitalism: The Institutional Foundations of Comparative Advantage*, Oxford: Oxford University Press.

Hall, T. 1996, 'The World System Perspective: A Small Sample from a Large Universe', *Sociological Inquiry*, 66(4), November: 440–54.

Hauerwas, S. 1986, 'Some Theological Reflections on Gutiérrez's Use of "Liberation" as a Theological Concept', *Modern Theology*, 3(1): 67–76.

—— 2000, *A Better Hope: Resources for a Church Confronting Capitalism, Democracy, and Postmodernity*, Michigan: Brazos Press.

Hauerwas, S. and W. Willimon 1989, *Resident Aliens: Life in the Christian Colony*, Nashville: Abingdon Press.

Hawthorn, G. 1991, *Plausible Worlds: Possibility and Understanding in History and the Social Sciences*, Cambridge: Cambridge University Press.

Hegel, G.W.F. 1956, *The Philosophy of History*, Preface by C. Hegel, trans. and preface by J. Sibree, introduction by E.J. Friedrich, New York: Dover.

Held, D. 1987, *Models of Democracy*, Stanford, CA: Stanford University Press.

Hennelly, A. 1979, *Theologies in Conflict: The Challenge of Juan Luis Segundo*, Maryknoll, NY: Orbis Books.

Hennelly A.T. 1990, *Liberation Theology: A Documentary History*, Maryknoll, NY: Orbis Books.

Hewitt, M. 1990, *From Theology to Social Theory: Juan Luis Segundo and the Theology of Liberation*, New York: Peter Lang.

—— 1992, 'Liberation Theology and the Emancipation of Religion', *The Scottish Journal of Religious Studies*, XIII(1), Spring: 21–38.

—— 1995, *Critical Theory of Religion: A Feminist Analysis*, Minneapolis: Fortress Press.

Hewitt, W. 1991, *Base Christian Communities and Social Change in Brazil*, Lincoln: University of Nebraska Press.

Hinkelammert, F. 1981, 'Socialdemocracia y Democracia Cristiana: Las Reformas y las Limitaciones', in *El Juego de los Reformismos frente a la Revolución en Centroamerica*, ed. H. Assmann, San José: DEI.

—— 1986, *The Ideological Weapons of Death: A Theological Critique of Capitalism*, Maryknoll, NY: Orbis Books.

—— 1990, *Crítica a la Razón Utópica*, San José: DEI.

—— 1990, 'Democracia y nueva derecha en América Latina', in *Ecuador: Coyuntura Politica*, Quito: CEDEP, 71–92.

—— 1990, *Democracia y Totalitarismo*, San José: DEI.

—— 1990, 'La Crítica de la religion en nombre del cristianismo: Dietrich Bonhoeffer', in *Teología Alemána y Teología latinoamericana de la Liberación: Un esfuerzo de Diálogo*, San José: DEI, 45–66.

—— 1993, 'Capitalismo y Socialismo: La Posibilidad de Alternativas', *Pasos*, 48 (July–August): 10–15.

—— 1993, 'Determinación y Autoconstitución del Sujeto: Las Leyes que se Imponen a Espaldas de los Actores y el Orden por el Desorden', *Pasos*, 64 (March–April): 18–31.

—— 1994, 'Changes in the Relationships Between Third World and First World Countries', in *Spirituality of the Third World*, ed. K. Abraham and B. Mbuy-Beya, Maryknoll, NY: Orbis.

—— 1995, *Cultura de la esperanza y sociedad sin exclusión*, San José, Costa Rica: DEI.

—— 1997, 'Liberation Theology in the Economic and Social Context of Latin America: Economy and Theology, or the Irrationality of the Rationalized', in *Liberation Theologies, Postmodernity, and the Americas*, ed. D. Batstone, E. Mendieta, L.A. Lorenzten and D.N. Hopkins, New York: Routledge, 25–52.

—— (ed.) 1999, *El Huracán de la Globalización*, San José: DEI.

Hirst, P. and J. Zeitlin 1992, 'Flexible Specialization Versus Post-Fordism: Theory, evidence, and policy implications', in *Pathways to Industrialization and Regional Development*, ed. M. Storper and A. Scott, New York: Routledge, 70–115.

Hodgson, G. 1998, 'Varieties of Capitalism and Varieties of Economic Theory', in *Institutions and Economic Change: New Perspectives on Markets, Firms, and Technology*, ed. B. Johnson, Nielsen, and Klaus, Cheltenham, UK: Edward Elgar Publishing Ltd, 215–42.

—— 1999, *Economics and Utopia: Why the learning economy is not the end of history*, London: Routledge.

Hohfeld, W. 1913, 'Some Fundamental Legal Conceptions as Applied in Judicial Reasoning', *Yale Law Journal*, 23: 28–59.

Hollenbach, D. 1992, 'Christian Social Ethics after the Cold War', *Theological Studies*, 53(1), March: 75–95.

Holmes, S. 1993, *An Anatomy of Anti-Liberalism*, Cambridge: Harvard University Press.

Hopkins, D. 1993, 'Black Theology and a Second Generation: New Scholarship and New Challenges', in *Black Theology, A Documentary History: Volume II 1980–1992*, ed. J. Cone and G. Wilmore, Maryknoll, NY: Orbis Books, 61–75.

—— 1993, *Shoes that Fit Our Feet*, Maryknoll, NY: Orbis Books.

—— 1997, 'Postmodernity, Black Theology of Liberation and the USA: Michel Foucault and James H. Cone', in *Liberation Theologies, Postmodernity, and the Americas*, ed. D. Batstone, E. Mendieta, L.A. Lorentzen and D. Hopkins, New York: Routledge, 205–21.

—— 1999, *Introducing Black Theology of Liberation*, Maryknoll, NY: Orbis Books.

—— 2002, *Heart and Head: Black Theology – Past, Present and Future*, New York: Palgrave.

Hopkins, D. and L. Thomas 2001, 'Womanist Theology and Black Theology: Conversational Envisioning of an Unfinished Dream', in *A Dream Unfinished: Theological Reflections on America from the Margins*, ed. E. Fernandez and F. Segovia, Maryknoll, NY: Orbis Books, 72–86.

Hopkins, T., I. Wallerstein *et al.* 1982, *World Systems Analysis: Theory and Methodology*, Beverly Hills: Sage.

Horwitz, M. 1992, *The Transformation of American Law, 1870–1960: The Crisis of Legal Orthodoxy*, Oxford: Oxford University Press.

Hout, W. 1993, *Capitalism and the Third World: Development, Dependence and the World System*, Aldershot: Edward Elgar Publishing Limited.

Human Development Report 1998, 1998, United Nations Development Programme.

Huntington, S. 1968, *Political Order in Changing Societies*, New Haven: Yale University Press.

—— 1984, 'Will more countries become democratic?', *Political Science Quarterly*, 99(2): 193–218.

—— 1989, 'The Modest Meaning of Democracy', in *Democracy in the Americas: Stopping the Pendulum*, ed. R.A. Pastor, New York: Holmes & Meier, 11–28.

—— 1991, *The Third Wave: Democratization in the Late Twentieth Century*, Norman: University of Oklahoma Press.

Hutchinson, A. and P. Monahan 1984, 'Law, Politics, and the Critical Legal Scholars: The Unfolding Drama of American Legal Thought', *Stanford Law Review*, 36.

Irarrazaval, D. 1996, 'Nuevas Rutas de la Teología Latinoamericana', *Revista Latinoamericana de Teología*, 38 (May–August): 183–97.

Kant, I. 1949, 'What is Enlightenment?', in *The Philosophy of Kant: Moral and Political Writings*, ed. C. Friedrich, New York: The Modern Library, 132–39.

Kaufman, G. 1993, *In Face of Mystery: A Constructive Theology*, Cambridge: Harvard University Press.

Kay, C. 1989, *Latin American Theories of Development and Underdevelopment*, New York: Routledge.

—— 1990, 'Reflections on the Latin American Contribution to Development Theory', CDS occasional paper no.7, Centre for Development Studies: University of Glasgow.

—— 1993, 'For a Renewal of Development Studies: Latin American Theories and Neoliberalism in the Era of Structural Adjustment', *Third World Quarterly*, 14(4): 691–702.

Kee, A. 1990, *Marx and the Failure of Liberation Theology*, Philadelphia, PA: Trinity Press International.

—— 2000, 'The Conservatism of Liberation Theology: Four Questions for Jon Sobrino', *Political Theology: The Journal of Christian Socialism*, 3 (November): 30–43.

Kennedy, D. 1993, *Sexy Dressing Etc.: Essays on the Power and Politics of Cultural Identity*, Cambridge, MA: Harvard University Press.

—— 1997, *A Critique of Adjudication*, Cambridge, MA: Harvard University Press.

Kiely, R. 1995, *Sociology and Development: The impasse and beyond*, London: UCL Press Limited.

—— 1998, *Industrialization and Development: A comparative analysis*, London: UCL Press Limited.

Kitschelt, H., P. Lange, G. Marks and J. Stephens 1999, 'Convergence and Divergence in Advanced Capitalist Democracies', in *Continuity and Change in Contemporary Capitalism*, ed. H. Kitschelt, P. Lange, G. Marks and J. Stephens, Cambridge: Cambridge University Press, 427–60.

Klare, K. 1994, 'Legal Theory and Democratic Reconstruction: Reflections on 1989', in *A Fourth Way? Privatization, Property, and the Emergence of New Market Economies*, ed. G. Alexander and G. Skapska, New York: Routledge, 310–33.

Kochuthara, T. 1993, *Theology of Liberation and Ideology Critique: A Study on the Praxis of Liberation in the Light of Critical Theory*, New Delhi: Intercultural Publications.

Kosofsky Sedgwick, E. 1990, *Epistemology of the Closet*, Berkeley and Los Angeles: University of California Press.

—— 1993, *Tendencies*, Durham: Duke University Press.

Krischke, P. 1991, 'Church Base Communities and Democratic Change in Brazilian Society', *Comparative Political Studies*, 24: 186–210.

Kronman, A. 1993, *The Lost Lawyer: Failing Ideals of the Legal Profession*, Cambridge, MA: Harvard University Press.

Laclau, E. 1990, *New Reflections on the Revolution of Our Time*, New York: Verso.

Laclau, E. and C. Mouffe 1985, *Hegemony and Socialist Strategy: Towards a Radical Democratic Politics*, New York: Verso.

Langdell, C. 1879, *A Selection of Cases on the Law of Contracts: With a summary of the topics covered by the cases*, Boston: Little, Brown.

—— 1880, *Summary of the Law of Contracts*, Boston: Little, Brown.

Larrain, J. 1989, *Theories of Development: Capitalism, Colonialism and Dependency*, Cambridge: Polity Press.

Leftwich, A. 1998, 'Forms of the Democratic Developmental State: Democratic Practices and Developmental Capacity', in *The Democratic Developmental State: Politics and Institutional Design*, ed. M. Robinson and G. White, Oxford: Oxford University Press, 52–83.

Lehmann, D. 1990, *Democracy and Development in Latin America: Economics, Politics and Religion in the Post-War Period*, Philadelphia: Temple University Press.

Levine, D. 1981, *Religion and Politics in Latin America*, Princeton, NJ: Princeton University Press.

—— (ed.) 1986, *Religion and Political Conflict in Latin America*, Chapel Hill: University of North Carolina Press.

Libânio, J.B. 1989, *Teología de la Liberación: Guia didactica para su estudio*, Santander: Sal Terrae.

—— 1993, 'Panorama de la Teología de América Latina en los ultimos veinte años', in *Cambio social y pensamiento cristiano en América Latina*, ed. J. Comblin, J. González Faul and J. Sobrino, Madrid: Editorial Trotta, 57–78.

Linden, I. 2000, 'Liberation Theology: Coming of Age?', *Political Theology: The Journal of Christian Socialism*, 3 (November): 11–29.

Linz, J. 1996, *Problems of Democratic Transition and Consolidation: Southern Europe, South America, and Postcommunist Europe*, Baltimore: Johns Hopkins University Press.

Linz, J. and A. Valenzuela 1994, *The Failure of Presidential Democracy*, Baltimore: Johns Hopkins University Press.

Long, S.D. 2000, *Divine Economy: Theology and the market*, NY: Routledge.

Lothian, T. 1995, 'The Democratized Market Economy in Latin America (and elsewhere): An Exercise in Institutional Thinking Within Law and Economy', *Cornell International Law Journal*, 28(1), Winter: 169–217.

Love, J. 1980, 'Raul Prebisch and the Origins of the Doctrine of Unequal Exchange', *Latin American Research Review*, 15(3): 45–72.

—— 1990, 'The Origins of Dependency Analysis', *Journal of Latin American Studies*, 22(1): 143–68.

Lovin, R. and M. Perry (eds) 1990, *Critique and Construction: A Symposium on Roberto Unger's Politics*, Cambridge: Cambridge University Press.

Löwy, M. 1996, *The War of Gods: Religion and Politics in Latin America*, New York: Verso.

Lynch, E.A. 1994, 'Beyond Liberation Theology?', *Journal of Interdisciplinary Studies*, 6(1–2): 147–64.

Maclean, I. 1998, 'Participatory Democracy – the Case of the Brazilian Ecclesial Base Communties: 1981–1991', *Religion and Theology*, 5(1).

—— 1999, *Opting for Democracy: Liberation Theology and the Struggle for Democracy in Brazil*, New York: Peter Lang.

Maduro, O. 1987, 'Christian Democracy and the Choice in Latin American Catholicism of Liberating the Oppressed', *Concilium*, 5.

Mainwaring, S. 1986, *The Catholic Church and Politics in Brazil: 1916–1985*, Stanford: Stanford University Press.

Mainwaring, S. and A. Valenzuela (eds) 1998, *Politics, Society, and Democracy*, Boulder, Colorado: Westview Press.

Mainwaring, S. and A. Wilde (eds), 1989, *The Progressive Church in Latin America*, Notre Dame, IN: University of Notre Dame Press.

Maritain, J. 1968, *Integral Humanism: Temporal and spiritual problems of a new Christendom*, New York: Charles Scribner's Sons.

Marx, K. 1955, *The Class Struggles in France*, New York: International Publishers.

—— 1966, *The Eighteenth Brumaire of Louis Bonaparte*, New York: International Publishers.

—— 1974, *The Karl Marx library*, vol. 5, *On religion*, ed. and trans. S. Padover, New York: McGraw-Hill.

Mathews, S. 1931, *The Growth of the Idea of God*, New York: The Macmillan Company.

—— 1971, *Jesus on Social Institutions*, ed. and introd. Kenneth Cauthen, 'Lives of Jesus', Philadelphia: Fortress Press.

McGovern, A. 1987, 'Latin America and Dependency Theory', in *Liberation Theology and the Liberal Society*, Washington DC: American Enterprise Institute, 106–32.

—— 1988, 'Dependency Theory, Marxist Analysis, and Liberation Theology', in *Expanding the View: Gustavo Gutiérrez and the Future of Liberation Theology*, ed. M. Ellis and O. Maduro, Maryknoll, NY: Orbis Books, 77–93.

—— 1989, *Liberation Theology and its Critics: Toward an Assessment*, Maryknoll, NY: Orbis Books.

Mejido, M. 2001, 'A Critique of the "Aesthetic Turn" in U.S. Hispanic Theology: A Dialogue with Roberto Goizueta and the Positing of a New Paradigm', *Journal of Hispanic/Latino Theology*, 8(3): 18–48.

Metz, J.B. 1969, *Theology of the World*, New York: Herder and Herder.

—— 1975, 'Political Theology', in *Encylopedia of Theology*, ed. K. Rahner, New York: Seabury Press, 1238–43.

—— 1998, *A Passion for God: The Mystical-Political Dimension of Christianity*, New York: Paulist Press.

Metz, J.B. and J. Moltmann 1995, *Faith and the Future: Essays on theology, solidarity, and modernity*, Maryknoll, NY: Orbis Books.

Milbank, J. 1990, *Theology and Social Theory: Beyond Secular Reason*, Oxford: Blackwell.

—— 1997, *The Word Made Strange: Theology, Language, Culture*, Cambridge, MA: Blackwell Publishers.

Mishra, R. 1999, *Globalization and the Welfare State*, Cheltenham: Edward Elgar Publishing Limited.

Moltmann, J. 1967, *Theology of hope: On the ground and the implications of a Christian eschatology*, trans. J.W. Leitch, New York: Harper and Row, Harper Torchbooks/Library.

—— 1974, *The crucified God: The cross of Christ as the foundation and criticism of Christian theology*, trans. R.A. Wilson and J. Bowden, New York: Harper and Row.

—— 1977, *The church in the power of the spirit: A contribution to Messianic ecclesiology*, New York: Harper and Row.

—— 1990, 'An Open Letter to José Míguez Bonino', in *Liberation Theology: A Documentary History*, ed. A. Hennelly, Maryknoll, NY: Orbis Books, 195–204.

Moreno Menendez, A. 1999, *Political Cleavages: Issues, parties and the consolidation of democracy*, Boulder, Colorado: Westview Press.

Mouffe, C. (ed.) 1996, *Deconstruction and Pragmatism*, New York: Routledge.

Nanko, C.M. 2002, 'Justice Across the Border: The Preferential Option for the Poor in the United States', in *A Reader in Latina Feminist Theology: Religion and*

Justice, ed. M.P. Aquino, D. Machado and J. Rodriguez, Austin: University of Texas Press, 177–203.

Novak, M. 1984, *Freedom with Justice: Catholic Social Thought and Liberal Institutions*, San Francisco: Harper and Row.

—— (ed.) 1987, *Liberation Theology and the Liberal Society*, Washington, DC: American Enterprise Institute.

—— 1991, *Will it Liberate? Questions about Liberation Theology*, Lanham, Maryland: Madison Books.

Nun, J. 2000, *Democracia: Gobierno del pueblo o gobierno de los políticos?*, Buenos Aires: Fondo de Cultura Economica.

O'Donnell, G. 1994, 'Delegative Democracy', *Journal of Democracy*, 5(1), January: 55–69.

O'Donnell, G. and P. Schmitter 1986, *Transitions from Authoritarian Rule: Tentative Conclusions About Uncertain Democracies*, Baltimore: Johns Hopkins University Press.

Oman, C. and G. Wignaraja 1991, *The Postwar Evolution of Development Thinking*, London: Macmillan Academic and Professional LTD.

Oxhorn, P. and P. Starr (eds) 1999, *Markets and Democracy in Latin America: Conflict or Convergence?*, London: Lynne Rienner Publishers.

Palma, G. 1978, 'Dependency: A Formal Theory of Underdevelopment or a Methodology for the Analysis of Concrete Situations of Underdevelopment?', *World Development*, 6: 881–924.

Peeler, J. 1998, *Building Democracy in Latin America*, London: Lynne Rienner Publishers.

Peet, R. and E. Hartwick 1999, *Theories of Development*, New York: The Guilford Press.

Petrella, I. 2000, 'Liberation Theology and Democracy: Toward a New Historical Project', *Journal of Hispanic/Latino Theology*, 7(4), May: 50–67.

—— 2002, 'Latin American Liberation Theology, Globalization, and Historical Projects: From Critique to Construction', in *Latin American Perspectives on Globalization: Ethics, Politics, and Alternative Visions*, ed. M. Saenz, Lanham, MD: Rowman and Littlefield Publishers.

Phan, P. 2000, 'Method in Liberation Theologies', *Theological Studies*, 61(1): 40–63.

Piore, M. and C. Sabel 1984, *The Second Industrial Divide: Possibilities for Prosperity*, New York: Basic Books.

Pottenger, J. 1989, *The Political Theory of Liberation Theology: Toward a Reconvergence of Social Values and Social Science*, Albany, NY: State University of New York Press, Albany.

Putnam, R. 1993, *Making Democracy Work: Civic Traditions in Modern Italy*, Princeton: Princeton University Press.

Ratzinger, J. 1988, *Church, Ecumenism and Politics: New Essays in Ecclesiology*, New York: Crossroads.

—— 1997, 'Relación sobre la Situación Actual de la Fe y la Teología', in *Fe y Teología en América Latina*, Santa Fe de Bogota, Colombia: CELAM, 13–36.

Rauschenbusch, W. 1907, *Christianity and the Social Crisis*, New York: Macmillan Co.

—— 1912, *Christianizing the Social Order*, Boston: The Pilgrim Press.

—— 1945, *A Theology for the Social Gospel*, Nashville: Abingdon Press.

Razeto, L. 1986, *Economía popular de solidaridad*, Santiago: Area pastoral social de la conferencia episcopal de Chile.

—— 1994, *Crítica de la economía, mercado democratico y crecimiento*, Santiago: Programa de Economía del trabajo.

Resnick, S. and R. Wolff 1987, *Knowledge and Class: A Marxian Critique of Political Economy*, Chicago: University of Chicago Press.

Richard, P. 1987, 'The Political Organization of Christians in Latin America', *Concilium*, 5.

—— 1995, 'Caos o esperanza. Fundamentos y alternativas para el siglo XXI', *Diakonia*, 74 (June): 59–67.

—— 1999, 'Teología de la solidaridad en el contexto actual de economía neoliberal de mercado', in *El Huracán de la Globalización*, ed. F. Hinkelammert, San José, Costa Rica: DEI, 223–38.

Richard, P. *et al.* 1983, *The Idols of Death and the God of Life*, Mayknoll, New York: Orbis Books.

Rieger, J. (ed.) 1998, *Liberating the Future: God, Mammon and Theology*, Minneapolis, MN: Augsburg Press.

Robertson, R. 1988, 'Liberation Theology, Latin America, and Third World Underdevelopment', in *The Politics of Latin American Liberation Theology: The Challenge to U.S. Public Policy*, ed. R. Rubenstein and J. Roth, Washington, DC: Washington Institute Press, 117–34.

Robles Robles, J.A. 1998, 'Postmodernidad y Teología de la Liberación', *Cristianismo y Sociedad*, 137: 49–66.

Rorty, R. 1979, *Philosophy and the Mirror of Nature*, Princeton, NJ: Princeton University Press.

—— 1982, *Consequences of Pragmatism (Essays: 1972–1980)*, Minneapolis: University of Minnesota Press.

—— 1991, *Essays on Heidegger and Others*, Cambridge: Cambridge University Press.

—— 1991, *Objectivity, Relativism, and Truth*, Cambridge: Cambridge University Press.

—— 1998, *Truth and Progress*, Cambridge: Cambridge University Press.

Rostow, W. 1960, *The Stages of Economic Growth: A Non-Communist Manifesto*, Cambridge: Cambridge University Press.

Roth, J. 1988, 'The Great Enemy? How Latin American Liberation Theology Sees the United States and the USSR', in *The Politics of Latin American Liberation Theology: The Challenge to U.S. Public Policy*, ed. R. Rubenstein and J. Roth, Washington, DC: Washington Institute Press, 225–46.

Rowland, C., ed. 1999. *The Cambridge Companion to Liberation Theology*. Cambridge: Cambridge University Press.

Rubenstein R. and J. Roth (eds) 1988, *The Politics of Latin American Liberation Theology: The Challenge to U.S. Public Policy*, Washington, DC: Washington Institute Press.

Sabel, C. 1982, *Work and Politics: The Division of Labor in Industry*, Cambridge: Cambridge University Press.

Sabel, C. and J. Zeitlin 1997, 'Stories, Strategies, Structures: Rethinking Historical Alternatives to Mass Production', in *World of Possibilities: Flexibility and Mass Production in Western Industrialization*, ed. C. Sabel and J. Zeitlin, Cambridge: Cambridge University Press.

Sawyer, F. 1992, *The Poor are Many: Political Ethics in the Social Encyclicals, Christian Democracy and Liberation Theology in Latin America*, Kampen, The Netherlands: Uitgeversmaatschappij J.H. Kok.

Scannone SJ, J. C. 1996, 'El comunitarismo como alternativa viable', in *El futuro de la reflexion teologica en América Latina*, Colombia: CELAM, 195–242.

Schumpeter, J. 1950, *Capitalism, Socialism and Democracy*, New York: Harper and Row.

Schüssler Fiorenza, E. 1984, *Bread not Stone: The Challenge of Feminist Biblical Interpretation*, Boston: Beacon Press.

—— 1984, *Foundational Theology: Jesus and the Church*, New York: Crossroad.

—— 1991, 'Systematic Theology: Tasks and Methods', in *Systematic Theology: Roman Catholic Perspectives*, ed. F. Schüssler Fiorenza and J. Galvin, Minneapolis: Fortress Press, 4–87.

Schuurman, F. 1993, 'Introduction: Development Theory in the 1990s', in *Beyond the Impasse: New Directions in Development Theory*, Atlantic Highlands, NJ: Zed Books, 1–48.

Scott, P. 2001, '"Global Capitalism" vs "End of Socialism": Crux Theologica? Engaging Liberation Theology and Theological Postliberalism', *Political Theology*, 4 (May): 36–54.

Segundo, J.L. 1974, 'Capitalism-Socialism: A Theological Crux', in *The Mystical and Political Dimension of the Christian Faith*, ed. C. Geffre and G. Gutiérrez, New York: Herder and Herder, 105–26.

—— 1974, 'Fe e ideología', *Perspectivas de Diálogo*, November, 227–33.

—— 1979, *Liberation of theology*, trans. J. Drury, Maryknoll, NY: Orbis Books.

—— 1982, *El Hombre de Hoy ante Jesus de Nazaret: Fe y Ideologia*, Madrid: Cristiandad.

—— 1982, *Faith and Ideologies*, Maryknoll, NY: Orbis Books.

—— 1985, *The Liberation of Theology*, Maryknoll, NY: Orbis Books.

—— 1993, *Signs of the Times: Theological Reflections*, ed. A. Hennelly, Maryknoll, NY: Orbis Books.

Shannon, T. 1992, *An Introduction to the World-System Perspective*, Boulder, Colorado: Westview Press.

Sigmund, P. 1990, *Liberation Theology at the Crossroads: Democracy or Revolution?*, New York: Oxford University Press.

Silva, P. 1999, 'The New Political Order in Latin America: Towards Technocratic Democracies?', in *Latin America Transformed: Globalization and Modernity*, ed. R.N. Gwynne and C. Kay, London: Arnold, 51–66.

Singer, J.W. 1988, 'Legal Realism Now', *California Law Review*, 76: 465–544.

Singer, J. 1988, 'The Reliance Interest in Property' *Stanford Law Review*, 40: 614–726.

Skocpol, T. 1977, 'Wallerstein's World Capitalist System: A Theoretical and Historical Critique', *American Journal of Sociology*, 82(5): 1075–90.

Smith, B. 1982, *The Church and Politics in Chile*, Princeton, NJ: Princeton University Press.

Smith, C. 1991, *The Emergence of Liberation Theology: Radical Religion and Social Movement Theory*, Chicago: University of Chicago Press.

—— 1995, 'The Spirit of Democracy: Base Communities, Protestantism, and Democratization in Latin America', in *Religion and Democracy in Latin America*, ed. W. Swatos, New Brunswick: Transaction Publishers, 1–25.

So, A. 1990, *Social Change and Development: Modernization, Dependency, and World-System Theories*, London: Sage Publications.

Sobrino, J. 1984, *The true church and the poor*, trans. M.J. O'Connell, Maryknoll, NY: Orbis Books.

—— 1995, 'La Teología y el "Principio Liberación"', *Revista Latinoamericana de Teología*, 35 (May–August): 115–40.

—— 1997, 'Que queda de la Teología de la Liberación', *Exodo*, 38 (April): 48–53.

Soskice, D. 1990, 'Reinterpreting Corporatism and Explaining Unemployment: Coordinated and Uncoordinated Market Economies', in *Labour Relations and Economic Performance*, ed. R. Brunetta and C. Dell'Aringa, London: Macmillan.

—— 1991, 'The Institutional Infrastructure for International Competitiveness: A Comparative Analysis of the UK and Germany', in *The Economics of the New Europe*, ed. A. Atkinson and R. Brunetta, London: Macmillan.

—— 1997, 'German Technology Policy, Innovation and National Institutional Frameworks', *Industry and Innovation*, 4: 75–96.

—— 1999, 'Divergent Production Regimes: Coordinated and Uncoordinated Market Economies in the 1980s and 1990s', in *Continuity and Change in Contemporary Capitalism*, ed. H. Kitschelt, P. Lange, G. Marks and J. Stephens, Cambridge: Cambridge University Press, 101–34.

Stackhouse, M. 1990, 'Now that the Revolution is Over', *The Reformed Journal*, 40(7), September: 16–20.

Storper, M. and R. Salais 1997, *Worlds of Production: The Action Frameworks of the Economy*, Cambridge, MA: Harvard University Press.

Sung, J.M. 1991, *La Idolatría del capital y la muerte de los pobres*, San José, Costa Rica: DEI.

—— 1993, *Neoliberalismo y pobreza*, San José, Costa Rica: DEI.

—— 1994, *Economía: Tema Ausente en la Teología de la Liberación*, San José, Costa Rica: DEI.

—— 1998, 'Economía y Teología: Reflexiones sobre Mercado, Globalización y Reino de Dios', *Alternativas*, 9: 97–118.

—— 1998, 'Idolatría: Una clave de lectura de la Economía contemporanea', *Alternativas*, 5(10): 19–38.

—— 1999, *Deseo, Mercado y Religion*, Santander: Editorial Sal Terrae.

—— 2000, 'Economics and Theology: Reflections on the Market, Globalization and the Kingdom of God', in *Global Capitalism, Liberation Theology and the Social Sciences*, ed. A. Muller, A. Tausch and P. Zulehner, New York: Nova Science Publishers, 47–60.

Swatos, W. 1995, *Religion and Democracy in Latin America*, New Brunswick: Transaction Publishers.

Toye, J. 1993, *Dilemmas of Development*, Oxford: Blackwell Publishers.

Trigo, P. 1992, 'Imaginario alternativo al imaginario vigente y al revolucionario', *Iter. Revista de Teología (Caracas)*, 3: 61–99.

—— 1993, 'El futuro de la Teología de la Liberación', in *Cambio social y pensamiento cristiano en América Latina*, ed. J. Comblin, J.I. González Faus and J. Sobrino, Madrid: Editorial Trotta, 297–317.

Unger, R.M. 1987, *Plasticity into power: Comparative–Historical studies on the institutional conditions of economic and military success: Variations on themes*, Cambridge: Cambridge University Press.

—— 1987, *Politics: A work in constructive social theory*, Cambridge: Cambridge University Press.

—— 1996, *What Should Legal Analysis Become?*, New York: Verso.

—— 1998, *Democracy Realized: The Progressive Alternative*, New York: Verso.

Unger, R.M. and C. West 1998, *The Future of American Progressivism*, Boston: Beacon Press.

Valdivieso, G. 1989, *Comunidades de Base*, Santiago: CISOC.

Valentin, B. 2001, 'Strangers no More: An Introduction to, and an Interpretation of, U.S. Hispanic/Latino/a Theology', in *The Ties that Bind: African American and Hispanic American/Latino/a Theologies in Dialogue*, ed. A. Pinn and B. Valentin, New York: Continuum, 38–53.

Vidales, R. 1979, 'Methodological Issues in Liberation Theology', in *Frontiers of Theology in Latin America*, ed. R. Gibellini, Maryknoll, NY: Orbis Books, 34–57.

Vigil, J.M. 1997, 'Cambio de Paradigma en la Teología de la Liberación?', *Alternativas*, 8: 27–46.

von Mettenheim, K. and J. Malloy (eds), 1998, *Deepening Democracy in Latin America*, Pittsburgh: University of Pittsburgh Press.

Wade, R. 1990, *Governing the Market: Economic Theory and the Role of Government in East Asian Industrialization*, Princeton, NJ: Princeton University Press.

—— 1996, 'Globalization and its Limits: Reports of the Death of the National Economy Are Greatly Exaggerated', in *National Diversity and Global Capitalism*, ed. S. Berger and R. Dore, Ithaca: Cornell University Press, 60–89.

—— 1999, 'A Clash of Capitalisms', *APSA-CP*, 10(1), Winter: 23–6.

Wallerstein, I. 1974, *The modern-world system: Capitalist agriculture and the origins of the European world-economy in the sixteenth century*, Studies in Social Discontinuity, New York: Academic Press.

—— 1979, *The capitalist world economy: Essays*, Cambridge: Cambridge University Press.

—— 1980, *The modern world system II: Mercantilism and the consolidation of the European world-economy, 1600–1750*, Social Studies in Discontinuity, New York: Academic Press.

—— 1983, *Historical Capitalism and Capitalist Civilization*, New York: Verso.

—— 1984, *The Politics of the World-Economy: The States, the Movements, and the Civilizations*, Cambridge: Cambridge University Press.

—— 1991, *Unthinking Social Science: The Limits of Nineteenth-Century Paradigms*, Cambridge: Polity Press.

—— 1995, *After Liberalism*, New York: The New Press.

—— 1999, *The End of the World as We Know It*, Minneapolis: University of Minnesota Press.

Weber, M. 1978, *Economy and society: An outline of interpretive sociology*, eds G. Roth and C. Wittich, Berkeley: University of California Press.

Weintraub E.R. 1991, *Stabilizing Dynamics*, New York: Cambridge University Press.

West, C. 1982, *Prophesy deliverance: An Afro-American revolutionary Christianity*, Philadelphia: Westminster Press.

—— 1993, 'Black Theology and Marxist Thought', in *Black Theology: A Documentary History, Vol. I 1966–1979*, ed. J. Cone and G. Wilmore, Maryknoll, NY: Orbis Books, 409–24.

—— 1993, 'Black Theology of Liberation as Critique of Capitalist Civilization', in *Black Theology, A Documentary History: Volume II 1980–1992*, ed. J. Cone and G. Wilmore, Maryknoll, NY: Orbis Books, 410–26.

Index

Adorno, Theodor 121
affluence 136
African American Church 135
Alfonsin, Raul 56
Allende, Salvador 55, 82
Alliance for Progress 1, 71
anarchy 55
anthropology 32
  Greek 33
  Semitic biblical 33
  unified 33, 146
  unitary 33, 125, 129
apathy, political 7, 52
Aquino, Maria Pilar ix, 132–4, 135, 136
  see also theology, Latina
Argentina 56, 71
Arroyo, Gonzalo 73, 74
Assmann, Hugo 14, 16, 30, 58, 73, 76,
  127–8
  Theology for a Nomad Church 75
Augustine 129
Australia 101
Austria 101

background rules 106, 108, 124
bankers, wealthy foreign 123
banks, public 100
base communities viii, 56, 59, 60, 129
Bell, Daniel Jr 128, 129–32 see also
  radical orthodoxy
Berlin Wall, fall of 2, 3, 24, 34, 82, 147
Betto, Frei 59, 60
Bible, the 34, 124, 135
  political nature of 28
  rereading 28, 33
  systematization 31
body, the 33
  as locus of salvation 37, 38, 146
Boff, Clodovis 25, 26–30, 31, 32, 33, 34,
  36, 76, 96
Boff, Leonardo 25, 38, 58–9, 60, 63, 76,
  77, 80, 82, 95–6, 108, 109–10, 124
Bolivia 54
Bonino, José Míguez 11–14, 16, 52–3, 54,

72, 73, 74–5, 76, 83, 110, 111
  Doing Theology in a Revolutionary
  Situation 11, 74
Bonino–Moltmann debate 12, 53
Borges, Jorge Luis 144–5
Brazil 1, 54, 56, 60, 71, 109
Brazilian Worker's Party 60
Burns, Peter 24, 38

Camdessus, Michael 8–9
Canada 101
capital
  accumulation 78
  investment 100
capitalism viii, ix, 1, 10, 38, 51, 54, 72, 75,
  76, 77, 80, 81, 104, 108, 122, 127,
  129, 131, 147, 148, 149
  alternatives to 7
  and the church 130
  and the market 96
  as a system 79
  as the devil 82
  definition of 100
  global 71, 73, 74, 78
  idolatrous nature 124
  industrial 97
  internal contradictions 9
  law of profit in 123
  reform of 76
  varieties of 101, 105, 111, 115 n.38
Cardoso, Fernando Henrique 73, 76, 83
Catholic Action 53
Catholic renewal 72
Catholic social teaching 53, 128
CEBs (comunidades eclesiales de base)
  59–60
  fourth Intereclesial 60
  membership 60–61
charity 38, 130
Chile 53, 54–6, 56, 72
Chinese shareholding cooperative system
  (SCS) 106–7
Christ 33
Christian Democracy 53, 54

Christian utopia 4
Christianity 129, 146
Christians for Socialism movement 75
church 81, 130, 131, 149
  and politics 129
  and state 127
  Black 135
  model of 130
citizenship 56
colonialism 1, 72
collective action 59
Comblin, José 61, 74, 111, 121–2
common good 47
communion 63
communist movement, worldwide 70
communitarian ownership 53, 54
community 6, 124, 130, 148
comparative institutional advantage 102
Concilium, 1974 special edition 10
conscientization 12, 59
contingency in society 97
cooperative competition 109
cooption of liberation theology's
    terminology 10, 11, 17, 105, 121,
    122, 128
core countries 71
corruption 130
Costa Rica 30
critical legal studies movement (CLSers)
    97, 98–9
critical legal thought 109, 111
criticism 104–7, 111
Cuban revolution 1, 71
culture 135
  focus on 134
  global 148
  role of popular 6

debt servicing 123
DEI (Departamento Ecuménico de
    Investigaciones) 30
de las Casas, Batolome 15
de Tocqueville 62
deideologizing 36
democracy vii, viii, 46–63, 104, 105
  conditions for survival 48
  critique of 127
  delegative 51
  economic 60
  electoral 53
  formal 52, 109
  from above 62

in the developing world 48
in modern industrial nations 48
institutional form 112
liberal 127
parliamentary 60, 96, 148
participatory 46, 56–60, 109, 110
political 58, 60, 61
present-day Latin American 61
presidential 148
procedural model 49, 96
social 60, 67 n.79
stagnant viii, 46, 60–62, 93, 96, 109
democratization 60
dependency theory ix, 69, 70, 71–7, 78, 79,
    80, 81, 82, 83, 85, 86 n.10
desire 129
development 71, 73, 74, 75, 76, 77, 123
  'associated-dependent' 73
  economic 27
Dewey, John 105
Diamond, Linz and Lipset: *Democracy in
    Developing Countries* 49
'Document of Latin American Theologians
    for the Second General Assembly of
    Third World Theologians' 57
Dominican Republic 71
dualisms ix, 107
Dussel, Enrique 25, 57, 73, 109, 110

East Asia 103
Eastern bloc 108
Economic Commission on Latin America
    (ECLA) 71, 74
economic vanguardism 109
economics 34, 37, 62, 125, 130, 146
  link with theology 33, 34
  mainstream 33
  popular 5
economy, the
  global 75
  in transition 97
  market 95, 105, 109, 127
  understanding of 97
efficiency 9, 46
Egypt 33
el pueblo (the people) 5, 83
elections, presidential 56
elite privilege 61
elites 62
Ellacuría, Ignacio 79–80
England 101
equality 50, 58

eschatology 126, 127
Escorial conference 1972 73
Eurocentrism 127
Europe 54, 70, 127, 148
'everyday life' 6
exclusion 46
   of Latina women from theological
      activity 132
   social 132
exploitation
   capitalist 52, 57, 75
   economic 129
   foreign 1
   of the poor 54

faith 80, 135
   commitment 26
   false 34
   in the market 33, 34
   live 36
   material reality 129
   political dimension 14
   relation with ideology 35
Feuerbach 125
'First World' 127
flexible specialization regimes 109
forgiveness 131
France 103
Frank, Andre Gunder 72–3, 74, 75, 77–8,
   83
   *Capitalism and Underdevelopment in
     Latin America* 72
freedom 10
   Christian 10
   for all human beings 135
   'revolution in' 53, 54
   the individual's 126
Frei, Eduardo 53, 55
Freire, Paulo 59
Friedman, Milton 107
Friedmann, Georges 137
Fujimori 56

Galilea, Segundo 74
Geffre, Claude 110
Germany 100, 101
global constraints 74
globalization 83, 103, 116 n.42, 116 n.50
   capitalist neoliberal 133
   economic 102
God
   a God of concrete bodily life 146

a God of life 32, 33, 37, 123, 125, 129,
   131
a God of peace 130–131
plan for all people 146
reign of 4, 6, 8, 9, 10, 13, 81, 111, 121,
   122, 125, 126
grace 130
Graham, Julie 104
growth, economic 79
Gutiérrez, Gustavo 3, 4, 5, 14–16, 17, 24,
   29, 33, 38, 52, 53, 61, 73, 75, 76,
   80, 81, 82, 85, 94, 96, 108, 109,
   136
   A Theology of Liberation 15, 75, 81, 94,
     108
   The God of Life 81

Hall, Peter 101, 102, 103, 104
Hauerwas, Stanley 128, 130 *see also*
   radical orthodoxy
Hayek, Friedrich 107
Hewitt, Marsha 29, 80–81, 82
Hinkelammert, Franz 8, 9, 10, 11, 62, 79,
   82, 123
historical projects vii, viii, 11–16, 35–40,
   83, 94, 107–10, 111, 112, 122,
   123–6, 136, 138 n.18, 144, 146
history 32, 37, 79, 130
   dualistic view 130, 131
   underside of 5, 6, 146
   unified understanding 146
   unitary 33, 125, 129
Hodgson, Geoffrey 100
Hopkins, Dwight ix, 132, 134–6 *see also*
   theology, black
Horkheimer, Max 34–5
human sacrifices 34
humanity 5–6
Huntington, Samuel 48, 49, 62
   The Third Wave 49
Hutchinson, Allan 98

ideals 104–5
identity
   Black 135
   Christian 149
   safeguarding 147
ideology 35–7, 121, 126, 133
   national security 61
   sociology of 37
idol(s) 8, 10, 11, 34, 85, 93, 123, 124
idolatry 16, 127

critiquing viii, 8–11, 34, 38, 40, 123,
		124, 125
	market 38
	of capitalism 124
	of economics 33
	totalitarianism 126
	unmasking 85
IMF *see* International Monetary Fund
income, distribution of 105
India 109
industrialization 71, 100
inequality 58, 78, 132
	global 127
	structural 56
import substitution
	industrialization (ISI) 72
	models of development 1, 18 n.2
injustice 40, 36, 134
institutional fetishism 94, 95–6, 103, 105,
		108, 130
institutional imagination ix, 94, 96,
		107–10, 111, 124
institutions 105
	contingent nature 104, 111
	thinking about 17, 104
International Development Bank 55
International Monetary Fund viii, ix, 8, 9,
		10, 38, 61, 121, 123, 128, 147
'international of life' 7
Ireland 101
Italy 103

James, William 84
Japan 100, 101
Jesus 35, 36, 40, 81
judges 98
justice 131

Kee, Alistair 125, 126
Kennedy, Duncan 105
Kierkegaard, Soren 144
King, Martin Luther Jr 136

Laclau, Ernesto 97, 99
law 39, 50, 98–9, 105, 114 n.22, 130
legal rules 105, 106
legal theory 133, 134, 147, 149
liberation 3–4, 6, 9, 11, 37, 39, 81, 105,
		121, 122, 125, 129, 134, 135, 136,
		146–7, 149
	ethical-social 29
	ethico-political 26

from capitalism 74
	from dependence 74
	goal 39, 40
	material 146
	social 26, 29, 36, 146
	soteriological 26
	three levels 15
	Vatican use of word 41 n.12
liberation theology 24, 81, 128
	and the historical project 11–16, 35–40,
		123–6
	and North American theology 111
	and the social sciences viii, 25–6, 129
	approaches to capitalism viii, ix, 144
	basic categories 5–8, 122
	canonical view 25, 26–30, 33, 38, 39, 40
	changes in historical context 2, 93, 147
	concept of property 106
	core ideas 3–5, 6, 93, 122, 124
	foundational texts 1
	goal of 29, 122
	in name only vii
	main dilemmas 17
	manifesto 146–9
	marginal view 25, 30–35, 38, 39, 40
	political paralysis 129
	practice of 26–30
	present situation of 121–3, 146–7
	responses to fall of socialism vii, viii,
		2–11
	understanding of capitalism 69–85, 95,
		106, 107, 129
	understanding of democracy viii, 46–63,
		144
	understanding of society 94
	view of history 33
	with different emphases 132
Libertatis Conscientiae 29, 122
Libertatis Nuntius 122
life
	as absolute criterion 11
	as precondition 131
	chances 37, 96
	concrete bodily 146
	material human 33
	sustainability of human 123
Lord's Prayer, commentary on 82
love commandment, the 35–6

Maclean, Iain 82
Magisterium, the 134
Malaysia 109

Malcolm X 136
mapping 104–7, 111
marginalization 6, 46, 133, 134
Maritain, Jacques 53
market, the 10, 40, 83, 104
    deregulation 102
    economies
        coordinated (CMEs) 101–2, 103
        liberal (LMEs) 101–2, 103
    idolatry 38
    model 5, 6
    reconstruction 124
    systems 95, 97, 100
    utopianization 9
marketplace, the 5
Marx 85, 112 n.5, 125
Marxism 3, 25, 31, 77, 80, 81, 82, 122
meaning structure 35
Medellin 1
mediation
    hermeneutic 30, 124
    practical 28–30, 124
    social scientific 122, 124
    sociocultural 122
Metz, Johann Baptist ix, 13, 126–8 *see
    also* theology, political
micro-democracies 59
middle class 133, 134, 141 n.59, 147
Milbank, John 128, 130, 131 *see also*
    radical orthodoxy
military coups 1, 54, 59, 71
military regimes 48, 54
modernity 10, 123, 127
modernization theory 70, 71, 72, 74, 86 n.4
Moltmann, Jürgen 12, 13, 53 *see also*
    theology, political
    The Crucified God 13
Monahan, Patrick 98
money 81
Mouffe, Chantal 97, 99
multinational companies 103
Mysterium Liberationis 26, 30

naturalistic premise, the 94
Nazi Germany 127
New Testament 126
non-human, the 17, 136
non-person, the 17, 40, 125, 136, 146, 148
North American Social Gospel movement
    41 n.7
North Atlantic philosophy 148
Norway 101

O'Donnell and Schmitter 49, 51
    *Transitions from Authoritarian Rule:
        Prospects for Democracy* 48
oppression 36, 42 n.18, 124
    causes of viii, 27, 124, 125, 146
    mechanisms of 58
    poverty as 76
orthodoxy
    radical 121, 128–32
    religious 135
    theological 147
    within liberation theology 26
ownership, socialist mode of 108

papal encyclicals 1
Paul 33
    'Letter to the Romans' 9
Pentecostal groups, rise of 2
peripheral countries 71, 74
Peru 54, 56
piecemeal change 7, 122
Pinochet, General 56
Piore, Michael 97
plebiscites 110
pluralisms, alternative ix, 96, 107, 111
political economy 39, 101, 108, 133, 134,
    135, 136, 147, 149
political science 130, 146
political theory
    Marxist 99
    post-Marxist 97
politicization 12
politics 1, 38, 94, 95, 99, 124, 129, 149
    cultural 134
    God's 130
    identity 147, 149
    pragmatic accommodation 54
    radical 135
poor, the
    as a unified subject 7
    as objects of pity 27
    as primary agents of social change 1
    as revolutionary subject 6, 122
    as subjects of political power 110
    idealization of 6
    material 136
    preferential option for viii, 3, 4, 6, 11,
        37, 39, 105, 121, 122, 123, 125, 129,
        135, 146, 147
Popular Unity party 55
popular will 47
poverty 10, 31, 46, 125

explanations for 27, 76
global 132, 134
  in the United States 132, 134
  physical 136
  routine 136
  short term increase 123
  socioeconomic 27
power
  political 83
  state 7
Prebisch, Raul 71
profitability 9, 10
property 106
  as an exclusionary power 109
  collective 108
disaggregated rights 106, 109, 119 n.84
private 100, 108
rights 108
shared 109
social 108, 109
Puebla 61

radical orthodoxy ix, 121, 128–9, 130, 131
Ratzinger, Joseph 25, 139 n.24
reconstruction, social 147
redemocratization 56–7, 60
referenda 110
reform 122
  agrarian 55
  gradual 53, 77
  revolutionary 108, 118 n.77
  social 54
  societal 132
resistance ix, 111
  Christian strategy of 131
resources
  distribution in society 105
  scarce 96
  social 37
  the world's, distribution of 17, 136
resurrection 33
revision 128
revolution ix, 1, 5, 7, 84, 18, 122
  failure of 124
  socialist 73, 83
Richard, Pablo 83, 103
rights, distribution of 131

Sabel, Charles 97, 98, 99
salvation 37, 133, 146

Scannone, Juan Carlos 7, 73
Schumpeter, Joseph 46, 47–8, 49, 50, 51,
  52, 62, 63
  Capitalism, Socialism and Democracy
  47
scripture 36, 59, 130, 147
Second General Conference of Latin
  American Bishops (CELAM) 1
Second Vatican Council 1
Segundo, Juan Luis 35–7, 44 n.75, 72, 73,
  106
Sobrino, Jon 3–4, 4, 84–5
social sciences viii, 24, 25, 27, 29, 30, 33,
  34, 37, 39, 40, 41 n.6, 62, 124, 125,
  129, 130, 146
socialism 1, 10, 38, 53, 54, 55, 60, 73, 77,
  78, 81, 93, 99, 122
  as a historical project 17
  fall of vii, ix, 2, 51, 82, 95, 107, 108,
  124, 144
  national 78
  revolutionary viii, 46, 56
socialization 49, 50, 53
society
  as frozen politics 97–9, 104, 107, 111
  civil 6, 7, 122, 123, 124
  economic foundation of 49, 51, 52
  institutional reconstruction 127
  mixed nature 107
  negative critique of 126, 127
  political 99
  social 99
sociology 37, 146
sociopolitical analysis 24, 25
solidarity 5, 7, 124
Soskice, David 101, 102, 103, 104
standard of living 51, 62, 136
state, the
  as unit of analysis 79
  reconstruction of 124
state(s)
  nation 70, 78
  national security 53, 55, 57, 61, 62, 82
statism 108
status quo vii, ix, 1, 13, 16
suffering 126, 127, 128, 131, 132
Sung, Jung Mo 30–35, 36, 37, 81, 82, 124,
  125
Sweden 101
Switzerland 101

theologians
  pastoral 28
  popular 28
  professional 28, 30
theology
  African American 112
  Black ix, 121, 132, 134–6, 141 n.49
  German political 111
  imperial 9, 10
  Latina ix, 121, 132–4
  North American 111, 147
  North Atlantic 146, 148
  of land 30
  political ix, 12, 16, 121, 128
  Vatican 26, 29
theory, social 84, 144, 149
  deep structure 94–5
'Third Italy' 109, 119 n.83
'Third Wave' of democratization 48, 50
Third World 34, 72, 103, 125, 138 n.5
tradition 31, 33, 34, 124, 130, 135, 146,
  147
Trigo, Pedro 5–7

underdevelopment 70, 72, 73, 74, 75, 77,
  78
undertheorizing of capitalism ix, 69,
  80–83, 84
Unger, Roberto viii, ix, 93–7, 100–101,
  103, 104–5, 107, 109, 110, 112 n.1,
  144
United States 55, 61, 70, 71, 101, 127, 132,
  136, 148

vagueness 128, 135
value(s) 35, 39, 47, 130
  North American and European 70
Vatican ix, 26, 29, 93, 121, 129, 133
  clampdown on liberation theology 2
  criticism of liberation theology 60
  *Instruction on Certain Aspects of the
    Theology of Liberation* 82, 122
  *Instruction on Christian Freedom and
    Liberation* 82, 139 n.24
Vatican II 1
Vietnam War, opposition to 71
Vigil, José Maria 4
violence 131
  inherent to capitalism 131
  institutionalized 1
  revolutionary 6

Wallerstein, Immanuel 78–9
welfare, social 50
welfare state 50
West, Cornel 112, 134 *see also* theology,
  black
Western civilization 79, 84, 85
Western philosophy and theology 127
word of God, the 27; *see also* the Bible
working class 60, 61
World Bank 55
world system 78, 137, 143 n.76
  capitalist 78
  theory ix, 69, 70, 77–80, 84

Zeitlin, Jonathan 97, 98